Undeclared War

THE KING (in disguise): Methinks I could not die anywhere so contented as in the King's company, his cause being just . . .

WILLIAMS (a soldier): But if the cause be not good, the King himself hath a heavy reckoning to make when all those legs and arms and heads, chopped off in a battle, shall join together at the latter day and cry all, 'We died at such a place,' some swearing, some crying for a surgeon, some upon their wives left poor behind them . . .

—Shakespeare's *King Henry V*: in the English camp,
the night before the battle of Agincourt

UNDECLARED WAR

Twilight Zone of Constitutional Power

Edward Keynes

The Pennsylvania State University Press
University Park and London

Chapter 3, "Democracy, Judicial Review, and the War Powers," appeared in a slightly altered form under the same title in *Ohio Northern University Law Review* 8 (January 1981): 69–101, and is reprinted here with permission.

Library of Congress Cataloging in Publication Data

Keynes, Edward.
   Undeclared war.

Includes index.
   1. War and emergency powers—United States.   I. Title.
KF5060.K48   1982   342.73′062   82–9854
ISBN 0–271–00327–8   347.30262   AACR2

For Diane, Stephen, Michael, and David

Contents

Acknowledgments

Every book has an intellectual history, every author an intellectual debt. My fascination with public law can be attributed to the fine teaching and scholarship of Professor David Fellman, who awakened and stimulated my interest in constitutional government during the early days of the Vietnam War. Along with my generation, I witnessed the nation's growing entanglement in Vietnam. This book has emerged from my concern for the future of constitutional government in an era of undeclared war.

Like every other author, I am responsible for this book's content but am indebted to many people for their advice and assistance. I thank my colleague Robert S. Friedman for his criticism and encouragement at every stage in this book's development. I am grateful to Meyer A. Bushman, Esq., of Philadelphia, for a lawyer's critique of the manuscript. Professor Harold J. Spaeth of Michigan State University and Professor C. Herman Pritchett of the University of California at Santa Barbara offered their thoughtful advice in revising the manuscript for publication. John M. Pickering and Peter Ross Sieger of the Pennsylvania State University Press shepherded the manuscript through the many stages of publication.

I am also grateful to Susan Anthes, Diane Smith, John Sulzer, and Ruth Senior, librarians in the Pennsylvania State University's Pattee Library, for their patient and creative assistance in documenting the manuscript. To my former students, Robert Elias, Christopher McNally, Kip Sturgis, and Marc Witzig, I owe a special debt for laboring tirelessly and performing the many research tasks that were essential. Finally, I thank Barbara Hendershot and Susan Sheridan for their superb typing and preparation of the manuscript.

Introduction

During the twentieth century aggressive Presidents and supine Congresses have transformed the President's constitutional authority to defend the nation against attack into a virtually unlimited power to initiate undeclared war and military hostilities. Responding to international crises, Theodore Roosevelt, William Howard Taft, and Woodrow Wilson dispatched American armed forces abroad to further their foreign policies. In 1941, before the United States entered the Second World War, Franklin Roosevelt ordered American troops to occupy Iceland and Greenland to protect national security in the Western Atlantic. Since the Second World War, Harry Truman, Dwight Eisenhower, John Kennedy, Lyndon Johnson, Richard Nixon, Gerald Ford, and Jimmy Carter have deployed armed forces to promote foreign policy, national security, and the diverse security interests of the nation's allies.[1] With the federal judiciary's blessing, Congress and the President have fused their respective and constitutionally distinct powers into a national war power that the commander in chief exercises with very few limitations.

Despite congressional attempts to limit presidential warmaking following the Vietnam War, recent Congresses have responded pliantly to the President's diplomatic and military initiatives in such diverse places as southern Africa, the Middle East, and Central America. With the Vietnam War receding from the national consciousness, the Reagan Administration has challenged Soviet and Cuban support for revolutionary regimes and liberation movements in Angola, Nicaragua, and El Salvador. In August 1981 U.S. combat aircraft destroyed two Libyan jet fighters over the Gulf of Sidra. The Reagan Administration has also committed U.S. armed forces to a Sinai peacekeeping force and made a national commitment to defend Israel against Soviet aggression. While these developments do not raise serious constitutional questions concerning presidential or congressional power to initiate and conduct military hostilities, American diplomatic and military engagement in unstable regions creates the potential for such hostilities, for the sacrifice of blood and treasure in future undeclared wars.

Although recent Presidents have acknowledged the congressional power to declare war, their administrative subordinates have minted a constitutional theory that confers inherent power on the President to dispatch American armed forces around the globe and commit them to combat without congressional approval or consultation. Testifying before a joint hearing of the Senate Committees on Foreign Relations and Armed Services in 1951, Secretary of State Dean Acheson claimed: "Not only has the President the authority to use the Armed Forces in carrying out the broad foreign policy of the United States and implementing treaties, but it is equally clear that this authority may not be interfered with by the Congress in the exercise of power which it has under the Constitution."[2] Fifteen years later, the State Department's legal advisor, Leonard Meeker, claimed that President Johnson had inherent power to commit U.S. armed forces to defend South Vietnam. "The grant of authority to the President in article II of the Constitution," observed Meeker, "extends to the actions of the United States currently undertaken in Viet-Nam."[3] Administration spokesmen from President Truman to President Nixon reiterated this view so frequently that many Americans accept the argument that the President has inherent constitutional authority to make war.[4]

In contrast to the modern view of the President as a king-general who exercises prerogative or discretionary power to make foreign policy, initiate war, and conclude peace treaties, the Framers had a limited conception of executive authority. Since the Constitution's authors believed that governmental power would threaten liberty, they separated and shared various powers of war, defense, and foreign affairs between Congress and the President. By separating and balancing governmental authority among competing institutions, apparently, the Framers believed that the Constitution would check governmental power, promote the rule of law, limit each branch to the performance of its constitutional functions, and keep Congress as well as the President accountable to the people. The Framers also believed that the new Constitution would provide government with the power necessary to promote external security and domestic peace without threatening either liberty or constitutional government.

Unlike the eighteenth-century British Constitution, which vested prerogative in the Crown to initate war and conclude peace, the Framers conferred only defensive powers on the President.[5] As civilian commander in chief, the President is responsible for superintending the armed forces in war and peace, defending the nation, its armed forces, and its citizens and their property against attack, and directing military operations in wartime.[6] The Framers did not confer authority on the President to initiate war or military hostilities, to transform defensive actions into aggressive wars, or to defend U.S. allies against attack. From the Framers' eighteenth-century perspective, only Congress could change the nation's condition from peace to war.[7]

While the Framers attempted to distinguish the congressional war powers from the commander in chief's defensive power, they did not and could not define precisely the scope and boundaries of legislative and executive authority. Against a background of royal prerogative, what powers did the Constitution's authors intend Congress and the President to exercise? Without a declaration of war or other legislation authorizing limited war or military hostilities, how far can the President go in taking defensive action before he exceeds the authority that the Constitution confers on his office? In authorizing limited war or military hostilities, how far can Congress restrict presidential military action without invading the authority that the Constitution vests in the presidency? Neither the language of the Constitution nor the record of the Federal Convention provides a conclusive definition of the congressional power to initiate war or the presidential power to defend the nation against attack.[8]

Despite the Framers' attempt to distinguish legislative from executive authority, changes in the international system and the conduct of warfare have virtually erased the distinction between defensive and offensive war upon which the separation of the congressional war powers from the President's defensive power rests. International terrorism, the Vietnam War, guerrilla and insurgency warfare, wars of "national liberation," and the global conflict between the United States and the Soviet Union resist the Framers' distinction between defensive and offensive war.[9] Is the deployment of U.S. intermediate-range missiles in Turkey or the stationing of Soviet combat troops in Cuba a defensive or an offensive measure? In an era of supersonic intercontinental strategic weapons, is a preemptive first strike defensive or offensive according to the Framers' classification? Is the Soviet invasion of Afghanistan or the U.S. invasion of Cambodia an aggressive war prohibited by the United

Nations Charter or a defensive action permitted by international practice? The answers to these questions will vary according to the international actors' perceptions of one another's motivations, intentions, and behavior rather than the Framers' classification of defensive and offensive conduct.

In addition to the difficulty of applying eighteenth-century theories of warfare to twentieth-century conditions, the Framers created ambiguity by conferring authority concurrently on Congress and the President.[10] The President and the Senate, for example, share authority in negotiating, accepting, and ratifying treaties and nominating, confirming, and appointing U.S. diplomatic personnel. Since many important treaties are not self-executing, the President requires legislative authority and appropriations to execute the terms of international agreements.[11] Although the President has exclusive authority to receive foreign ambassadors and, thereby, to recognize other nations, Congress has the power to authorize and appropriate the funds necessary to accomplish the President's recognition policy. These overlapping powers create the potential for legislative-executive conflict and demonstrate the need for cooperation in formulating, authorizing, and conducting national-security policy.[12]

The contemporary system of regional alliances and mutual-security agreements such as the North Atlantic Treaty illustrates the rapid growth of a twilight zone, a zone of concurrent authority in which the distribution of power and responsibility is uncertain.[13] Although Article 5 of the NATO treaty provides that an attack on any signatory is considered an attack on all, Article 11 reserves to each member the right to decide how it will respond in accordance with its domestic constitutional processes.[14] The reserve clause implies that Congress retains its constitutional authority to declare war or authorize limited military hostilities. However, President Truman's decision to station four U.S. Army divisions in Western Europe eroded the congressional power to initiate military hostilities.[15] The presence of an American "hostage army" in Western Europe virtually guarantees that Congress will face a military *fait accompli* if the Soviet Union attacks a NATO ally. The NATO alliance expands presidential power into a twilight zone of concurrent authority that includes protecting the territorial integrity and security interests of U.S. allies. These mutual-security agreements also transform the President's defensive power into an indeterminate power to protect the diverse security interests of the nation's allies.

As the distinction between defensive and offensive warfare has eroded, the twilight zone of concurrent authority has expanded, the zones of exclusive legislative and executive authority have become less distinguishable, and the boundaries between congressional and presidential power have become more difficult to locate.[16] The absence of clear boundaries creates the potential for serious conflict between Congress and the President. Under most circumstances, Congress and the President have reconciled competing claims of power to initiate and sustain military hostilities through negotiation and compromise. However, when such conflict becomes resolute or irreconcilable, the legislature and executive invite judicial intervention and resolution of disputes that otherwise would remain beyond the judiciary's competence.[17]

Although Congress and the President may not be able to reconcile conflicting claims of power to initiate war and military hostilities, there are important theoretical, constitutional, and prudential reasons for judicial abstention from war-powers controversies. Democratic theory recommends that decisions to commence war and hostilities belong exclusively to the people's elected representatives. Therefore, federal judges, who are neither responsive nor responsible to the American electorate, should not interject themselves into the politics of the people. Judicial intervention also interferes with the democratic process through which the people hold their representatives accountable for the government's decisions to go to war.[18]

The constitutional separation of powers also recommends judicial self-restraint. Since the Constitution commits decisions to initiate war and defend the nation to Congress and the President, respectively, the courts cannot decide war-powers cases without breaching the separation of powers. By deciding war-powers controversies, the Federal courts inevitably exceed their jurisdiction and judicial function. Inasmuch as the Constitution demonstrably commits questions of war, peace, and national defense to Congress and the President, the courts cannot decide war-powers controversies without invading and, perhaps, impairing the legislative and executive functions.[19]

In addition to the foregoing theoretical and constitutional considerations, prudence dictates judicial self-restraint. Since the judiciary lacks the diplomatic and military information available to the executive, courts cannot evaluate questions of military necessity. Judges also lack the training and expertise to evaluate foreign intelligence and the military options available to the commander in chief. Even if the judiciary had access to and could evaluate the information available to the President and his military subordinates, the courts cannot control the international consequences of their decisions. The judiciary simply lacks the military, political, economic, and other instruments necessary to influence the international system. Furthermore, the danger exists that the President will ignore judicial decisions that challenge his conduct of military operations or that Congress will restrict the Federal courts' jurisdiction to entertain future war-powers cases. In either event, judicial intervention can only impair the judiciary's effectiveness, i.e., its ability to protect the citizen's constitutional rights.[20]

Despite the persuasive theoretical, constitutional, and prudential rationale for self-restraint, there are compelling reasons for the judiciary to entertain war-powers controversies. While the separation of powers precludes judicial determination of political questions, i.e., questions that the Constitution commits exclusively to either the legislature or the executive, in the twilight zone of concurrent authority no such textual commitment exists. In the face of constitutional ambiguity, the courts have the jurisdiction and judicial power to determine the scope of congressional and presidential authority to wage undeclared war. Such controversies involve classical questions of constitutional and statutory adjudication rather than policy questions that are beyond judicial competence.[21]

Although the courts lack the authority to determine the wisdom, propriety, or desirability of waging undeclared war, in cases that meet jurisdictional and other procedural requirements, the federal judiciary can determine (1) the scope of authority that the Constitution vests exclusively in Congress or the President, (2) whether their actions fall in the zones of authority that the Constitution confers on the legislature and the executive, (3) whether their actions breach one another's authority, or (4) whether congressional and presidential actions fall in a twilight zone of concurrent authority. If the judiciary determines that the commander in chief's military conduct falls in a twilight zone, the courts can proceed to determine whether (1) there is a need for joint legislative-executive action, (2) Congress has taken any action to support the President, and (3) congressional authorization passes constitutional muster.

Insofar as the foregoing determinations involve questions of constitutional and statutory interpretation, they do not breach the separation of powers or represent political questions. The foregoing determinations do not call for nonjudicial policy decisions, imply disrespect for a coordinate branch of the national government, or constitute conflicting pronouncements on the same question. If interpreting the Constitution is a judicial function, the courts do not lack judicially discoverable and manageable standards to resolve war-powers controversies. In the event that conflict exists between Congress and the President over the allocation and exercise of the war powers, judicial intervention does not risk questioning established policy. By definition, legislative-executive conflict implies the absence of a single uniform policy. Indeed, judicial intervention may be necessary to restore the unity in foreign affairs that otherwise dictates judicial abstention.[22]

If the courts can surmount such threshold barriers as jurisdiction, sovereign immunity, standing to sue, and the political-question doctrine, the Federal judiciary has a constitutional obligation to decide war-powers controversies on their merits. In determining whether Congress and the President, separately or jointly, have acted according to their constitutional mandate, the Federal judiciary should proceed cautiously, however. Before marching into the political thicket, the courts should first determine how broadly and deeply their decisions cut into the other departments' functions. When the Federal courts intervene to protect an individual's constitutional rights or the citizen's right to constitutional government, they should not impair the national government's ability to protect national security. In defining the boundaries between legislative and executive authority to initiate and sustain military hostilities, the courts should search for formulas that least restrict the other branches from performing their responsibility to protect national security.[23]

The conscientious objector, the draft registrant, the inductee, the serviceman, or any other plaintiff who challenges congressional authority to initiate or presidential authority to conduct an undeclared war should recognize that the judiciary does not favor such suits. In fact, the Federal courts employ various procedural techniques to abstain from deciding war-powers cases on their merits. When the courts dispose of such cases on their merits, usually, they sustain congressional and presidential actions. During the Vietnam War, for example, only two Federal district courts challenged the President's power to conduct military actions in Southeast Asia without explicit congressional authorization.[24] The courts of appeals subsequently overruled the district courts.[25] In all but one case, the Supreme Court simply denied petitions for writs of certiorari.[26] The contemporary record of the Federal courts suggests that the government is free to initiate and conduct undeclared wars and military hostility with very few constitutional limitations.

Although the Federal courts were loath to decide war-powers controversies during the Vietnam War, the existence of irreconcilable conflict between Congress and the President created the opportunity for judicial intervention. As the Vietnam War recedes from the national consciousness, the time is ripe to examine the role that the courts have played in adjudicating such controversies. The time is also propitious to examine dispassionately the judiciary's role in adapting the Framers' intentions to the exigencies of modern warfare. Is there an unbreachable chasm between the Framers' intentions and contemporary practice? As the nation approaches the Constitution's second centennial, what is the effect of judicial intervention in war-powers cases on the continuing development of American constitutional government? The following chapters examine the origin, development, and contemporary status of the war powers in the United States.

1

The Constitutional Background

THE FRAMERS' PHILOSOPHICAL MILIEU

Although the Constitution's authors were eighteenth-century liberals who accepted the need to protect such values as popular sovereignty and individual liberty, they also recognized the compelling need to protect the new nation's independence, external security, and domestic peace. The Framers' philosophical commitments, political experience during successive periods of British imperial government and post-revolutionary floundering under the Articles of Confederation, and their knowledge of British and European history reveal a commitment to reconciling the values of liberty and popular sovereignty with the desiderata of national security and domestic peace. In resolving this co-nundrum, the Framers developed a uniquely American version of con-stitutionalism, a written constitution that incorporates the partial sepa-ration of powers, a system of checks and balances, and limitations on the exercise of governmental power. The separation of the constitu-tional office of commander in chief of the nation's armed forces from the congressional war powers reflects the Framers' dual commitment to con-stitutional government and national security.

As eighteenth-century liberals, the Framers apparently believed that by limiting and fragmenting governmental power they could protect national security without endangering the individual's liberty. Their ra-tionale for the separation of power and balanced government (i.e., the simpler English term for checks and balances) is the inevitable tension or friction that arises from the interaction of these two closely related but different principles of American government. While the separation of the war powers from the office of commander in chief creates the conditions for struggle between Congress and the President, balanced government, or so the Framers apparently thought, would promote the cooperation necessary to formulate and execute effective national-security policies. Separation of power and balanced government, they also believed, would result in the legitimation and popular consensus that national-security policies require in a constitutional system that incorporates the principle of popular sovereignty. However sanguine the Framers' views appear to a generation recovering from the Indochina War (1964–1973), the Constitution's authors anticipated that such major decisions as committing the nation to war and restoring peace would require extensive legislative-executive consultation, cooperation, and discussion.

In contrast to these expectations of governmental accountability, the Framers also recognized the need for secrecy in conducting foreign negotiations, dispatch in conducting foreign and military policies, and flexibility in meeting foreign military threats whose contingency cannot always be anticipated. By committing the conduct of foreign and military policy to the President, the Framers hoped to achieve the requisites of an effective national-security policy without endangering the nation's domestic liberties by creating the potential for governmental tyranny. By committing defensive powers to the President, as the armed forces' civilian commander in chief, and to the states, they attempted to provide for the contingency of a sudden attack on the United States. Despite a long history of presidential *faits accomplis* in committing U.S. armed forces to foreign hostilities, the Framers did not, however, assign prerogative powers of war and peace to the President.

Throughout the nation's history, the exercise of congressional war powers and presidential power as commander in chief has generated lively controversy among constitutional scholars, political commentators, and political activists. In the absence of a clear and exclusive textual constitutional commitment of all powers of war and national defense to either Congress or the President, the Framers created a twilight zone, at times, a no man's land, between the legislative and executive branches. However patiently the constitutional scholar examines the Constitution's text or the Constitutional Convention's records, he can not turn a constitutional doubt, created by the absence of an exclusive commitment of power, into a logical certainty. Not only are such textual exegeses futile, but they are more applicable to scriptural than constitutional interpretation. Insofar as one can interpret the Framers' intent regarding the congressional war powers and the office of commander in chief, one must examine the Framers' philosophical tradition and values, their views at the time of the Constitutional Convention, and their subsequent debates during the states' ratifying conventions and the decade of the 1790s.

BRITISH CONSTITUTIONAL THEORY AND DEVELOPMENT

Eighteenth-century American views on the war powers and the powers of external sovereignty represent a significant departure from British political theory and practice. Although the British view, as represented in John Locke's *Two Treatises of Government* (1681), recognizes the people as sovereign in domestic affairs and the executive as subordinate to the legislative power in foreign affairs,[1] Locke introduced two concepts that American constitutionalists later rejected, namely, prerogative and federative power. Federative power, as Richard Cox observes, represents the conjunction or fusion of executive and legislative power in conducting foreign affairs.[2] Federative power is the power of every nation "to act for its own preservation . . . vis-à-vis other commonwealths. . . . In short, the federative power 'contains the power of war and peace, leagues and alliances, and all the transactions with all persons and communities without the commonwealth. . . .'"[3] Since federative power is exercised only in external or foreign affairs, such power is not subject to the same limitations as various domestic powers.[4] In the international community, the only limitation on federative power is international practice and the ultimate rationale for such power is success, i.e., self-preservation.

From the international community's perspective, the nation exercises federative power or external sovereignty as a unitary body.[5] From a domestic perspective, however, the executive, which conducts foreign affairs, theoretically is subordinate to the legislature. In fact, the executive's conduct and the primacy of foreign affairs—of war and peace—in Locke's writings, suggests that in practice the ultimate power of decision devolves on the executive.[6] In other words, the executive must necessarily exercise great discretionary power in foreign affairs, unlimited by the nation's standing laws and constitution,[7] since the legislature cannot predict other nations' behavior or the imprecise contingencies upon which the executive's decisions and actions depend.

The executive's discretion in foreign and domestic affairs is enhanced by Locke's recognition of prerogative, which is "nothing but the power of doing public good without a rule,"[8] although he recognizes that the "public good" constitutes a limit on royal prerogative.[9] Prerogative (which is essentially an executive power according to Locke) is the power to determine the public good or interest in circumstances that were unforeseen or unforeseeable by the legislature. Prerogative encompasses the power to act contrary to standing law as well as the power to act in the face of the standing law's silence in order to preserve the nation from external military threat or internal violence. President Abraham Lincoln's exercise of extraordinary powers between April 19 and July 4, 1861, was a clear exercise of prerogative in the face of compelling emergency. Lincoln exercised powers that were unauthorized by Congress and that were vested in Congress rather than the President.[10]

Locke's test for the legitimate exercise of prerogative is of little value since it merely defers but does not answer "the 'old question' of what *is* for the public good, and who, in any case, is going to judge."[11] Locke's answer to this "old question," as Richard Cox argues, is:

> Between an executive power in being, with such a prerogative, and a legislative that depends upon his will for their convening, there can be no judge on earth. . . . The people have no other remedy in this, as in all other cases where they have no judge on earth, but to appeal to heaven. . . .[12]

In a postrevolutionary society searching for domestic political stability and national security without endangering political liberty, however, "appeal to the sword" seems a more likely alternative than an appeal to heaven.[13] In a constitutional system that incorporates the principle of popular sovereignty, such concepts as federative and prerogative powers are invitations to revolution by a weary people whose blood and treasure have been spent in the foreign wars and military adventures that such theories encourage.

While the Framers rejected English theories of royal prerogative and governmental sovereignty, they were indebted to the Whigs and the British Crown's other opponents whose views on balanced government and the separation of powers justified their separation of congressional war powers from the office of commander in chief. British constitutionalism, which incorporated such ideas as balanced government, separation of powers, limits on all governmental power, and the rule of law, first evolved in the 1640s as an attempt to resolve the basic conundrum that Heroclitus of Ephesus had posed (ca. 470 B.C.). "The major problem of human society," wrote Heroclitus, "is to combine that degree of liberty without which law is tyranny with that degree of law without which liberty becomes license."[14] Although modern American constitutionalism owes an intellectual debt to Greek and Roman theories of mixed government and the supremacy of law,[15] the modern version of constitutionalism, upon which the Framers relied, evolved in England during successive periods of Civil War (1642–1648), the Interregnum (1649–1660), and the Glorious Revolution (1688–1689).

During the English Civil War and the Interregnum the theory of the separation of powers developed as a response to arguments that England already possessed a balanced and mixed constitution whose monarchic, aristocratic, and democratic elements were represented by the King, the House of Lords, and the House of Commons.[16] Since the Stuart monarchs controlled the courts and, through their ministers, influenced both houses of Parliament, critics of royal prerogative argued that new constitutional principles were necessary to restrain the monarchy.[17] The Levellers, who had opposed unlimited parliamentary power during the Interregnum, were equally convinced that unqualified legislative power posed a similar danger to liberty.[18] The theoretical separation of legislative from executive power and, later in the seventeenth century, judicial from executive power were introduced as the "grand secret of liberty and good government."[19] By 1645 such diverse opponents of unlimited governmental power as the Levellers and religious dissenters argued that the separation of executive from legislative functions and personnel were necessary restraints on arbitrary government, on both royal and parliamentary abuses that threatened the individual's liberties. Such figures as Sir Robert Filmer, James Harrington, John Lilburne, and John Milton accepted the separation of powers as a basic concomitant of English constitutionalism and limited government.[20]

Between the monarchy's restoration in 1660 and the Glorious Revolution (1688–1689), a second basic tenet of English constitutionalism developed: balanced government.[21] With the monarchy's restoration, the King's participation in Parliament and the courts appeared to the Whigs as a glaring contradiction to constitutional government.[22] Partially in response to the restoration, Whig theories of legislative supremacy eclipsed the separation of powers as a means of preserving popular sovereignty and political liberty. To Whig theorists, a representative national legislature, acting in the people's name, served as a real check on arbitrary government. John Locke's *Second Treatise* (probably written in 1681), which is representative of the period, accepted legislative supremacy, but recognized the necessity for royal prerogative and federative power. Although Parliament represents the Commonwealth's supreme will (namely, the people), limited by law and in function, external security and internal peace require a unitary, vigorous executive. For Locke, legislative supremacy and the law's binding quality (except, of course, regarding prerogative and federative power), however, were inadequate assurances of constitutional government.[23]

Theoretically, both royal prerogative and federative power vitiated legislative supremacy and constitutional government. After 1688, the growing presence of the King's "placemen" or ministerial officers in the House of Commons vitiated legislative independence.[24] Royal control of the judiciary further compromised English constitutionalism. Without an independent judiciary to curb "licentious ministers," the only restraint on the executive was the parliamentary power to impeach and remove the King's ministers. Between 1688 and 1700 English constitutionalists concluded that the separation of executive from legislative power could not alone prevent ambitious men from undermining liberty, constitutional government, popular sovereignty, or the rule of law.

Locke accepted the need for an independent judiciary that could administer justice impartially.[25] By separating the function of interpreting from enforcing law, both the Crown and Parliament could be confined to their constitutionally prescribed functions of making and enforcing public policy. An impartial judiciary with independent tenure could also protect the individual's liberty from governmental encroachment, and could intervene in struggles between King and Parliament.[26] Thus, the judiciary might at times support Parliament against the King's exercising his absolute veto power. Political disaffection with the judiciary's subordination to the Crown eventually resulted in a guarantee of judicial independence in the Act of Settlement of 1701.[27]

By 1700, advocates of constitutional government realized that the complete separation of powers was both impossible and undesirable.[28] The practical fusion of legislative and executive power also threatened constitutional government. While judicial independence might promote the rule of law as a constitutional standard for judging the government's behavior, the judiciary lacked the power to enforce its decisions. John Trenchard, Walter Moyle, and, later, Henry St. John, Viscount Bolingbroke arued that balanced government (checks and balances) or mutual restraints on power were necessary to preserve both liberty and order.[29] Otherwise, naturally ambitious men might concentrate governmental power, serve their private ends, and pervert the public interest. Trenchard, for example, argued that checks and balances were necessary to hold the Crown and Parliament responsible to one another and to the nation.[30] By exercising their respective veto, impeachment, and removal powers, the King and Parliament would restrain one another, limit the scope of governmental power, promote responsible government, safeguard liberty, and assure the cooperation necessary to enact and execute domestic and foreign policy.[31]

James Pitt, who also feared arbitrary government, nevertheless appreciated the internal order and external security that government provides, and without which liberty cannot long survive. As Pitt realized, the problem is to provide government with adequate power to preserve order without posing a threat to liberty. Pitt's answer to the "old problem" was to separate legislative, executive, and judicial power and, simultaneously, to make the power holders mutually dependent. Constitutional government or "government by law," as Pitt called the rule of law, is best preserved by separating and balancing various powers against one another. In an unsigned article of April 11, 1730, Pitt summed up the doctrine of English constitutional theory that Montesquieu later restated and elaborated and that the Framers of the U.S. Constitution incorporated into the American governmental system:

> Our [the English] Constitution consists indeed of Three Powers [executive, legislative, and judicial] *absolutely distinct*; but if they were also as *absolutely independent*, no Business would ever be done: There would be everlasting Contention and Dispute till one had got the better of the other. 'Tis necessary, therefore, in Order to the due Exercise of Government, that these Powers which are *distinct*, and have a Negative on each other, should also have a *mutual Dependence, and mutual Expectations.*[32]

Although the Constitution's authors undoubtedly derived their views on constitutional government from numerous English sources, including Joseph Addison, Viscount Bolingbroke, and Sir William Blackstone, whose *Commentaries on the Laws of England* (1765) emphasized the importance of an independent judiciary in limiting arbitrary executive and legislative power,[33] Charles Louis de Secondat, Baron de Montesquieu also provided a persuasive case for constitutionalism. As President of the Parlement de Bordeaux, a judicial office, Montesquieu became an advocate of independent judicial authority and an opponent of centralized, unlimited legislative and executive (royal) power. In his *Spirit of the Laws* (1748), Montesquieu elaborated his views on constitutionalism (individual liberty, mixed monarchy, the rule of law, separation of powers, and balanced and limited government), which characterized early eighteenth-century English constitutional development.

Despite Montesquieu's failure to distinguish clearly between balanced government and the separation of powers, he relied upon checks and balances to maintain the separation of powers.[34] According to Montesquieu, balanced government and the separation of powers were two closely related but different principles of liberty and constitutionalism.[35] Operating in counterpoise, both principles promote moderate, temperate, and limited government. The separation of powers, according to Montesquieu, promotes liberty by limiting or preventing governmental action. Checks and balances assure that important governmental policies result from basic consensus among the organs of government. Together, Montesquieu believed, these principles would maintain a "constitution of liberty" and the rule of law, which were his primary objectives.[36]

Since a complete separation of powers risked deadlock and paralysis, Montesquieu also relied on balanced government to promote cooperation and interaction between the legislature and the executive. When governmental power is shared and fragmented, governmental action requires legislative and executive consent and cooperation. Legislative and executive power, wrote Montesquieu, " . . . naturally form a state of repose or inaction. But as there is a necessity for movement in the course of human affairs, they are forced to move, but still in concert."[37] Montesquieu may have been too optimistic about legislative and executive cooperation in making public policy, but his understanding of the inherent tension between the separation of powers and checks and balances as principles of constitutionalism is his most important contribution to American constitutional development after 1776.[38]

Taken together, Locke, Montesquieu, and other commentators on British constitutionalism relied on institutional means to prevent naturally aggressive and ambitious men from destroying liberty. As Montesquieu observed, liberty could be " . . . found in moderate governments." To prevent the abuse of power, Montesquieu concluded:

> [I]t is necessary from the very nature of things that power should be a check to power. A government may be so constituted, as no man shall be compelled to do things to which the law does not oblige him, nor forced to abstain from things which the law permits.[39]

If one could not change human nature, one could at least counteract vice with vice, power with power, and ambition with ambition, a view that American federalists and other constitutionalists articulated in 1787–1788 during the debates over ratification of the United States Constitution.

THE AMERICAN SETTING

In addition to studying British constitutional thought and development, the Framers were attentive to their own recent history, a history of colonial government, revolutionary crisis, and postrevolutionary floundering. Prior to the Revolution, separation of powers and checks and balances were justified as means of opposing royal power and prerogative. Colonial legislatures occasionally used their tax powers as a check on the British Crown's judges and governors.[40] Such revolutionary figures as James Otis, John Adams, and Thomas Jefferson advocated balanced government and the separation of powers as defenses against tyranny.[41] "It is by balancing each of these powers [legislative, executive, and judicial] against the other two," observed John Adams, "that the efforts in human nature towards tyranny can alone be checked and restrained."[42]

In 1775 and 1776, amidst revolutionary, antimonarchical fervor, American revolutionaries turned away from balanced government and toward legislative supremacy as a defense against tyranny. Once they had overthrown British imperial government, there was no longer a need for balanced government and the separation of powers as weapons against the Crown. Revolutionary congresses and committees of public safety seized all governmental power during this period. Without the monarchy and a hereditary aristocracy, direct legislative responsibility to a sovereign people seemed to provide adequate safeguards against tyranny.[43]

From 1776 to 1787, neither balanced government nor the separation of powers was universally accepted in the United States. Written hastily in 1776, several state constitutions rejected both doctrines.[44] While every state constitution written thereafter incorporated some form of separation of powers, most ignored or gave little emphasis to checks and balances.[45] The Articles of Confederation, which governed the new nation from 1781 to 1789, completely ignored both the separation of powers and checks and balances. Whatever limited power the states vested in the United States they delegated to Congress. Thus, Congress exercised only quasilegislative power and such former prerogatives as the powers to conduct foreign affairs, declare war and peace, and supervise General George Washington's conduct of the Revolutionary War.[46]

Although every state constitution written after 1776 incorporated the separation of powers and some state constitutions provided for balanced government, constitutional limitations on the exercise of power were often ignored by state legislatures. Despite the New Hampshire Constitution's explicit reference to the separation of powers, for example, from 1784 to 1792, " . . . the state legislature freely vacated judicial proceedings, suspended judicial actions, annulled or modified judgments, cancelled executions, reopened controversies, authorized appeals, granted exemptions from the standing law, expounded the law for pending cases, and even determined the merits of disputes."[47] Eager " . . . to take a short course with enemies of the new regime [English Loyalists],"[48] the Massachusetts General Court enacted "pains and penalties" against loyalists that amounted to legislative confiscation of property without due process. Separation of powers to the contrary, the General Court exercised both judicial and administrative powers during the postrevolutionary period.[49]

By 1787 legislative abuses of power or "legislative despotism," as Jefferson called such abuses, had become so prevalent that John Adams, James Wilson, John Jay, James Madison, and Thomas Jefferson advocated separation of powers to protect liberty against legislative power.[50] In light of recent controversies over presidential power, it is enlightening to remember that the Constitution's authors and various other leading political figures of the time feared legislative as well as executive caprice. Since man's genius for the abuse of power is universal, as the Constitution's authors assumed, the very creation of government, the delegation of power by the people to their representatives, requires great limitations on the use of power.[51]

"It is not surprising," observes Malcolm Sharp, " . . . that the principle of the separation of powers was accepted without any debate whatever by the members of the convention. It had become an axiom; and the only question was of applying it."[52] Indeed, every plan submitted to the Constitutional Convention incorporated this principle.[53] While James Wilson called for complete separation of legislative, executive, and judicial power, James Madison tempered separation of powers with balanced government, that is, with checks and balances.[54] Within this broad framework there were, nevertheless, serious disagreements about the scope and limit of each branch's power.

THE CONSTITUTIONAL ALLOCATION OF POWER

In contrast to an earlier generation of revolutionaries who were concerned with dissolving governmental power, the Constitution's authors focused on the allocation and limitation of governmental powers. The convention's debates, the debates of the state ratifying conventions, contemporaneous writings, and the constitutional text reveal that the Framers' major concern was a more reasonable allocation of power between the national and state governments than had existed under the Articles of Confederation. While limited defensive powers were allocated to the states (including the powers to maintain a militia and respond to sudden attack or imminent danger of invasion),[55] the final powers of decision were vested exclusively in the national government. In fact, the states were explicitly prohibited from exercising various war and foreign-affairs powers,[56] which had been a source of national embarrassment under the Articles of Confederation.

Despite the Tenth Amendment's reservation of domestic powers to the states, the new national government enjoyed important governmental powers—regarding taxation, the money and banking system, foreign and interstate commerce, and immigration and naturalization—that the Confederation's government had lacked. In addition to these enumerated powers, which strengthened the national government vis-à-vis the states in foreign as well as domestic affairs, the Constitution's necessary-and-proper clause (Art. 1, Sec. 8, Cl. 18) would later provide a fecund source of national power. The Tenth Amendment to the Constitution to the contrary notwithstanding, the federal judiciary's broad reading of the necessary-and-proper clause along with the Constitution's affirmative grants of power to the national government and the supremacy clause (Art. 6, Cl. 2) would subsequently promote centralized national power in war, foreign affairs, and domestic policymaking.

In domestic affairs, the Framers vested the national government's affirmative grants of power in Congress rather than in the President. The Framers did not, however, vest unlimited power in Congress. In addition to delegating enumerated and implied powers to Congress, they prohibited the legislature from exercising such specific powers as taxing exports, passing bills of attainder and ex post facto laws, and granting titles of nobility. These and other limitations on legislative power reflect the Framers' distrust of unlimited congressional power. In recent debates on the exercise of presidential authority to control foreign affairs and command the nation's armed forces, partisans of both unlimited congressional and presidential power seem to have forgotten that the Framers suspected all governmental power.

If the Framers suspected legislative power, they distrusted executive power. Motivated by their recent colonial history and Whig criticism of the Stuart kings, they denied the President most of the prerogatives that the Stuarts had exercised. The absolute royal veto was reduced to a conditional veto that Congress could override. The sovereign's inherent and exclusive power to conduct foreign affairs was shared with the Senate by requiring the President to seek senatorial advice and consent in making treaties and appointing diplomatic personnel. The President, however, retained the exclusive power to receive foreign ambassadors and ministers and, thereby, the implicit right to recognize other nations.

In addition to dividing and sharing power over foreign affairs, the Framers also divided the war and defensive powers between Congress and the President so that it would be more difficult to make war than to conclude peace.[57] While the Constitution makes the President commander in chief of the nation's armed forces, it grants Congress power to "provide for the common Defence," "declare War, grant Letters of Marque and Reprisal, and make Rules concerning Captures on Land and Water," "raise and support Armies," "provide and maintain a Navy," "make Rules for the Government and Regulation of the land and naval Forces," "provide for calling forth the militia to execute the laws of the Union, suppress insurrections, and repel invasions," and "provide for organizing, arming, and disciplining the Militia."[58] While the President is civilian commander in chief, there is considerable debate about his constitutional authority to commit the nation to foreign wars.[59] The nation's first general and first admiral has the responsibility to repel sudden attacks on the nation's territory and armed forces, protect citizens' lives and property, supervise military strategy, and superintend the armed forces that Congress provides, but the Framers did not envision the President's committing troops to foreign wars without prior congressional consent.

In contrast to the specific legislative powers that the Constitution vests in Congress and in contrast to the checks and balances that it places on the President's war, veto, and foreign-affairs powers, the Constitution's authors failed to define the executive power vested in the President. By defining executive power broadly and by wedding the commander in chief clause to the take-care clause, such aggressive presidents as Lincoln, Wilson, the two Roosevelts, Johnson, and Nixon have converted the Constitution's silence on the meaning of executive power into a claim for unlimited executive power to make foreign and military policy. It is difficult to believe that the Framers, who suspected power, opposed tyranny, advocated liberty, and labored to limit royal prerogative, would accept such a view of executive power. Despite the Constitution's textual silence, one of its principal authors and leading advocates, James Madison, expressed his opposition to both unlimited executive and legislative power:

> In a government where numerous and extensive prerogatives are placed in the hands of an hereditary monarch, the executive department is very justly regarded as the source of danger, and

watched with all the jealousy which a zeal for liberty ought to inspire. . . . But in a representative republic, where the executive magistracy is carefully limited, both in the extent and duration of its power, . . . it is against the enterprising ambition of [the legislature] that the people ought to indulge all their jealousy and exhaust all their precautions.[60]

Even Alexander Hamilton, a forceful advocate of a strong and energetic executive, admitted the need to limit presidential power. According to Hamilton, the Constitution solved the problem by balancing the need for an energetic executive against " . . . other ingredients which constitute safety in the republican sense[.]"[61] Thus, Hamilton, Madison, Charles Pinckney, and the other Framers who expressed their views on the presidency defined executive power in a limited sense as the administration of government. Unlike the British Crown, which exercises prerogative, (1) the President has an obligation to remain within the Constitution's limits in exercising his powers, (2) has an obligation to execute law, and (3) within these limits the President may exercise discretion in carrying out the law and constitutional commands.[62] In the United States, executive power is basically discretionary within the limits of the law and the Constitution.[63]

As another means of limiting legislative and executive power, balancing and adjusting competing claims of power, and promoting constitutional government, Hamilton, Madison, and Charles Pinckney favored creating an independent judiciary. Or, as Hamilton stated the case in the seventy-eighth *Federalist*, "The complete independence of the courts of justice is peculiarly essential in a limited Constitution."[64] By a limited Constitution, Hamilton meant a governmental system that limits legislative and executive power. The potential for the abuse of power was so great, the Framers apparently believed, that neither the separation of powers nor legislative and executive checks and balances could adequately protect constitutional government and political liberty. " '[T] here is no liberty,' " Hamilton approvingly quoted Montesquieu, " 'if the power of judging be not separated from the legislative and executive powers.' "[65]

The Framers' creation of an independent judiciary represents a significant contribution to eighteenth-century constitutionalism. Unlike British constitutionalism, which by the 1790s relied upon parliamentary self-restraint and ministerial responsibility, the U.S. model accepts the legitimacy of judicial restraint on governmental power and popular sovereignty.[66] Beyond these yeoman tasks, some of the Framers expected the federal judiciary to resolve competing claims of executive and legislative power. By adjusting and balancing competing claims, the judiciary would also contribute to the general equilibrium upon which the American constitutional model rests. Thus, the Framers regarded the judiciary as a guardian of constitutional government.

American constitutional government is a product of seventeenth- and eighteenth-century political thought and struggle. As eighteenth-century liberals, the Framers relied on balanced government and the separation of powers to promote liberty. The Constitution's authors apparently believed that by separating and balancing governmental power, they could prevent arbitrary and capricious government. While the Framers' philosophical commitment to liberty explains their reliance on balanced government and the separation of powers, the logic of separating the congressional war powers from the constitutional office of commander in chief lies in the British development of prerogative power and the subsequent American reaction to and rejection of theories that emergencies justify the exercise of extraordinary power beyond the Constitution and standing laws, particularly in times of war and hostilities.

SEPARATING AND SHARING POWER: THE CONGRESSIONAL WAR POWERS AND THE COMMANDER IN CHIEF

Unlike some European nations such as the German and the Austro-Hungarian empires, in the Anglo-American political systems, the commencement and conduct of war do not imply the displacement of civilian with military government and martial law. By commencing war, therefore, the executive does not assume the powers of an emperor or "general-king." [67] The executive may make (conduct) war, but war does not make the executive an absolute monarch whose conduct is beyond the Constitution and the standing law. The contemporary Anglo-American view represents a taming or domestication of prerogative, which began in England during the seventeenth century.

British Theory and Practice
In his *Commentaries on the Laws of England* (1765), Sir William Blackstone noted that in foreign affairs, prerogative includes the plenary or exclusive powers of sending and receiving ambassadors, which implies the power to recognize and withdraw recognition from foreign states. [68] "It is also the king's prerogative," continued Blackstone, "to make treaties, leagues, and alliances with foreign states and princes." [69] In other

words, since sovereign power is vested in the King, he alone has the power to bind the whole community to international agreements. Should the King's judgment regarding the national interest be incorrect, the only parliamentary checks on the abuse of royal prerogative are the powers to impeach and remove the King's ministers who have led the sovereign astray.[70]

Royal prerogative also includes "the sole prerogative of making war and peace."[71] Only the King, as sovereign, can commit the whole community to public war.[72] In the eighteenth century, as Blackstone emphasized, a major purpose of declaring war was to inform the nation as well as other sovereigns that, henceforth, the people are called to a higher duty and sacrifice than at other times in their national existence. In addition to authorizing public war, the sovereign has exclusive power to grant letters of marque and reprisal, i.e., to authorize private measures against piracy and other depredations against commerce and navigation.[73] By implication, the power to commence public war and to authorize measures short of public war includes the power to terminate war and hostilities. The only checks on "improper or inglorious conduct, in beginning, conducting, or concluding a national war" are Parliament's powers to impeach and remove the Crown's errant ministers.[74]

As sovereign, the King has the power to conduct war as well as the power to determine foreign and military policy. "The king is considered," writes Blackstone, " . . . as the generalissimo, or the first in military command, within the kingdom."[75] As the nation's first general and first admiral, the King is responsible for raising and regulating the army and navy, conscripting and governing the armed forces, commanding the militia, and constructing, manning, and governing military installations.[76] To assure the revenues necessary for naval defense, the King has the power to license ports and harbors.[77] Although Blackstone includes the power to embargo arms and ammunition among the King's prerogatives, this power can be traced to two parliamentary statutes (12 Car. II, c. 4 and 29 Geo. II, c. 16). The King also can prevent his subjects from leaving the realm to escape their military obligations and can require their return to defend the nation against invasion.[78] In other words, royal prerogative includes all the powers necessary to protect the national security and to wage war successfully.

Although Blackstone recognized the broad scope of prerogative vested in the Crown, he was well aware of the successful parliamentary struggles against Charles I (1625–1649), Charles II (1660–1685), and James II (1685–1688), which had resulted in limiting and domesticating royal prerogative. Indeed, as early as the middle of the fourteenth century Parliament had begun limiting the royal war powers. Under Ed-

ward I (1272–1307), in the Confirmation of the Charters (1297), the
Crown first recognized parliamentary power to tax and appropriate
money.[79] The first specific parliamentary tax and appropriation for war,
along with an audit of the King's account books, occurred in 1353, but
exclusive parliamentary right to control such appropriations remained
in doubt until the seventeenth century.[80]

Charles I's struggle and failure to obtain funds to wage war in 1626
led to the Petition of Right (1628), which denied the sovereign's power
to tax without parliamentary consent.[81] In 1665 Parliament first speci-
fied how tax monies were to be spent. That same year Parliament began
voting annual military appropriations, which increased parliamentary
control over the standing army.[82] In 1678 Parliament reduced severely
a military-appropriations request and in 1679 voted a special appropriation to disband the army.[83] Both measures were intended to veto or
nullify the King's power as commander in chief. The Bill of Rights
(1688), which reaffirmed parliamentary control over the purse, represented another important limitation on royal prerogative.[84]

In addition to gaining the power of the purse, by the eighteenth century Parliament secured the right to oversee the military. Although the
Crown theoretically retained command over the army, Parliament had
the power to grant and abolish military commissions. During the War of
the Spanish Succession (1702) the King lost personal command of the
army to Lord Marlborough, who was made captain general. After 1714
the Cabinet Council became the captain general's source of authority.[85]
Thus, well before Blackstone's first volume of the *Commentaries* appeared in 1765, Parliament had restricted the scope of royal prerogative to determine and conduct war.

Within these limits, the British theory of prerogative in war and foreign affairs, nonetheless, means that the Crown retains residual power
to act in the national interest in the face of emergency. Although the
executive did not have power to dispense with or suspend law under the
eighteenth-century British Constitution, the standing laws left the executive considerable plenary power in war and foreign affairs. In an
address to the House of Lords (1766), Lord Mansfield summarized the
Whig view of prerogative as "that share of the government which, by
the constitution, is vested in the king alone."[86]

Although Mansfield argues that the exercise of prerogative represents a public trust whose limits are the public good or interest,[87] in war
and foreign affairs, he accepts Blackstone's enumeration of plenary
powers including the power to determine war and peace.[88] Insofar as
the standing laws do not limit the sovereign's conduct, he has discretion
to act to preserve the national security. Internationally, the only restric-

tions on the sovereign's powers are the law and practice of nations. Domestically, Mansfield relies on parliamentary powers to impeach and remove the King's errant ministers as an effective restraint on plenary power that is beyond the standing law's reach.[89]

American Theory and Practice

Despite the British Whigs' efforts to domesticate royal prerogative, American constitutionalists adopted a more limited concept of executive power, which, as Raoul Berger comments, is a postrevolutionary term virtually unknown in British and colonial history.[90] Indeed, the term "executive power" represents a repudiation of the theory of prerogative or inherent, extraconstitutional power to preserve the nation against external threat. Or, as Justice Davis noted in *Ex parte Milligan* (1866), " . . . the government, within the Constitution, has all the powers granted to it which are necessary to preserve its existence, . . . "[91] In contrast to British constitutional theory, which vests an undefined residue of power in the Crown, American constitutional theory presumes that the Constitution's broad, affirmative grants of power to the national government are adequate in confronting all emergencies, in times of war and times of peace.

Congressional primacy in war and foreign affairs under the Articles of Confederation also belies the argument that inherent, prerogative, or sovereign power devolved from the British Crown to the President of the United States in an unbroken chain of events between 1776 and 1789. Under the Articles of Confederation, the powers of war and foreign affairs were vested in Congress.[92] Article 9 vested "the sole and exclusive right and power of determining on peace and war" in Congress, except that (under Article 6) the states retained the power to respond to sudden attack or when the danger of such attack was imminent. In addition to determining war and peace, Congress had the power to appoint and receive ambassadors, enter into treaties and alliances, determine rules on captures and prizes, grant letters of marque and reprisal, establish courts for trying piracy and maritime crimes, appoint army officers above the rank of major, appoint all naval officers, commission all officers in the U.S. military service, make rules for governing and regulating the land and naval forces, and direct military operations.[93]

Congressional power to wage war, however, was actually limited by the states' retention of fiscal powers, i.e., the powers to tax and supply funds to the Confederation's treasury. During congressional recesses, a Committee of the States had the power to ascertain the funds necessary to defray public expenditures, but the states retained the powers to tax and arm, equip, and supply troops.[94] Theoretically, the committee was authorized to "build and equip a navy," determine "the number of land forces," "make requisitions from each state for its quota" of forces, and direct such forces to assemble for the Confederation's defense.[95] Similarly, the Articles empowered the committee to borrow on the credit of the United States, but the national credit rating depended on the states' behaving in a fiscally responsible way toward the Confederation.

These limited powers of war and foreign affairs were further qualified by the requirement that:

> The united states in congress assembled shall never engage in a war, nor grant letters of marque and reprisal in time of peace, nor enter into any treaties or alliances, . . . nor ascertain the sums and expences necessary for the defense and welfare of the united states, . . . nor borrow money on the credit of the united states, nor appropriate money, nor agree upon the number of vessels of war, to be built or purchased, or the number of land or sea forces to be raised, nor appoint a commander in chief of the army or navy, unless nine states assent to the same. . . .[96]

In other words, nine states' congressional representatives were empowered to call upon their respective states to support congressional recommendations concerning war and peace. Congressional power to make recommendations to the states concerning war and peace hardly represents the exercise of inherent, plenary, sovereign or any other governmental power. The Articles of Confederation constitute a broken link in the mystical chain of events between the American Revolution and the Federal Convention.[97]

Whether one concludes that the United States was born in the twinkling of an eye in a revolutionary moment or that the states retained their international sovereignty under the Articles of Confederation,[98] there is no evidence to suggest that American constitutionalists equated "executive power" with the British Crown's prerogatives of war and peace.[99] Neither the state governments nor the Confederation government exercised an undefined residual power to determine war, conduct hostilities, and conclude peace. Under the Articles no such power was vested in Congress or its Committee of the States. As a plural executive, with something like ministerial responsibility to Congress, the Committee of the States had only qualified powers of war and peace. In 1775, the Second Continental Congress had delegated the powers of military command to General George Washington. Prior to and under the Articles of Confederation, General Washington held his commission as commander in chief from Congress. Between 1775 and 1783, when he returned his commission to Congress, Washington conducted the Revolutionary War according to congressional direction.[100] Whatever war powers the Confederation government possessed were vested in Congress.

The Articles of Confederation were a defensive alliance accepted by the states during the Revolutionary War, when most men viewed themselves as Virginians, Pennsylvanians or New Yorkers rather than as Americans. At the time the Articles were drafted and accepted by the states there was little feeling of national consciousness. The idea of a national state, of Americanism, was emerging, but would not be realized for some time.[101] When compared to abstract constitutional theories of national sovereignty, which are more relevant to nineteenth-century than eighteenth-century constitutional and political thought, the individual states represented a concrete reality that their citizens could understand, and with which they could identify. In an age with rudimentary communications and transportation systems, one should not be surprised that the generation of the 1770s and the 1780s expected the states to respond first to external threats to their security and newly acquired independence.

The Articles of Confederation represented a first, uncertain attempt at limited self-government whose principal purpose was securing the states against foreign invasion. The Articles' principal defect was the states' refusal to surrender adequate powers to the Confederation over war, foreign affairs, and fiscal policy, i.e., the powers necessary to maintain the states' survival in the international community. Besides ignoring congressional requests for money, Virginia, for example, ratified a treaty with France, concluded a loan with Spain, and pledged its credit to purchase arms. Other states laid embargoes, fitted out navies, authorized privateers, drafted armies, and negotiated with the Indian tribes.[102] The Articles of Confederation established an organization of thirteen states, but a fourteenth state, the United States, did not exist since the states retained their sovereignty.[103]

During the 1780s, the defects of the Articles became increasingly obvious to leading politicians, statesmen, and Revolutionary War heroes. Robert Morris, Alexander Hamilton, James Wilson, Edmund Randolph, Richard Henry Lee, James Madison, and Thomas Jefferson were aware of the Confederation's lack of domestic power vis-à-vis the states, which vitiated its sovereignty in external affairs.[104] Governor John Hancock of Massachusetts concluded that the Confederation had to be strengthened.[105] The fear of disunion, as Charles Warren writes, prompted George Washington to reply to a letter from John Jay in July 1786:

> Your sentiments that our affairs are drawing rapidly to a crisis accord with my own. . . . I do not conceive we can exist long as a nation without having lodged somewhere a power, which will pervade the whole Union in as energetic a manner as the authority of the State Governments extends over the several States. . . . requisitions are a perfect nullity where thirteen sovereign, independent, disunited States are in the habit of discussing and refusing compliance with them at their option. Requisitions are actually little better than a jest and a byword throughout the land. If you tell the Legislatures they have violated the treaty of peace [of 1783 with Great Britian] and invaded the prerogatives of the confederacy, they will laugh in your face.[106]

Jay and Washington feared, of course, that the people, especially "the better kind of people, . . . who are orderly and industrious, who are content with their situations, and not uneasy in their circumstances, . . . "[107] would surrender their liberty to obtain domestic order and international security. Jay and Washington feared that the people, in their anxiety, would restore monarchical government.[108]

In contrast to these concerns about national power, the Articles' failure to provide for a single executive with independent tenure who would conduct military and foreign policy was not generally viewed as an irremediable defect. In fact, Congress had begun to establish committees, commissions, and departments that were directly responsible to the legislature. As early as June 12, 1776, Congress had established a Board of War Ordinance to superintend the military's provisioning and maintenance.[109] Under the Articles, Congress was beginning to develop ministerial responsibility, not unlike the British system of cabinet government then evolving.[110]

If the executive was weak, Congress could easily have remedied the defect by establishing a cabinet, a single coordinating committee to supervise the government's administration.[111] Congressional criticism usually came from contemporary proponents of the separation of executive from legislative power such as Alexander Hamilton, who believed that national power, particularly in foreign affairs, should be focused in an independent executive ministry.[112] While Hamilton argued for executive independence in formulating and conducting foreign policy, he believed that Congress should control the military.[113] Although Hamilton probably overstated congressional administrative weakness, he recognized that the Articles' basic flaw was the relationship between Congress and the states.[114] In any event, alleged congressional inadequacies under the Articles of Confederation did not suggest the need to reestablish a monarchy with prerogatives of war and peace.

Recognizing these problems, a congressional committee headed by Charles Pinckney recommended (on August 7, 1786) calling a convention to amend the Articles, but no subsequent action was taken because Virginia called for a meeting in September at Annapolis.[115] When representatives of all the states failed to appear, the Annapolis Convention adjourned, issuing a report that called on the states to send commissioners to meet in Philadelphia on the second Monday in May 1787.[116] The compelling need to revise the Articles was strengthened by Shays' Rebellion, a popular insurrection that occurred in Massachusetts between September 1786 and February 1787.[117] The writings of General Henry Knox, George Washington, John Marshall, and James Madison reflect the contemporary fears of disunion and domestic strife. Writing in his diary on February 21, 1787, Madison commented, "All [members of Congress] agreed and owned that the Federal government, in its existing shape, was inefficient and could not last long."[118]

The Constitutional Convention, which deliberated almost continuously from May 25 to September 17, 1787, confronted three major problems. First, how could the delegates create a national government without imperiling the states' existence? Their solution represented a delicate exercise in transferring governmental power from the states to the national government by asserting that sovereign authority resides in the people who happen to be organized into states.[119] Second, how could the delegates restrain the national government's authority so that it could not exercise its powers over war and foreign affairs arbitrarily, which, inevitably, would threaten liberty? The delegates' solution involved well-known constitutional limitations on all governmental power, separating national governmental institutions, and checks and balances. Third, how could the delegates create an independent executive without vitiating congressional power?

As the Convention developed, the delegates' solution to the problem of executive power took shape. Their creation of a unitary executive with independent tenure who shared limited power over war and foreign affairs with Congress reflected the Framers' general fear of governmental power and their particular fear of prerogative. Anyone who studies the Convention's proceedings, wrote Harold Laski, is struck by the Framers' fear of executive despotism.[120] Anyone who studies these proceedings is also struck by the Framers' fear of legislative and judicial despotism.[121] Indeed, the very delegation of governmental power by a sovereign people creates the potential for despotism. The Framers were, after all, eighteenth-century liberals who believed that in a republic the best way to preserve liberty is by countering vice with vice, power with power, and ambition with ambition.[122]

2

The Constitutional Framework

INTERPRETING THE CONSTITUTION OF 1787

Interpreting the constitutional separation of the congressional war powers from the presidential office of commander in chief is a difficult art that requires the skills of a historian, constitutional lawyer, political scientist, social psychologist, and the Oracle of Apollo at Delphi. Although some scholars interpret the Constitution with the binding precision of a life-insurance contract or a municipal-housing code, others argue that its vague language is virtually irrelevant in confronting contemporary problems of war and peace.[1] Between the logical certainty of Scylla and the crude pragmatism of Charybdis one can chart a more rational course, however. The Constitution is a general charter of government whose broad divisions of power lack the precision of either a municipal code or the law of contracts. Its general commands, therefore, require patient analysis of contemporaneous sources as well as an appreciation of the Framers' intellectual milieu.

The constitutional scholar must confront, evaluate, and weigh the evidence in a manner that gives positive effect to the Framers' broad purpose and does not make their work a nullity. In interpreting the separation of the congressional war powers from the presidential office of commander in chief, the scholar's task is complicated by the fact that the Framers were concerned primarily with the distribution of power between the state and national governments rather than the separation and sharing of legislative and executive powers. The fragmentary evidence available suggests that the Framers attempted to make Congress more effective vis-à-vis the states than it had been under the Articles of Confederation so that the national government could discharge its international responsibilities.[2] Their fears of executive military power, for example, were motivated largely by expectations of domestic tyranny rather than engagement in foreign military adventures. Some antifederalists also feared that an aggressive president would engage the nation in foreign military adventures in order to aggrandize his office and powers.[3] Nonetheless, it is difficult to project the Framers' conceptions of the eighteenth-century international system onto the twentieth century, in which inchoate international security concerns have displaced limited, defensive territorial preoccupations.

In addition to the fact that the distribution of power between Congress and the President was not the convention's primary focus, the fragmentary nature of the evidence compounds the task of interpreting the Constitution's meaning and the Framers' intent. As the fragmentary record of the Federal Convention's secret proceedings indicates, the delegates often disagreed on important constitutional provisions. While Pierce Butler of South Carolina, for example, favored "vesting the [war] power in the President," Elbridge Gerry of Massachusetts strenuously objected, arguing that he "never expected to hear in a republic a motion to empower the Executive alone to declare war."[4] Aside from Butler and Gerry, only Charles Pinckney, James Madison, Roger Sherman, Oliver Ellsworth, and George Mason expressed cursory views before the states voted (8–1) to vest the power to declare war in Congress while leaving the President the power to repel sudden attacks.[5] The *Record* is fragmentary precisely because it preserves the Convention's official actions rather than the delegates' views on the many compromises to which they agreed in order to resolve their differences.

The evidence also suggests, notes W. Taylor Reveley, " . . . that the Framers may have drafted the Constitution with a measure of deliberate ambiguity,"[6] which reflects the difficulty of allocating the war powers precisely between Congress and the President. The Framers were also more interested in stating governmental principles than in drafting "detailed codes." "[T]he Constitutional Fathers," Reveley writes, "were practical men, and their laconic drafting technique no doubt reflected awareness of the difficulty of laying down rules to govern situations whose dimensions were at best dimly grasped."[7] As practical men, they realized that experience rather than abstract logic would embody the Constitution. Indeed, they anticipated that struggle between Congress and the President would define the boundaries of legislative and exec-

utive power. A cynical observer might conclude that the Framers deliberately employed ambiguity as a technique of compromise to dissolve
seemingly irreconcilable conflicts, to reduce differences of principle to
matters of interest. Or, as Gouverneur Morris later wrote, "[I]t became
necessary to select phrases which, expressing my own notions, would
not alarm others. . . ."[8]

In attempting to construe the Framers' intent or the Constitution's
meaning, one should remember that the presidency was a new institution that did not exist prior to the Constitution. Although some of the
Framers argued for a strong, energetic executive, few envisioned that
the presidency would become the engine of an interventionist foreign
policy that would rely on exercising global military power. In 1787–
1788, the war powers were viewed as the defensive powers of a new
nation attempting to disengage itself from European conflicts. At most,
the new nation would require a small standing army of several thousand
professional soldiers, a militia on its northern and western frontiers, and
a coastal navy to protect American commerce and navigation in the
Atlantic and the Caribbean. The Framers simply did not envision a
large standing army in their midst. Given their inability to predict future contingencies and their primary concern with the states' exercising
war and foreign-affairs powers under the Articles, the Framers left
many questions of presidential-congressional relations to be settled in
practice, through the inevitable conflicts that the separation and sharing
of legislative and executive powers would generate.

Ambiguity and parsimony characterize the Constitution's broad affirmative grants of power to Congress and the President over war, defense, and foreign affairs. There is no clear, exclusive textual commitment of all the war, defense, and foreign-affairs powers to either
Congress or the President. Rather, these powers are anchored in a constitutional system that fragments governmental power. While the records of the Federal Convention and the state ratifying conventions as
well as contemporaneous writings and commentaries are important in
interpreting the Framers' intentions, these materials are more useful in
describing the conflicting views of the Constitution's authors, advocates,
and opponents than in reconciling their conflicts. The fragmentary record also warrants a generous rather than a niggardly interpretation of
the Constitution's text and the Framers' intentions. Such a rule of construction neither ignores the existence of a written constitution nor
treats it as the ark of the convenant. Insofar as one can construe the
Framers' intent, it is relevant in interpreting the constitutional text
when confronting contemporary problems of war and peace.

THE POWER TO DECLARE WAR UNDER THE CONSTITUTION OF 1787

In direct contrast to the Articles of Confederation, under which the government's limited war powers were vested exclusively in Congress, the Framers deliberately divided the national government's war and defense powers between Congress and the President. Their division of the congressional war powers from the presidential office of commander in chief rests on a fundamental distinction between offensive and defensive war and hostilities. Only Congress can change the nation's condition from one of peace to war, but the President, as civilian commander in chief, can repel sudden attacks on U.S. territory, the nation's armed forces, and its public ships at sea. The President can also employ the armed forces to protect citizens' lives and property.[9] The Framers did not specify, however, how far the President could go in resisting military threats to national security and independence.

The fundamental distinction between offensive and defensive war and hostilities appears in the convention's proceedings. In the draft that the convention referred to its Committee of Detail, the power "[t]o make war" was vested exclusively in Congress. As commander in chief of the armed forces, including the militia, the President was authorized "to direct their discipline" and direct the states' executives to call their respective militias into the national service.[10] The report of the Committee of Detail (on August 6, 1787) contains similar language, vesting the power "[t]o make war" in Congress[11] and making the President "commander in chief of the Army and Navy of the United States, and of the Militia of the Several States."[12] On Friday, August 17, a motion was offered " . . . to strike out the word 'make' and to insert the word 'declare' . . ." in the clause vesting the war power in Congress. Although the motion was at first defeated (5–4), on a second ballot immediately thereafter the delegates accepted the substitution (8–1).[13]

In the debate that preceded the vote on August 17, the rationale for the distinction between "make" and "declare" war is evident. Charles Pinckney apparently believed that Congress would be "too slow" in responding to sudden attacks on the United States. According to Madison's *Notes*:

> Mr. Pinkney opposed the vesting [of] this power in the Legislature. Its proceedings were too slow. It would meet but once a year. The House of Representatives would be too numerous for such deliberations. The Senate would be the best depository, being more acquainted with foreign affairs, and most capable of

proper resolutions. If the States are equally represented in [the] Senate, so as to give no advantage to large States, the power will notwithstanding be safe, as the small have their all at stake in such cases as well as the large States. It would be singular for one—authority to make war, and another peace.[14]

In contrast to Pinckney's confidence in the Senate to "make war," Pierce Butler's objections to vesting this power in the legislature were directed toward the Senate rather than the House of Representatives. Butler " . . . was for vesting the power in the President, who will have all the requisite qualities, and will not make war but when the Nation will support it."[15]

At this point in the debate, Madison and Gerry offered a compromise, moving to " . . . insert 'declare,' striking out 'make' war; leaving to the Executive the power to repel sudden attacks." While Gerry adamantly opposed giving the President alone the power to declare war, Roger Sherman thought the original motion "stood very well." "The Executive," Sherman concluded, "should be able to repel and not to commence war." He believed that the term "make" was better than "declare," however, since the latter was too restrictive.[16] As the debate continued, it became apparent that the substitution of "declare" for "make" war was not designed to subtly transfer the power of commencing war from Congress to the President. Both Oliver Ellsworth and George Mason, for example, expressed the view that it should be more difficult to commence war than to conclude peace. Immediately before voting, Mason expressed his opposition to vesting the war power in the President because he could not be safely "trusted with it," or to the Senate alone, which was not entitled to exercise such power. Mason was " . . . for clogging rather than facilitating war; but for facilitating peace." Therefore, "He preferred 'declare' to 'make'."[17]

Responding to Ellsworth's objections to substituting "declare" for "make" war, Rufus King further clarified the amendment's purpose. The term " . . . 'make' war might be understood to [be] 'conduct' it which was an Executive function, . . . "[18] At this point, Ellsworth apparently gave up his objection to the substitution. The motion was then carried eight to one.

As Madison's parsimonious account of the debate indicates, there was considerable animated disagreement on vesting the power to declare war in Congress. Nonetheless, the fragmentary record warrants several conclusions. Only one delegate who expressed his views on the subject, Pierce Butler, favored vesting the power to commence war exclusively in the President. The stylistic change from "make" to "declare" was intended to allow the President, as commander in chief, to respond to sudden attacks rather than to commence offensive war. Insofar as the Framers intended to vest *any* war powers in the President, these powers were defensive. Declaring or commencing offensive war is a fundamental decision that requires consensus between Congress and the President as well as broad popular support, or so the Framers apparently believed. Their laconic language, however, defines neither the scope of presidential authority in ordering defensive measures nor the point at which defensive measures become offensive warfare.

By adopting this stylistic change, the Framers also attempted to avoid potential confusion about presidential power to conduct military operations. Once Congress publicly declares war or authorizes hostilities short of war, the President, as commander in chief, is responsible for the actual conduct of any war or hostilities that Congress has previously authorized. Within the limits of congressional legislative power (in Article 1, Section 8), the President assumes command of whatever armed forces Congress places at his disposal. Obviously, the distinction between the commencement and conduct of war and hostilities is not a neat, logical dichotomy. An aggressive President can pursue a foreign policy that presents Congress with a military *fait accompli* while a contentious Congress can interfere with the President's effective and efficient conduct of military operations.[19]

Although the separation of congressional war powers from the President's office of commander in chief rests on the Framers' distinction between offensive and defensive war, some contemporary scholars argue that below the threshold of a declared war, which is governed by the declaration-of-war clause (Art. 1, Sec. 8, Cl. 11), the President has power to commit armed forces unilaterally to material war, i.e., to de facto war or military hostilities below this threshold. The Framers understood the distinction between declared and material war, which is an important one in international law since a declaration of war authorizes measures (e.g., blockade) that affect the rights and obligations of neutrals and belligerents. In addition to recognizing the legal and theoretical distinctions between declared and material war, the Framers had experienced undeclared, limited or imperfect wars, i.e., hostilities below the threshold of publicly declared war. Prior to 1787 there were numerous undeclared wars and military hostilities fought among the European powers, some of which had involved the North American colonies. In 1754, for example, George Washington commanded Virginian troops, under the British, against the French. Indeed, the French defeated Washington on July 3, 1754 at Great Meadows in the Ohio Valley.

These hostilities, leading to the Seven Years War (1756–1763), were conducted without a declaration of war.[20]

Despite their familiarity with undeclared war and military hostilities below the threshold of declared war, the Constitution's authors did not provide for presidential commitment of the nation's armed forces to war, whether declared or material, other than recognizing presidential power or responsibility to repel sudden attacks.[21] In fact, the Constitution (Art. 1, Sec. 8, Cl. 11) specifically vests the power to grant letters of marque and reprisal in Congress. By vesting this power in Congress, the Framers recognized congressional power to determine the use of limited force against other nations to redress grievances. From this grant of power, one can infer that the Framers intended to vest limited as well as general war-making power in Congress rather than the President.

The Constitution also vests the power to "make Rules concerning Captures on Land and Water" in Congress (Art. 1, Sec. 8, Cl. 11). Thus, Congress can authorize U.S. public and private ships to take prizes at sea and can provide for their condemnation in domestic courts. During 1798–1799 Congress passed more than twenty laws authorizing limited naval war with France,[22] including the taking of prizes under certain conditions. In *Bas* v. *Tingy*, which sustained these seizures, Justice Bushrod Washington distinguished between declared (perfect) and limited (imperfect) war. Justice Washington also recognized congressional power to authorize declared or general war and authorize and control limited war.[23] In a second concurring opinion, Justice Chase commented:

> Congress is empowered to declare a general war, or congress may wage a limited war; limited in place, in objects, and in time. If a general war is declared, its extent and operations are only restricted and regulated by the *jus belli*, forming a part of the law of nations; but if a partial [war] is waged, its extent and operation depend on our municipal laws.[24]

In a separate concurring opinion, Justice Patterson sustained the congressional power to regulate the scope of a limited war, writing, "As far as Congress tolerated and authorized the war on our part, so far may we proceed in hostile operations." The naval war with France, Patterson concluded, was a limited war " . . . qualified, on our part, in the manner prescribed by the constitutional organ of our country."[25]

In contrast to a limited war, when Congress declares war, the international law of war, the *jus belli*, as well as domestic statutes limit the subsequent conduct of war. If Congress authorizes measures below this threshold, these authorizations limit the scope, intensity, and duration of subsequent hostilities.[26] In the absence of any congressional action below the threshold, however, is the President free to act, to commit the nation to military hostilities or limited, undeclared wars? Does the President have the constitutional power to commit U.S. armed forces to combat when an ally's security interests are jeopardized? As commander in chief, can the President make executive agreements to defend allies against future threats to their security in exchange for the right to station U.S. armed forces in another nation's territory? In other words, below the threshold of a declaration of war, can the President infer prerogative or plenary power from congressional silence?

When the President acts in the face of congressional legislation to the contrary, such action poses a clear confrontation to Congress and violates the constitutional separation of powers. In the absence of congressional legislation to the contrary, however, presidential commitment of armed forces to offensive military hostilities or limited war poses a similar threat to the separation of powers.[27] Inasmuch as these powers are vested in Congress, congressional failure to exercise constitutional power does not confer it on the President. The decision to engage the nation in offensive hostilities or limited war is a congressional decision. Any other conclusion would vitiate the separation of powers and justify the exercise of presidential prerogative.

If there is any doubt about the exclusive textual commitment of offensive war powers to Congress, the doubt arises from the difficulty of distinguishing between offensive and defensive war and hostilities as well as determining the scope of permissible defensive measures necessary to protect national-security interests. The lack of a clear-cut demarcation between offensive and defensive warfare was evident rather early in U.S. military history during the wars with the Barbary Powers (1801–1805). In his order dispatching a small U.S. naval squadron to protect American navigation and commerce in the Mediterranean against depredations, President Jefferson acknowledged the distinction between offensive and defensive war and hostilities.[28] Responding to the Bashaw of Tripoli's ultimatum to the United States, Jefferson reported to Congress on December 8, 1801:

> Unauthorized by the Constitution, without the sanction of Congress, to go beyond the line of defense, the vessel, being disabled from committing further hostilities, was liberated with its crew. The Legislature will doubtless consider whether, by authorizing measures of offense also, they will place our force on an equal

footing with that of its adversaries. I communicate all material information on this subject, that in the exercise of this important function confided by the Constitution to the Legislature exclusively their judgment may form itself on a knowledge and consideration of every circumstance of weight.[29]

Although Jefferson clearly paid deference to congressional power, there is considerable dispute about the actual scope of the naval measures that the President authorized in the nine months before requesting and receiving congressional authority.[30] Jefferson apparently began the now well-established pattern of post hoc communication with Congress, and Congress responded pliantly to presidential initiative.[31] Toward the end of the Barbary Wars, the U.S. consul, General William Eaton, led a military expedition against the Bey of Tripoli. Between March 8 and April 25, 1805, Eaton led a 6,000-man force from Alexandria, Egypt, almost 1,000 miles across the Libyan desert to Derna.[32] Eaton was largely responsible for planning and executing this aggressive military policy, but some evidence suggests that the Jefferson Administration approved of Eaton's plans.[33] In any event, General Eaton's military adventure concluded a defensive war on an offensive note.[34]

In the twentieth century, threats to national security, independence, and survival extend far beyond the limited territorial defense that the Framers contemplated. The development of strategic thermonuclear capabilities, including supersonic intercontinental delivery systems, has radically altered national defense requirements. Aside from blurring the line between offensive and defensive warfare, the loss of U.S. thermonuclear monopoly and, later, superiority as well as the diffusion of strategic-weapons systems have necessitated the creation of an extensive mutual-security alliance system. By the mid-1960s, the United States had entered into bilateral and multilateral agreements with forty-two other nations, which represented a minimum commitment to consult with these nations in the event of an attack or threat to their security. At the same time, the United States developed approximately 375 major military bases and 3,000 minor military installations in some sixty nations.[35] Furthermore, various Presidents entered into executive agreements such as the Spanish bases agreement, which involved a national commitment to defend Spain against external threats.[36]

While these alliances, agreements, and commitments reflect threats to national survival in the thermonuclear age, they also undermine the distinction upon which the Framers' separation of defensive from offensive war powers rests. The stationing of U.S. armed forces and sophisticated weapons in Western Europe, for example, increases their exposure to attack. In the event of an attack on a NATO ally such as the Federal Republic of Germany, U.S. armed forces may have little choice about responding to military hostilities.

Although Article 5 of the North Atlantic Treaty provides that an attack on one or more of the parties "shall be considered an attack against them all," the Treaty does not alter the constitutional relationship between Congress and the President, i.e., the allocation of offensive war powers to Congress and defensive powers to the President.[37] Nonetheless, the stationing of some 324,511 U.S. troops in Western Europe alters the President's responsibilities as commander in chief as well as his relation to Congress.[38] Through the treaty clause, the President and the Senate have transformed presidential power to defend the nation against attack into a power to defend inchoate national-security interests, including the security interests of allies.

Despite presidential assertions of power to initiate war and hostilities and congressional deference to the commander in chief, the Framers vested the power to declare or initiate war and hostilities exclusively in Congress. Analysis of the constitutional text, the convention's record, and contemporaneous views support the argument that the Framers deliberately limited the royal prerogative to initiate war. The Framers' intentions to the contrary, however, there is no clear-cut distinction between defensive and offensive warfare. In the twentieth century, extensive alliance systems, thermonuclear warfare, and supersonic delivery systems vitiate such eighteenth-century dichotomies.

THE AUXILIARY WAR POWERS UNDER THE CONSTITUTION OF 1787

In addition to granting Congress the power to declare war, the Constitution vests specific auxiliary or ancillary war powers in Congress. These affirmative grants of legislative power provide the national government with the means to wage war effectively. Compared with the Articles of Confederation, the Constitution permits the national government to exercise its auxiliary war powers directly on the people rather than through the states. Furthermore, the expansive or sweeping language of the necessary-and-proper clause (Art. 1, Sec. 8, Cl. 18) gives Congress broad, but not unlimited discretion in selecting the appropriate means or mode of carrying out the national government's various auxiliary war powers.

Several important factors explain the Framers' enumeration of the auxiliary war powers in Article 1. Although the Constitution's authors expected the President to be a vigorous national leader, they did not want to reestablish royal prerogative.[39] By specifically depriving the President of prerogatives in war and foreign affairs, prerogatives that had been enjoyed by the British Crown, and by specifically conferring these powers on Congress, the Framers left little doubt about the limits of executive power.[40] In separating presidential command of the armed forces from congressional power to provide such forces, as Elias Huzar writes, the Constitution attempts to avoid domestic military dictatorship. The Framers apparently believed that by separating the power of the purse (appropriations) from the power of the sword (military command), they could curb foreign military adventurism and domestic tyranny.[41]

Besides limiting executive power, the constitutional enumeration of the auxiliary war powers limits legislative power. Concerned with the possibility of a large standing army, the Framers restricted the Army's appropriations to no more than two years. Apparently, these fears did not extend to the Navy since there is no similar restriction on naval appropriations. Similarly, the Constitution's authors restricted the purposes for which the militia could be called into the Federal service ("to execute the Laws of the Union, suppress Insurrections and repel Invasions"). While the Framers expressed greater confidence in Congress than in the President by conferring these powers on the former rather than the latter, their confidence was prudently limited. Thus, congressional exercise of the auxiliary war powers is subject to constitutional limitations in times of war and peace.

Before evaluating each specific grant of the auxiliary war powers to Congress, several caveats are in order. First, the constitutional text vests these powers exclusively in Congress. Second, the auxiliary war powers are almost exclusively domestic or internal rather than external powers. Third, by exercising these powers, Congress controls the means—money, material, and manpower—necessary to defend the nation in peacetime, prepare for war, conduct military operations, and return the nation to peace. Fourth, Congress can delegate auxiliary war powers to the President within the same constitutional limitations that govern other domestic delegations. Fifth, the failure to delegate such powers to the executive does not confer constitutional power on the President by default. Broadly construed, but within constitutional limitations, the auxiliary war powers are adequate to meet national security needs without appealing to theories of inherent, prerogative, or sovereign power.

"The Founding Fathers," notes Elias Huzar, "had a great deal of confidence in the financial powers of Congress as an instrument for controlling the executive agencies of the Government."[42] Foremost among these financial or fiscal powers is the constitutional power to raise revenues "to pay the Debts and provide for the common Defence and general Welfare of the United States." Not unlike other important constitutional provisions, the general-welfare clause is subject to considerable debate. Narrowly construed, the general-welfare clause limits governmental expenditures to the specific grants of power that follow in the first article and elsewhere.[43] Broadly construed, the clause implies that the national government can tax and spend for purposes that extend beyond the legislative powers of Congress.[44] Whether one construes the general-welfare clause narrowly or broadly, the powers to tax and spend undoubtedly include the great national purposes of defense, peacetime military preparations, and the conduct of war and hostilities inasmuch as these objectives clearly fall within the first article's legislative ambit.

Some of the Framers so feared a large standing army in peacetime as a threat to liberty that, in addition to separating the government's purse from its sword, they favored limiting the Army's appropriations to two years. Elbridge Gerry was so strenuously opposed to a standing army that he urged limiting the Army's size in peacetime to two or three thousand men. On August 18, 1787, Gerry noted that:

> . . . there was [no] check against standing armies in time of peace. . . . He thought an army dangerous in time of peace and could never consent to a power to keep up an indefinite number. He proposed that there shall not be kept up in time of peace more than   thousand troops. His idea was that the blank should be filled with two or three thousand.[45]

While Gerry and Luther Martin moved to limit the standing army's size in peacetime, Hugh Williamson of North Carolina believed that George Mason's motion to restrict the Army's appropriation to two years was an adequate restriction on congressional power.[46] Despite such assurances, on August 20, Charles Pinckney proposed that " 'No troops shall be kept up in time of peace, but by consent of the Legislature' and that ' . . . no grant of money shall be made by the Legislature for supporting military Land forces, for more than one year at a time.' "[47] As Pinckney's attempt to assuage the foes of a strong executive indicates, they feared that the President would employ a standing army to establish a military dictatorship.

When the Committee of Eleven (or postponed matters) recommended to the convention on September 5 that appropriations for the Army be limited to two years, Gerry once again objected that this provision " . . . implied there was to be a standing army which he inveighed against as dangerous to liberty, . . . "[48] Although the committee also recommended that "No money shall be drawn from the Treasury but in consequence of appropriations made by law,"[49] apparently Gerry was not satisified with this further restriction on executive power. Near the end of the convention, on September 15, Gerry indicated that he would "withhold his name from the Constitution" citing, among other reasons, the congressional power to "raise armies and money without limit."[50]

Gerry, Martin, and James McHenry of Maryland remained implacably opposed to "unlimited" congressional power to raise and support armies. On November 29, 1787, Luther Martin addressed his objections to the Maryland legislature, arguing that

> . . . the Congress have also the power given them to raise and support *armies*, without *any limitation* as to *numbers*, and without any restriction in *time of peace*. Thus, Sir, this plan of government, instead of *guarding against a standing* army, that *engine* of *arbitrary* power, which has so *often* and so *successfully* been used for the *subversion* of freedom, has in *its formation* given it an *express* and *constitutional sanction*. . . .[51]

In answering these objections to vesting discretionary power in Congress to provide for the common defense and to raise and support armies, Alexander Hamilton wrote in the twenty-fifth *Federalist* (December 21, 1787) that without the power to anticipate threats to the national security

> . . . the United States would then exhibit the most extraordinary spectacle which the world has yet seen—that of a nation incapacitated by its Constitution to prepare for defence, before it was actually invaded.[52]

Encircled by hostile powers, the United States would have to rely on the states' militia to protect the nattional security. Although the militia had fought valiantly during the Revolution, it was not equal to a professional military force. Prudence dictated, Hamilton concluded, that the national government have the power to determine future threats to national security and the armed forces necessary to counter such threats.[53]

As for the danger to liberty posed by a standing army, Hamilton argued " . . . that it is better to hazard the abuse of confidence than to embarrass the government and endanger the public safety by impolitic restrictions on the legislative authority."[54] While Hamilton recognized the dangers that a standing army had posed to English liberty under Charles II and James II, he argued that the source of danger was royal prerogative rather than the standing army's existence. The English Bill of Rights, however, limited royal prerogative by prohibiting the King from maintaining a standing army in the kingdom without parliamentary consent. The new Constitution restricted executive power even further since Congress alone had the power to tax and appropriate funds for the Army (for no longer than two years), which, Hamilton argued, would encourage congressional accountability to the states and their citizens.[55] Hamilton also discounted the probability that a legislative-executive conspiracy could mature sufficiently to threaten liberty or create a military dictatorship:

> Schemes to subvert the liberties of a great community require time to mature them for execution. An army, so large as seriously to menace those liberties, could only be formed by progressive augmentation, which would suppose, not merely a temporary combination between the legislature and executive, but a continued conspiracy for a series of time.[56]

If all else failed, the separation of powers, of the community's purse from its sword, would protect society against a return to prerogative or the creation of military dictatorship.

Obviously the Framers believed that Congress would employ its fiscal powers to control the executive, avoid foreign military adventurism, and prevent domestic military dictatorship. Despite their disagreement on the desirability of vesting such broad powers in Congress, both Gerry and Hamilton viewed the congressional powers to tax and to spend for national defense, to raise and support armies, and, when necessary, to conduct war and hostilities as discretionary powers. By separating the government's fiscal powers from the power to conduct war, at least some of the Constitution's authors believed that they had reconciled the requirements of national security and domestic peace with the values of liberty and popular sovereignty. The separation of the community's purse from its sword is an integral feature of the separation of powers through which the Framers hoped to preserve constitutionalism.

The congressional power "To make Rules for the Government and Regulation of the land and naval Forces," also reflects the Framers' attempt to preserve constitutional government and protect national security. Although the original draft of the Constitution did not contain this clause, on August 18 it was added without comment. The language (of Art. 1, Sec. 8, Cl. 14) is virtually identical to the Articles of Confederation (Art. 9), which granted Congress the power of "making rules for the government and regulation of the said land and naval forces. . . ."[57] The power to make such rules, Justice Story later commented, " . . . is a natural incident to the preceding powers to make war, to raise armies, and to provide and maintain a navy."[58]

Originally, the powers to enlist, govern, organize, and discipline the army were part of the King's prerogative as generalissimo or first general.[59] Under Charles I, the Long Parliament had challenged this prerogative, but a later parliament recognized Charles II's exclusive power to govern and command the army.[60] As Parliament increased its powers over the standing army, it began to pass annual acts "to punish mutiny and desertion." Besides providing for the stationing of the army in England, the mutiny acts were the genesis of modern military law. In the early mutiny acts Parliament defined military crimes punishable by death and delegated power to enact articles of war or to determine lesser military offenses and to constitute courts-martial with powers to try military crimes.[61] While Blackstone, for example, recognized parliamentary right to delegate such vast powers to the Crown, he urged Parliament to enact specific articles of war in order to limit arbitrary power over the citizen-soldier. The military state (i.e., the army), he concluded, should not " . . . be reduced to a state of servitude in the midst of a nation of freemen!"[62]

While the Framers did not discuss including this clause (granting Congress the power to make rules for the regulation and government of the armed forces), they were familiar with the history of the British mutiny acts. Vesting this power in Congress was another means of limiting and distinguishing executive power from royal prerogative. The citizen-soldier does not enjoy the Fifth Amendment's protection of indictment by grand jury or the Sixth Amendment's right to a jury trial in criminal cases, but he does enjoy certain protections that Congress affords through the Uniform Code of Military Justice, the contemporary version of the Articles of War. In the United States, the system of military command is subject to such congressional limitations. By separating the power to prescribe military law from the power to enforce it, the Constitution's authors provided one more safeguard for liberty while confronting the necessity for military discipline.

In contrast to the preceding clause, which generated little debate or apparent discord, the two clauses (Art. 1, Sec. 8, Cls. 15 and 16) that provide for calling forth the states' militia into the Federal service and for organizing, arming, disciplining, and governing the militia generated greater controversy than the provision for a standing army. Once again, the convention was divided between such nationalists as Alexander

Hamilton and advocates of state sovereignty as Elbridge Gerry, John Dickinson, Oliver Ellsworth, Luther Martin, and Roger Sherman. In the plan that Hamilton submitted to the convention on June 18, the states were prohibited from maintaining a regular army or navy. Hamilton favored placing the states' militia under "the sole and exclusive direction of the United States," which was empowered to appoint and commission their officers.[63] An obvious response to the inadequacies of the Articles of Confederation, Hamilton's plan called for nationalizing the armed forces and implied their professionalization.[64]

While Madison favored national regulation of the militia as an alternative to a large standing army, Gerry and Sherman viewed such regulation as an attempt to destroy the states. The opponents of the militia clauses feared that the national government would employ the militia to enforce national supremacy (under the supremacy clause, Art. 6, Cl. 2) and interfere with the states' internal organization (under Art. 4, Sec. 4, which guarantees a republican form of government to each state). Despite Wilson, Mason, Randolph, Gorham, and Carroll's assurances that the exclusive purposes of the guarantee clause were to protect domestic peace, representative government, and external security, Luther Martin insisted that the states should be left free to suppress rebellion themselves.[65] As the convention's record indicates, the nationalists feared a repetition of the disorders that had occurred in several states (e.g., Shays' Rebellion in Massachusetts and civil disturbances in Pennsylvania) under the Articles of Confederation. Advocates of state sovereignty feared the potential for national tyranny, which they inferred from the juxtaposition of the militia clauses and the supremacy and guarantee clauses.

During several months the Framers hammered out a series of compromises between the advocates of state and national power. Although Congress could call the militia into the national service, such a call would be limited to executing national law, suppressing rebellion, and repelling invasions. At other times, the states would control their respective militias. Congress was granted power to provide for organizing, arming, and disciplining the militia, but, unless called into the national service, the states would actually administer their respective militias. While Congress was granted power to govern the militia when actually in the national service, the states retained the power to appoint its officers and supervise military training within congressionally approved guidelines. Thus, the state and national governments were granted concurrent powers regarding the militia.

By conferring on Congress the powers to call the militia into the national service and to provide for governing, organizing, arming, and disciplining the militia, the Framers left little doubt that the President's executive power did not include the former royal prerogative of governing the militia. As commander in chief, the President has power to command the militia only during the time that it is actually in the national service. Despite various constitutional limitations on congressional power concerning the militia, early critics of national military power opposed the militia clauses as a source of national and presidential power and, therefore, as a threat to liberty, democratic government, and state sovereignty. At the same time, they opposed the creation of a professional standing army for similar reasons.[66]

Taken together, the auxiliary war powers furnish the national government the appropriate means to protect the nation's external and internal security. As the repository of national power to commence war and hostilities, Congress also possesses the constitutional power to determine the most effective means to wage war and hostilities successfully. Within the constitutional limitations imposed on legislative power, Congress rather than the President has the constitutional discretion to determine national defense policy. Although one can argue that the various auxiliary war powers, alone, imply broad congressional discretion, the necessary-and-proper clause also confers such discretion on Congress.[67]

Despite Thomas Jefferson's restrictive reading of the necessary-and-proper clause,[68] its location at the end of Article 1, Section 8, which enumerates congressional power, rather than in Section 9, which enumerates limitations on congressional power, suggests an expansive interpretation.[69] Compared to the Articles of Confederation, which prohibited Congress from exercising any power not "expressly delegated" to the United States, Madison noted, the Constitution contains no such explicit restriction on congressional power.[70] As a result, one can infer incidental legislative power from the necessary-and-proper clause. According to Hamilton's rather disarming analysis, this clause expresses little more than a self-evident truth. Given the impossibility of foreseeing every possible contingency or enumerating every power denied to the national government, the Framers entrusted discretionary power to Congress. In the event that Congress misconstrued its power, the executive, judiciary, and state governments could restrain the unconstitutional exercise of congressional power.[71] Thus, Hamilton and Madison relied on federalism, balanced government, and separation of powers to restrain an intemperate Congress.

Hamilton's, Madison's, and Jefferson's claims to the contrary notwithstanding, the Convention's record does not amplify the scope of the necessary-and-proper clause as a vertical sweeping clause, i.e., its effect on the legislative powers conferred on Congress. Nor does the record amplify the scope of the clause as a horizontal sweeping clause, i.e., its implication for congressional power to control the incidental powers vested in the President and the Federal judiciary. There was virtually no discussion of the language that the Committee of Detail reported to the Convention. "That it did not arouse any discussion, . . ." Charles Warren argues, "was probably due to the fact that the delegates understood that this clause, in reality, added nothing to the powers already granted."[72] Nevertheless, on September 15, Gerry listed the necessary-and-proper clause among his objections to the Constitution.[73] Mason also objected to the provision because " . . . the State legislatures have no security for the powers now presumed to remain to them, or the people for their rights."[74]

In a recent article that draws attention to the horizontal effect of the necessary-and-proper clause, William Van Alstyne concludes that "reasonable differences of opinion" exist on the scope of this clause. Insofar as the clause implies power to control the incidental (implied) powers of the President and the Federal courts, no less than five plausible interpretations exist! Each of these interpretations rests on several assumptions concerning legislative, executive, and judicial power. First, the second part of the necessary-and-proper clause authorizes Congress to make laws which shall be necessary and proper for carrying into execution the powers vested in the executive and the judiciary. Second, since neither the executive nor the judiciary article contains language that is similar to the necessary-and-proper clause, the President and the Federal judiciary cannot infer the same broad, incidental power from Articles 2 and 3. Third, the President and the Federal judiciary can infer only those powers that are "essential" or "indispensable" to the performance of their specific constitutional functions.[75] When the President and the judiciary require discretionary incidental power to perform their duties, Congress has the exclusive authority " . . . to determine and to make provision for incidental (but not indispensable) powers that in *its* view may promote greater efficiency in the executive or judicial branches."[76]

Narrowly construed, the necessary-and-proper clause is neither a vertical nor a horizontal sweeping clause. As Jefferson argued, the clause does not confer any greater authority on the national government than the Constitution specifically enumerates. Commenting on the constitutionality of the National Bank in 1791, Jefferson noted that the Constitution " . . . was intended to lace them [Congress] up straitly within the enumerated powers, and those without which, as means, these powers could not be carried into effect."[77] Only those means that are essential or indispensable to execute enumerated powers are constitutional.[78] Such a narrow interpretation would place a legislative strait-jacket on Congress similar to the Articles of Confederation.

By construing the necessary-and-proper clause more liberally as a horizontal sweeping clause and by interpreting presidential power narrowly, as Van Alstyne recognizes, Congress could employ its power to limit presidential discretion.[79] In the absence of a necessary-and-proper clause in the second article, the President possesses only those incidental powers absolutely indispensable to execute the specific powers vested in his office. Such a view of presidential power could reduce the office to a ministerial agency of Congress. However, if one construes the vesting, take-care, and commander-in-chief clauses broadly, these broad grants incorporate a plethora of essential incidental powers. At one end of the continuum, the President has inherent power to act for the public good, which includes discretionary as well as essential incidental power, unless the Constitution or laws prohibit presidential conduct. At the other end, the President cannot infer discretionary incidental power unless Congress authorizes presidential conduct.

However appealing such polar extremes seem to advocates or opponents of presidential power, there is little evidence to conclude that the Framers intended to elevate the Presidency to a divine providence or reduce the office to a congressional eunuch. Neither is there conclusive evidence that the Framers intended the necessary-and-proper clause as a basis for unlimited congressional power. Since the evidence is inconclusive, the broad language of the necessary-and-proper clause invites various interpretations of its horizontal effect. Like other broad grants of power such as the general-welfare clause and the executive and judicial vesting clauses, the necessary-and-proper clause invites struggle between Congress and the President. Finally, as Van Alstyne comments, " . . . there is . . . no sufficient evidence of any one 'original understanding' of the sweeping clause as to foreclose a large measure of wholly legitimate judicial discretion in its interpretation."[80]

As the foregoing analysis of the congressional war powers suggests, it is impossible to construe the Framers' intentions or the Constitution's text according to a rigorous analytical model. Although the Framers separated offensive from defensive war powers, the distinction between offensive and defensive war and hostilities, like perceptions of truth or beauty, is often in the eye of the beholder. Contemporary weapons systems also vitiate the Framers' analytical distinction between offensive and defensive war and hostilities. Constitutional text and the Framers' intentions to the contrary notwithstanding, the realities of war invite struggle between Congress and the President.

Compared to the logical ambiguities of the declaration-of-war clause, the auxiliary war powers, which the Constitution vests exclusively in the legislature, afford Congress the constitutional means to influence the scope, intensity, and duration of war and hostilities. Congress can withhold the means outright or it can restrict delegations to the executive in order to influence presidential warmaking. In other words, Congress can employ the necessary-and-proper clause as a vertical sweeping clause to limit or channel presidential policymaking. Furthermore, Congress can exploit the horizontal effect of this clause to limit incidental but not indispensable executive power, although its horizontal reach is debatable. As the legislature develops new techniques of executive control, however, it will confront countervailing presidential claims of constitutional powers over war and foreign affairs.

PRESIDENTIAL POWER UNDER THE CONSTITUTION OF 1787

The drafting of the executive article caused considerable controversy in the Federal Convention. Beginning on June 1, the delegates debated virtually every feature of the executive article, including the President's selection, tenure, title, compensation, powers, and removal from office. Since the Articles of Confederation lacked a separate, unitary executive, the Framers lacked a model for the new national executive other than the governors of the states, whose office and powers varied considerably. In some states the governor was little more than a military figure; in others he had administrative powers. The lack of a model probably explains the controversy and confusion that attended the delegates' debates on the executive article.

The controversy divided the delegates into two camps. In one camp James Wilson, Alexander Hamilton, Charles Pinckney, and John Rutledge, in varying degrees, favored a strong, singular, and energetic executive. In the other camp William Paterson, George Mason, and Edmund Randolph favored a plural executive with limited ministerial powers.[81] With the possible exception of Alexander Hamilton, none of the delegates favored a restoration of monarchy, although Randolph saw a single executive "as the foetus of monarchy."[82] Attempting to assuage Randolph's fears,

> Mr. Wilson said that Unity of the Executive instead of being the fetus of Monarchy would be the best safeguard against tyranny. He repeated that he was not governed by the British Model which was inapplicable to the situation of this Country; the ex-

tent of which was so great, and the manners so republican, that nothing but a great confederated Republic would do for it.[83]

Wilson believed in a strong executive but he also accepted legislative primacy and popular sovereignty.[84]

Despite Wilson's assurances, James McHenry feared that advocates of a strong executive were attempting to restore monarchy.[85] The executive that emerged from the convention's deliberations resembled the strong governors of Massachusetts and New York rather than the King of England.[86] The convention made a series of important decisions that resulted in a strong, independent President with more than ministerial power but less than prerogative. The Framers provided for a separate executive, which was a clear departure from the nascent ministerial system of the Articles. James Wilson apparently persuaded the Committee of Detail to recommend a single rather than a plural executive. After five votes in favor of legislative selection, Gouverneur Morris convinced the delegates to accept the electoral-college system of presidential election. The delegates also accepted fixed tenure of four years but provided for impeachment and removal, in direct contrast to the British monarchy. The Framers did not, however, foreclose presidential eligibility for reelection. By rejecting proposals for an executive council, the convention strengthened presidential independence and political accountability. The delegates also strengthened the separation of powers by prohibiting members of the executive from serving in Congress. Finally, the Framers conferred independent powers on the presidency. After considerable debate and compromise, the convention recommended a strong, independent, and politically responsible chief magistrate to the states' ratifying conventions.[87]

Foremost among the powers that the Constitution vests in the presidency is the executive power. Some scholars argue that the executive vesting clause merely provides for a single executive who exercises no more power than the second article specifically vests in the President, e.g., the powers to execute the law, to command the armed forces, or to receive foreign diplomatic personnel. According to this narrow ministerial view, the President also exercises additional incidental powers that are indispensable in carrying out his functions.[88] Although the ministerial view is consistent with the arguments of delegates who favored a weak presidency, even Charles Pinckney, who favored an energetic executive, had a limited view of executive power.[89]

Compared to the ministerial view of executive power, other scholars argue that the vesting clause is a broad grant that is limited only by the Constitution's specific exceptions, limitations, and prohibitions. Unlike the vesting clause of Article 1, which provides that "All legislative powers *herein granted* shall be vested in a Congress," the executive vesting clause contains no intrinsic limits on executive power. While Congress can exercise only the specific powers that the Constitution confers on the legislature, the President is free to exercise "executive power," restricted only by those constitutional limitations extrinsic to the vesting clause of Article 2.[90] In defining "executive power," the strong presidency's proponents argue, the law and practice of nations provide a constitutional standard.[91] The law and practice of other nations are in reality an extraconstitutional standard that defies the concept and purpose of a written constitution. Moreover, the Framers clearly departed from eighteenth-century international practice when they divested the presidency of the former royal prerogatives of determining war and peace and raising and supporting armed forces.

Neither the constitutional text nor the Convention's debates conclusively resolve the continuing controversy over the scope of executive power. While some of the Framers favored a vigorous President with broad executive powers, others favored a weak chief magistrate with limited ministerial powers. The former group emphasized the need for energy, unity, dispatch, and secrecy, especially in conducting war and foreign affairs. The latter group emphasized the dangers to liberty and popular sovereignty arising from military dictatorship. These arguments appeared during the convention's debates, the debates of the state ratifying conventions,[92] in the exchange between Hamilton and Madison over George Washington's Neutrality Proclamation of 1793,[93] during the limited naval war with France (1797–1801),[94] and in the wars with the Barbary Powers (1801–1805).[95] If a consensus emerged from the convention, which is rather doubtful, that consensus lies somewhere between prerogative and ministerial responsibility. The clause vesting executive power in the President is an ambiguous provision that papers over the unresolved controversy attending the creation of an independent executive.

As the opponents of a strong presidency realized, the vesting clause must be interpreted in relation to the other powers that the executive article confers on the President. Although their fears seem somewhat exaggerated in the context of the period, the opponents believed that an aggressive president could unite executive power with his office as commander in chief to enslave the nation. Thus, in the plan that Paterson presented to the convention on June 15, the executive was authorized " . . . to direct all military operations; provided that none of the persons composing the federal Executive shall on any occasion take command of any troops, so as personally to conduct any enterprise as

General, or in any other capacity."[96] The logic implicit in separating the higher direction of war from commanding troops in the field is explicit in Patrick Henry's speech to the Virginia Convention on June 5, 1788:

> Your President may easily become king. . . . If your American chief be a man of ambition and abilities, how easy is it for him to render himself absolute! The army is in his hands, and if he be a man of address, it will be attached to him, and it will be the subject of long meditation with him to seize the first auspicious moment to accomplish his design; . . . the President, in the field, at the head of his army, can prescribe the terms on which he shall reign master, so far that it will puzzle any American ever to get his neck from under the galling yoke. . . . If ever he violates the laws, one of two things will happen: he will come at the head of his army, to carry everything before him; . . . Can he not, at the head of his army, beat down every opposition? Away with your President! we shall have a king: the army will salute him monarch: your militia will leave you, and assist in making him king, and fight against you: and what have you to oppose this force? What will then become of you and your rights? Will not absolute despotism ensue?[97]

Despite the fear that the President might manipulate his office as commander in chief to establish a military dictatorship or plunge the nation into foreign wars in order to aggrandize his powers,[98] the Framers conferred the powers of command on the President. At the least, these powers include the direction of military operations. Both Paterson's and Hamilton's plans, for example, provided that the President have the power to direct military operations.[99] Recognizing the principle of presidential responsibility for supervising the armed forces, Gouverneur Morris, seconded by Charles Pinckney, recommended that the secretaries of war and marine (Navy) be appointed solely at the President's pleasure and that they be responsible for superintending their respective departments, including raising and equipping troops, caring for military and naval stores, equipment, and installations, and, in times of war, preparing plans of offense and defense.[100]

The convention did not, however, prescribe the President's duties as commander in chief. On August 6, the Committee of Detail reported that the President "shall be commander in chief of the Army and Navy . . . , and of the Militia of the Several States,"[101] which was later restricted to the time during which the militia actually is in the national service. The Framers also limited the President's power to command the militia by conferring the power to call it up on Congress rather than on the commander in chief.[102] In addition to these command functions, by implication, the Framers attributed defensive powers to the President but they did not, explicitly or implicitly, attribute any prerogatives that the British Crown had enjoyed. Indeed, several delegates denied explicitly that the President would enjoy the powers to commence war, raise and support armies, and determine peace.[103]

Although the Framers did not explicitly restrict the President's power to command the Army in the field, the logic of Paterson's recommendation bears further examination. By prohibiting the President from actually commanding an army, Paterson's proposal emphasizes a significant distinction between the higher direction of war and the actual conduct of military operations. As civilian commander in chief, the President is politically responsible to Congress and the electorate for the strategic and tactical decisions of his professional military subordinates.[104] The distinction between the higher direction of war and the conduct of military operations also emphasizes the responsibility and subordination of the uniformed military services to a politically responsible head of state.[105] On August 20, Pinckney recognized this chain of command by recommending that the Committee of Detail consider amending the executive article so that "'The military shall always be subordinate to the Civil power, . . . '"[106] In addition, separating the two functions emphasizes the military's loyalty and subordination to the office of commander in chief rather than the presidential incumbent as a personal generalissimo or captain general, which Patrick Henry and Luther Martin believed would degenerate into military dictatorship.[107]

In addition to the vesting and commander-in-chief clauses, considerable controversy surrounds the scope of the take-care clause as a basis for presidential military power. An orthodox interpretation of this clause is that the President's duty to execute the laws faithfully does not give him discretion in determining which laws he will enforce or the extent to which he will execute a law. However, various Presidents, including Andrew Johnson and Woodrow Wilson,[108] have refused to enforce laws they viewed as unconstitutional. Two strong Presidents, Andrew Jackson and Abraham Lincoln, however, argued that the President has no choice but to enforce the law.[109] In direct contrast to his predecessor, James Buchanan, who believed that without prior congressional authorization the President could not employ military force to execute the law,[110] Lincoln argued that, as commander in chief, the President had "no choice . . . but to call out the war power" to enforce federal law throughout the nation.[111]

Since various laws authorize the President to call the militia (National

Guard) into the Federal service or authorize the use of force to execute Federally protected rights, contemporary Presidents can cite specific statutory authority for employing military force.[112] In the absence of such contingent legislation, however, does the President have inherent power to employ military force in order to execute the law? Or, does the take-care clause afford the President considerable discretion in implementing law, including the use of military force? Is presidential discretion under the take-care clause as broad as congressional discretion under the necessary-and-proper clause?

Although the convention's record does not permit a conclusive construction of the take-care clause, several inferences seem justifiable. The power to execute the law faithfully does not include the power to make or dispense with law. As Lord Mansfield had argued in the House of Lords, not even the British Crown's prerogatives include the dispensing power.[113] Justice Black wrote in *Youngstown Sheet and Tube Co. v. Sawyer* (1952):

> In the framework of our Constitution, the President's power to see that the laws are faithfully executed refutes the idea that he is to be a lawmaker. The Constitution limits his functions in the lawmaking process to the recommending of laws he thinks wise and the vetoing of laws he thinks bad. And the Constitution is neither silent nor equivocal about who shall make the laws which the President is to execute.[114]

Inasmuch as the Court found President Harry S Truman's seizure policy contrary to congressional intent, the *Youngstown* decision denies presidential power to act contrary to standing law. In *Youngstown* the Court did not decide what the President could do in the absence of congressional policy in order to fulfill his constitutional responsibilities under the vesting, take-care, commander-in-chief or other clauses of Article 2. In the absence of a congressional delegation, how broad are these various grants of power and what is the scope of the President's incidental powers? When Congress delegates power to the executive in foreign and domestic affairs, the Court has provided rather broad standards for the constitutional exercise of such powers.

Viewed in relation to the foreign-affairs powers that the President exercises alone or shares with the Senate, the vesting, take-care, and commander-in-chief clauses provide extensive, but not unlimited, powers to conduct the nation's foreign affairs in war and peace. In the hands of an adroit and aggressive President, these constitutional powers more than counterbalance congressional claims of authority over war and for-

eign affairs. Although the Framers probably anticipated legislative-
executive cooperation in formulating and implementing foreign and
military policy, balanced government and the separation of powers create the potential for conflict and mutual frustration. Or, as Justice Louis
D. Brandeis wrote in a dissenting opinion in *Myers* v. *U.S.*,

> The separation of the powers of government did not make each
> branch completely autonomous. It left each, in some measure,
> dependent upon the others, as it left to each power to exercise,
> in some respects, functions in their nature executive, legislative
> and judicial. . . .

> Checks and balances were established in order that this should
> be "a government of laws and not of men." . . . The doctrine of
> the separation of powers was adopted by the Convention of
> 1787, not to promote efficiency but to preclude the exercise of
> arbitrary power. The purpose was not to avoid friction, but, by
> means of the inevitable friction incident to the distribution of the
> governmental powers among three departments, to save the
> people from autocracy.[115]

CONCLUSION

As the available evidence suggests, there is no clear and exclusive commitment of all the war and foreign-affairs powers to either Congress or
the President. Neither the Constitution's text nor the Framers' intentions, insofar as one can identify their views, reveal a commitment to
either legislative or executive supremacy and autonomy. Apparently,
the Framers so feared abuses of legislative and executive power that
they limited both congressional and presidential powers to determine
and conduct war and foreign affairs. These powers are anchored in a
constitutional system that shares and partially separates responsibility
between the legislative and executive branches.

Although the Framers realized that effective foreign and military
policymaking requires extensive legislative-executive cooperation, they
also realized that the separation and sharing of power create potential
for conflict, frustration, and stalemate. Balanced government and the
separation of powers, as Justice Brandeis observed, were designed to
promote liberty rather than efficiency. The Framers also realized that
the preservation of constitutional government requires granting the national government power adequate to promote domestic peace and ex-

ternal security. Thus, American constitutionalism represents a balance between the requirements of liberty and order.

Throughout the nation's history, domestic and international crises— civil war, international war and hostilities, and economic depression— have threatened the constitutional equilibrium between Congress and the President. The First and Second World Wars, for example, were characterized by congressional-presidential cooperation, by the sharing of power and responsibility. During these two international crises, a fundamental national consensus on winning the war led to the fusion of congressional and presidential powers into a national war power. Blessed by the courts, the national war power is subject to few limits other than the test of waging war successfully. By contrast to the First and Second World Wars, the Vietnam War was characterized by a collapse of national consensus and legislative-executive conflict over the scope of each branch's respective powers and responsibilities for initiating, conducting, and terminating war and hostilities.

During the Vietnam War, draftees, servicemen, taxpayers, and members of Congress urged the Federal courts to intervene in the growing conflict between Congress and the President over the initiation, conduct, and termination of military hostilities in Southeast Asia.[116] In addition to important questions of foreign and military policy, various litigants asked the Federal courts to determine fundamental questions of legislative and executive power, the separation of powers, and constitutional checks and balances. By asking the courts to adjudicate these constitutional questions, inevitably, the litigants were urging the Federal judiciary to resolve fundamental questions concerning their own power vis-à-vis Congress and the President. Although the Federal courts generally refused to approach the merits of the Vietnam litigants' claims, these cases raise issues that are important to the continuing development of constitutional government in the United States.

In the absence of a clear and exclusive textual commitment of all military power to Congress or the President, can the Federal judiciary play a constructive role in resolving legislative-executive conflict? Are there constitutional limitations on judicial power that preclude judicial intervention in war-powers controversies? Are there prudential reasons why the Federal judiciary should not intervene in legislative-executive conflicts over the war powers? Under what conditions are the Federal courts likely to intervene in and/or abstain from such controversies? What are the consequences of judicial abstention and/or intervention for the Federal courts as well as for Congress and the President? Which constitutional and political values do the Federal courts promote by intervening in and/or abstaining from war-powers controversies?

When Congress and the President concur in the exercise of the war powers can the Federal courts, nonetheless, play a constructive role in determining the scope of power that the other two branches exercise jointly or individually? Does joint congressional-presidential participation in war-powers decisions increase the probability that the Federal judiciary will legitimate the national government's conduct? Does congressional acquiescence to presidential decisionmaking assure judicial acquiescense to the exercise of governmental power? Are the Federal courts more likely to restrain joint congressional-presidential actions in cases involving individual rights than in cases involving more abstract questions of executive-legislative power?

Conventional wisdom suggests that the courts should not intervene in questions of external sovereignty. Prudence as well as respect for the constitutional separation of powers dictate that such questions should be committed exclusively to the political departments for resolution. In the event of conflict between the political departments, the courts should reserve judgment, giving Congress and the President time to resolve their differences. In the event that conflict persists, judicial intervention is not likely to succeed since the Federal courts possess limited power, which they should employ judiciously. When Congress and the President exercise their powers jointly, prudence also dictates that the Federal courts should exercise their powers cautiously, if at all. In other words, the conventional wisdom implies that the doctrine of the separation of powers does not apply to most questions of external sovereignty. Or, even if the doctrine applies, the courts should refrain from entertaining such cases.[117]

In contrast to conventional wisdom, some scholars have advocated judicial intervention in war-powers cases in order to protect individuals' rights and to enforce the constitutional separation of powers. Failure or refusal to entertain war-powers cases may avoid confrontations with Congress and the President, but judicial abstention severely restricts the exercise of judicial power and prevents the Federal courts from protecting judicially cognizable and enforceable rights. Despite the danger of confrontation with Congress or the President, in cases that are appropriately before the courts, the Federal judiciary has an obligation to decide constitutional issues.[118]

Whether one advocates judicial intervention in or abstention from constitutional issues concerning external sovereignty, the separation of the congressional war powers from the office of commander in chief creates the potential for separation-of-powers controversies. When such controversies develop into irreconcilable conflicts that threaten national security or constitutional government, the potential or occasion for judicial intervention exists. When Congress and the President act jointly to protect national-security interests, in the face of a national emergency, their temptation to ignore constitutional limitations also creates the occasion for judicial intervention. In a litigious society, citizens turn to the courts to resolve such thorny controversies and to protect their rights. The continuing debate over the constitutional allocation of the national government's war powers suggests a need to analyze the Federal judiciary's adjudication of cases involving the initiation, conduct, and termination of war and hostilities.

3

Democracy, Judicial Review, and the War Powers

JUDICIAL REVIEW IN A DEMOCRACY

Conventional wisdom suggests that in a democracy the judiciary should refrain from deciding "political questions."[1] Such decisions as initiating, conducting, and terminating war and hostilities require policy choices that are political rather than legal in character. Whether the nation sends its sons and daughters to war involves choices among fundamental values that only responsible, popularly elected public officials can and should decide. There is little justification for "a bevy of Platonic Guardians"[2] in judicial robes deciding whether a democratic nation goes to war or remains at peace.

Although democracy entrusts decisions of war and peace to responsive and responsible public officials, constitutionalism requires that such decisions be made according to known and accepted constitutional standards. The rule of law means that elected and appointed public officials act within their respective spheres of constitutional authority according to neutral decision rules.[3] In a constitutional system that shares and partially separates power and responsibility for decisions of war and peace between Congress and the President, the courts have a duty to enforce the rule of law by limiting the other branches to the exercise of their respective constitutional powers in cases that meet jurisdictional and procedural requirements. As Alexander Hamilton argued in the seventy-eighth *Federalist*, as constitutional guardians judges have a unique responsibility to defend constitutional government and the rights of individuals against executive and legislative usurpations.[4]

While opponents of judicial review argue that it is incompatible with popular sovereignty, advocates argue that judicial review promotes liberty and constitutional government. Relatively few partisans in the debate over judicial review acknowledge that the American constitutional system incorporates both liberal and democratic values, processes, and institutions.[5] Judicial review is an important element in a constitutional system that restrains democratic impulses through such institutional devices as federalism, bicameralism, checks and balances, the separation of powers, and the electoral-college system. Indeed, the very purpose of constitutionalism is to limit popular sovereignty and governmental power.[6]

Despite their commitment to constitutionalism, the Framers did not explicitly provide for judicial review, i.e., constitutional and statutory review of congressional and presidential actions. Their failure to vest such powers in the Federal courts has given rise to a continuing debate regarding the Federal judiciary's exercise of judicial review vis-à-vis Congress and the President.[7] Although there is no explicit grant of judicial power to review congressional and presidential actions, developments in political thought and practice between 1776 and 1787 suggest that the Framers accepted constitutional theories compatible with judicial review.[8] State constitutions providing for an independent judiciary, separation of legislative from executive power, and checks and balances eventually displaced legislative supremacy as an operating principle of government. Legislative interference with judicial independence (e.g., legislative attempts to intervene in pending cases) resulted in expressions of dissatisfaction with "legislative despotism."[9] By 1787 such leading political figures as John Adams, John Jay, James Madison, and James Wilson accepted the need to limit governmental power through such institutional devices as the separation of powers in order to protect liberty from legislative as well as executive encroachments.[10]

Despite the convention's failure to provide explicitly for judicial review, several delegates assumed that the Federal judiciary would exercise the power to review the constitutionality of congressional and presidential actions. Elbridge Gerry, Alexander Hamilton, Rufus King, Luther Martin, George Mason, Gouverneur Morris, John Francis Mercer, and James Wilson assumed that the Federal judiciary would have the power to enforce constitutional supremacy vis-à-vis congressional acts that violated the Constitution's command. Arguing against creating a Council of Revision that included the judiciary, with the power to veto

legislative acts, Luther Martin observed, " . . . as to the Constitutionality of laws, that point will come before the Judges in their proper official
character. In this character they have a negative on the laws."[11] Although Mason urged including the judiciary in a Council of Revision
with the power to veto unjust, oppressive or pernicious laws, he, too,
agreed that the Federal judiciary " . . . could declare an unconstitutional
law void."[12] On July 23, 1787, Madison noted that under a written constitution "A law violating a constitution established by the people themselves, would be considered by the Judges as null and void."[13] In a political system based on a hierarchy of law and constitutional supremacy,
in the event of conflict judges have a binding obligation to enforce the
organic law over mere legislative acts.

Neither the Constitution's text nor the records of the Federal Convention demonstrate conclusively that the Framers intended the federal
judiciary to exercise the power of constitutional review. "[The] people
who say the framers intended [judicial review] are talking nonsense,"
Edward Corwin once testified, adding, "and the people who say they
did not intend it are talking nonsense."[14] Despite a tenuous claim to the
power of judicial review, the Supreme Court lost little time in asserting
its authority to determine the constitutionality of congressional acts. In
these early cases, the Supreme Court sustained the congressional acts
in question while asserting its power of constitutional review.[15] The
Court tempered its claim to judicial review by sustaining congressional
acts unless they were clearly unconstitutional. Early in its history, the
Supreme Court recognized limits to its power of judicial review.[16]

The Case for Judicial Review of Legislative-Executive Conflict

Casting judicial caution to the winds, in *Marbury* v. *Madison* (1803),
John Marshall claimed the power of judicial review and declared Section 13 of the Judiciary Act of 1789 unconstitutional. Marshall's bold
assertion of judicial power rests on a series of syllogisms that provides
the basis for the classical theory of judicial review. Since the Constitution is the supreme and binding act of the people, in the event of a
conflict with a congressional statute, which is a lesser act of the people's
representatives, the latter must yield to the former. If the Court must
choose between a statute and the Constitution, it has no choice but to
set aside the statute in favor of the Constitution.[17] Marshall's second
syllogism assumes that the judicial oath to enforce the Constitution im-
poses a special duty on the judiciary since " . . . the language of the
constitution is addressed especially to the courts."[18] Finally, Marshall
argues that the fundamental purpose of a written constitution, which

includes various prohibitions on governmental power, is to limit each branch to the exercise of its constitutional authority.[19]

According to the classical (Marshall) view, when Congress or the President exceeds their constitutional powers, the courts must entertain and decide cases that meet their jurisdictional and procedural requirements.[20] Since the Constitution is a binding and enforceable organic law rather than a merely horatory document, the judiciary cannot abstain from deciding legal controversies that involve "political questions."[21] If questions of external sovereignty (i.e., the war powers and foreign affairs) arise in otherwise judicially cognizable cases, for which judicial remedies exist, the Federal courts must decide such cases on their merits. The classical doctrine of judicial review obliges the Federal judiciary to enforce the constitutional separation of powers.

Aside from the classical justification for judicial review, some contemporary scholars argue that judicial review promotes majority rule, popular sovereignty,[22] and other democratic values. In congressional and state legislative apportionment and districting cases, for example, judicial intervention has promoted equal representation, without which neither majority rule nor popular sovereignty could exist.[23] If democratic governments derive their legitimacy from the consent or acquiescence of popular majorities, judicial review of election practices that interfere with the citizen's right to vote, free from corruption and intimidation, promotes popular sovereignty. If popular sovereignty also requires informed consent and public choice, one can reconcile constitutional review of legislative or executive actions that abridge political speech or debate protected by the First Amendment with democratic values.[24] Criticism of constitutional review as undemocratic often ignores the Federal judiciary's role in protecting democratic values as well as undemocratic features of presidential elections and congressional organization that distort majority rule and popular sovereignty. The electoral-college system of presidential elections and the equal apportionment of senatorial seats among the states, for example, vitiate popular sovereignty.

Since a basic objective of American constitutionalism is to advance the individual's freedom or liberty, judicial review can serve to protect individuals and minorities against repressive and intemperate majorities. During periods of war and hostilities the courts should provide a forum in which individuals and minorities can vindicate their rights when Congress and the President exceed their constitutional war powers. Although the Supreme Court's record in defending the rights of unpopular minorities during the Second World War is somewhat wanting,[25] eventually, the Court restrained the exercise of congressional and presidential war powers.[26] Confronted with an international crisis, the Supreme Court tempered its obligation to protect the individual's liberty with a respect for national security, governmental power, and a sense of judicial self-restraint.

In addition to enforcing the rule of law, limiting governmental power, and protecting the rights of individuals and minorities, the courts can employ their powers of constitutional review to reconcile conflict between Congress and the President.[27] When Congress and the President fail to reconcile conflict through political negotation and compromise, as an arbiter of the separation of powers the Federal judiciary can intervene to resolve boundary disputes. By applying judicial standards of constitutional interpretation to war-powers controversies, the Federal courts can promote the American political system's equilibrium and adjustment to a changing international environment. Although judicial intervention in legislative-executive boundary disputes entails obvious political risks for the Federal courts, judicial review seems especially justifiable when such disputes jeopardize an individual's constitutional rights and society's interest in constitutional government.[28]

Both principle and pragmatism warrant judicial intervention in boundary disputes concerning the initiation, conduct, and termination of war and hostilities. The conservation of democratic values, constitutional government, individual liberty, and political equilibrium requires an arbiter of legislative and executive power. When such fundamental issues arise in cases that meet constitutional (jurisdictional and procedural) requirements, the Federal judiciary should decide cases on their merits. Insofar as Federal judges can apply constitutional standards and develop principled remedies, they should not employ theories of judicial self-restraint to avoid deciding judicially cognizable conflicts.[29]

The Case against Judicial Review of Legislative-Executive Conflict

In contrast to those who favor judicial intervention in war-powers controversies, opponents argue that judicial review is inherently undemocratic. Since democracy (i.e., popular sovereignty) requires that the people's representatives make fundamental policy choices, judicial intervention in the initiation, conduct, and termination of war and hostilities is an intolerable interference in the democratic process. Indeed, constitutional review of popular choice by an irresponsible (appointed) and unresponsive (independent) judiciary vitiates governmental accountability to the people. Or, as Alexander Bickel has written, " . . . judicial review is a deviant institution in the American democracy."[30]

Writing in the 1890s, James B. Thayer argued that the judiciary lacks the authority to reverse actions that the Constitution commits to congressional or presidential discretion.[31] Although Thayer's plea for judicial self-restraint denies the courts' power to review legislative and executive actions that are constitutionally committed to their discretion, his argument permits prudent judicial intervention in war-powers controversies between Congress and the President. In such controversies, the judiciary should not attempt to substitute its judgment for legislative or executive judgments on policy questions that are exclusively, textually committed to one or the other branch (e.g., the commencement or termination of war and hostilities). The courts may, however, initially determine whether such an exclusive commitment exists. Unless Congress is clearly mistaken about its constitutional authority (e.g., to delegate power to the executive to conduct military operations), the courts should refrain from entertaining such cases. Similarly, unless the President is clearly mistaken about the scope of his constitutional authority (e.g., to conduct defensive military operations) or the power that Congress has delegated to him (e.g., to allocate scarce material in wartime), the courts should not entertain such controversies.

Only when Congress or the President clearly exceeds the scope of their respective authority should the courts intervene in a viable case or controversy. Judicial intervention is permissible when legislative or executive actions clearly violate specific constitutional prohibitions (e.g., the Bill of Rights). By definition, abridgments of constitutional rights cannot be within the scope of discretionary authority committed to Congress or the President. Thus, Thayer's argument for judicial self-restraint provides rationale for judicial intervention in the relatively few cases in which the political departments exceed their constitutional authority and jeopardize the individual's liberty. At the same time, Thayer offers rationale for avoiding abstract boundary disputes that do not meet jurisdictional and procedural requirements.

Not unlike later theories of judicial self-restraint, Thayer also advances prudential reasons for judicial abstention that go beyond the doctrine of the clear mistake. Even when a case meets his requirements for exercising judicial power, Thayer suggests that the courts should refuse to entertain cases that provoke conflict with Congress.[32] Since Congress has ample disciplinary powers over the Federal courts, including the power to alter their jurisdiction, the judiciary should not invite legislative attacks on judicial independence. In addition to destroying judicial independence, legislative interference with the judiciary could impair its ability to defend individual liberty and constitutional government. Thayer's appeal for judicial self-restraint arises from constitutional principle as well as the principle of self-preservation.

Premature judicial intervention in boundary disputes between Congress and the President also could encourage their constitutional and political irresponsibility.[33] Rather than considering the constitutionality of their behavior, the legislature and executive might rely excessively on the judiciary to determine constitutional questions. By enacting constitutionally doubtful legislation, Congress and the President, in turn, could invite further judicial intervention. Eventually, the courts could become a convenient whipping boy for the political departments, which may refuse to assume responsibility for the constitutionality of their actions. Premature judicial resolution of constitutional questions invites cynical legislative and executive behavior that vitiates governmental responsibility to the electorate.

Aside from encouraging constitutional and political irresponsibility, premature judicial intervention denies Congress and the President the opportunity to reconcile their differences through negotiation and compromise. When the courts reconcile conflict between Congress and the President, the judiciary unnecessarily interrupts political controversy, the clash of political forces from which American democracy derives its vitality and creativity.[34] By interrupting political controversy and applying accepted legal rules to public conflict, the courts routinize conflict and reduce the level of political uncertainty.[35] As the outcome of political conflict becomes more predictable, political actors become less responsive to the clash of electoral politics. Congress and the President become more attentive and responsive to a judicial rather than a popular electoral constituency. Thus, judicial abortion of political conflict terminates the democratic process.

Advocates of judicial self-restraint also argue that the courts are inherently incapable of principled resolution of political conflict. War-powers controversies between Congress and the President, for example, present "political questions" that cannot be subjected to legal rules. The courts do not possess nor can they develop judicial standards to determine conflicts over the constitutional allocation of the war powers. War-powers controversies, therefore, pose nonjusticiable political questions that are more appropriately addressed to Congress or the President than to the Federal courts.[36]

War-powers conflicts involve policy determinations that are beyond judicial competence since the courts lack adequate information to decide questions of war, national defense, and foreign affairs. Indeed, the executive controls the very sources of information that the courts require. Under statutory authority, the executive is responsible for gathering and analyzing foreign intelligence upon which the President and his advisors make diplomatic, military, and national-security decisions.

Executive agencies are also responsible for protecting the secrecy of their foreign intelligence sources and operations. In contrast to executive agencies, the judiciary cannot guarantee the security of classified information. Even if the judiciary had access to such information, judges lack the training, temperament, and intellectual acumen to evaluate and employ intelligence information in making policy decisions.[37]

Beyond these barriers to judicial review of war-powers controversies, critics argue that the courts lack judicial remedies to resolve conflict and enforce their decisions.[38] Judicial enforcement requires continuing supervision of legislative and executive conduct, which demands an administrative temperament and techniques that judges lack. Continuing supervision or oversight of Congress and the President also threatens judicial independence and objectivity as well as popular sovereignty.[39] Moreover, the executive may simply ignore judicial decisions, which would impair judicial power as well as the judiciary's ability to protect individual rights since the courts rely on executive enforcement of their decisions when voluntary compliance fails.[40]

Advocates of judicial self-restraint make a persuasive prima facie case against constitutional review of war-powers controversies between Congress and the President. They are especially persuasive in arguing against judicial intervention in issues that touch directly on external sovereignty. Nonetheless, even ardent opponents of judicial review of war-powers controversies admit that, under certain conditions, the courts might resolve disputes that meet jurisdictional and procedural requirements in order to protect individual rights and constitutional government. However, such disputes must overcome the various jurisdictional and procedural barriers that stand in the way of judicial review.

TECHNIQUES OF JUDICIAL AVOIDANCE OF WAR-POWERS CONTROVERSIES

Among the barriers that war-powers controversies confront are judicial criteria of standing to sue, ripeness, jurisdiction, justiciability, and political questions. Despite significant changes that occurred during the Warren Court in judicial requirements for standing,[41] a particular litigant's failure to meet such criteria does not have the same implication as a judicial decision that an issue raises nonjusticiable, political questions. The decision that a particular litigant or even a class of litigants lacks standing to sue, for example, does not necessarily prevent future litigants who demonstrate sufficient adversarial interest from challeng-

ing governmental actions that are allegedly unconstitutional. Requirements for standing to sue attach to the litigants, as Fritz Scharpf argues,
rather than to a constitutional issue that may be ripe for adjudication.[42]

JUDICIAL AVOIDANCE OF "POLITICAL QUESTIONS"

A judicial decision that a dispute presents a nonjusticiable, political
question beyond a court's jurisdiction, according to Scharpf, erects a
categorically different and higher barrier than such criteria as standing,
ripeness, mootness, or the Supreme Court's denial of certiorari. In contrast to criteria that attach to a particular litigant or case, the "political
question" attaches to the *issue*.[43] A judicial decision that the recognition
of a foreign government, or the recognition of territorial sovereignty, or
the commencement of military hostilities constitute political questions
removes these *issues* from judicial determination until such time that a
future court decides otherwise. Until that time, no litigant can present
the same issue for judicial resolution since the question, theoretically, is
beyond judicial competence. Given judicial reluctance to set aside
precedent and overrule previous decisions, the doctrine of political
questions raises a significantly higher barrier to constitutional review of
otherwise cognizable disputes[44] than other techniques of self-restraint.
Insofar as the political-question doctrine has more serious, long-term
consequences for constitutional review of war-powers controversies
than other techniques of avoidance, its invocation requires careful
analysis and justification.

Since the early 1960s at least three different theories have been advanced to explain and justify the Supreme Court and the Federal judiciary's invocation of the political-question doctrine to avoid constitutional review. In addition to the "classical" and "prudential" theories,
Scharpf has developed a "functional" theory.[45] While each theory accepts the legitimacy of avoiding political questions, the classical, prudential, and functional theories rest on varying assumptions that justify
judicial invocation of the political-question barrier under different circumstances. The intellectual approach that one accepts, therefore, is
rather important in determining how high a barrier the political question poses to resolving disputes over the constitutional allocation and
exercise of the war powers.

The Classical View

According to the classical view, political questions are questions that the
Constitution commits exclusively to Congress or the President for reso-

lution. Either explicitly or implicitly, a clear textual commitment exists that removes the question from a court's determination.[46] In *Luther* v. *Borden* (1849), the Supreme Court could not determine whether Rhode Island's government was a lawful, "republican" government because the Constitution commits the definition of the term "republicanism" to the political departments.[47] The classical view, its proponents argue, rests squarely on the separation of powers, which confines the judiciary to the exercise of judicial power in cases that are within its constitutional or statutory jurisdiction.[48] Obviously, questions that are committed exclusively to congressional or presidential determination cannot be within the judiciary's jurisdiction.

Aside from being tautological, difficulty arises in applying the classical theory to the constitutional review of war-powers controversies. Although the Constitution clearly commits the power to declare war as well as various auxiliary war powers to Congress, it also commits defensive military powers to the President as commander in chief. In war, defense, and foreign affairs there is no clear, comprehensive, exclusive commitment of power to either Congress or the President. Absent a complete separation of powers, constitutional boundary disputes are likely to occur that call for judicial arbitration. When such conflict exists, when the power to make policy choices is at stake, the classical formulation of the political-question doctrine does not provide an adequate rationale for judicial abstention.[49]

When applied to presidential or congressional acts that transgress constitutional limitations on governmental powers (e.g., the Bill of Rights), the classical theory is wanting.[50] By definition, neither presidential nor congressional acts that exceed their respective constitutional powers or abridge an individual's constitutional rights involve political questions. In a constitutional system that limits the exercise of legislative and executive power, actions that overreach such limits cannot be within the scope of power committed to Congress or the President. Finally, the classical theory does not account for the fact that courts must make a preliminary determination that an exclusive textual commitment exists or that a governmental action jeopardizes an individual's constitutional rights. In any event, such preliminary judgments border on substantive adjudication.[51] The classical theory does not really account for the adjudication of boundary disputes or cases in which the exercise of governmental power is constitutionally marginal.

The Prudential View
In contrast to the classical view, which is anchored in the constitutional separation of powers, the prudential view rests on a pragmatic rather

than a dogmatic basis. When a court invokes the political question to avoid deciding a constitutional case that is otherwise within its jurisdiction, Alexander Bickel urges, it is attempting to reconcile constitutional principle with the principle of popular sovereignty.[52] By exercising self-restraint, the judiciary attempts to avoid conflicts with Congress or the President in cases where breaches of constitutional principle do not clearly, irrefutably threaten an individual's rights.[53] Although a case meets jurisdictional and procedural requirements, the courts exercise discretion in refusing to subject legislative or executive judgment to constitutional adjudication.[54] In relatively few cases, the Federal courts decide that judicial prudence or wisdom dictates respect for legislative or executive judgments. Since judicial prudence is not based on a single identifiable principle such as the separation of powers, it is necessary to specify the various prudential reasons for avoiding cases involving questions of external sovereignty.

Issues of war, national security, and international conflict are strange to judicial decisionmakers. Such issues call for the evaluation of data that are beyond judicial competence. Questions of external sovereignty are so important, complex, and unmanageable that they tend "to unbalance judicial judgment" and defy principled resolution.[55] By enmeshing themselves in controversial issues, the courts imperil their objectivity, their detached evaluation of legal issues.[56] Questions of external sovereignty require nonjudicial policy determinations based on the evaluation of information that cannot be reduced to judicial criteria or standards.

"The anxiety [exists]," Bickel observes, "not so much that the judicial judgment will be ignored, as that perhaps it should but will not be."[57] Lacking adequate information and judicial criteria of evaluation, judicial intervention risks embarrassing the executive's conduct of foreign, military, national-security or other external policies that require unity, dispatch, and secrecy. The danger exists that judicial intervention will promote public discord, confuse foreign governments, reveal information that can be useful to an enemy, jeopardize ongoing military or covert intelligence operations, and so forth. Since the judiciary cannot influence or control the international environment, judicial interference with democratic institutions responsible for deciding and conducting military and foreign policy is rarely justifiable "in a mature democracy."[58]

Although the Supreme Court has rejected the idea that emergencies create constitutional powers that do not otherwise exist, in a dissenting opinion in *Korematsu* v. *United States* (1944),[59] Justice Robert H. Jackson offered an important prudential rationale for refusing to decide the constitutionality of wartime military decisions. Faced with the military necessity of detaining some 112,000 Japanese and Japanese-Americans in the continental United States, the military could not " . . . conform to conventional tests of constitutionality." "The armed services," Jackson noted, "must protect a society, not merely its Constitution. . . ."[60] Jackson conceded the military necessity of detaining citizens and resident aliens, but he could not sustain the program's constitutionality.

As much as Jackson abhorred military expediency and could not justify the President's executive order as a constitutional exercise of the war powers, he argued that the civilian courts lacked the information and constitutional competence to judge military necessity. The Constitution, Jackson observed, commits such power to the military authorities who are responsible to the commander in chief and, through him, to the American people.[61] Unable to give the military order judicial blessing, Jackson apparently believed that the Court should have declined to review the order's constitutionality. When the Court can neither legitimate governmental policy nor deny the indispensability of the government's action to national security, prudence dictates judicial abstention. Exercising the passive virtues, as Bickel refers to techniques of judicial abstention, the judiciary declines either to check or to legitimate the exercise of congressional or presidential power.[62] During a wartime emergency the Court simply refuses to render a principled judgment (i.e., a judgment based on the principle of constitutional limitations on governmental power) in deference to the principle of popular sovereignty.

Justice Jackson's dissenting opinion also suggests that the judiciary does or should employ the political-question doctrine as well as other passive techniques to avoid confrontation with the political departments. In confronting the executive, the danger exists that the President will ignore, refuse to enforce, or actively oppose judicial decisions that challenge his authority as commander in chief.[63] In *Ex parte Merryman*,[64] for example, Lincoln simply ignored Chief Justice Taney's letter reminding the President of his constitutional duty and oath " . . . to enforce the laws, execute the judgment of the court, and release the prisoner."[65] Since the courts rely on voluntary compliance or executive enforcement of their decisions, confrontations with the President can endanger judicial power, prestige, popularity, and effectiveness.[66] A series of confrontations with a popular President who is conducting a popular war can jeopardize the judiciary's ability to protect constitutional rights, to render a principled judgment that challenges the principle of popular sovereignty.

In some cases, the legislature has failed to articulate the popular will with sufficient clarity so that the judiciary lacks rules upon which it can adjudicate.[67] Either the legislature has failed to make an initial policy determination or its determination is so vague and confusing that the courts cannot make a principled judgment. In other cases, litigants invite the courts to intervene in issues that are novel or unfamiliar to the judiciary.[68] During the Vietnam War, for example, various litigants asked the judiciary to determine a series of questions concerning the congressional war powers and presidential power as commander in chief that was unfamiliar to the Federal courts. As commander in chief, does the President have the constitutional authority to conduct prolonged military hostilities without a congressional declaration of war? Is the Southeast Asia Resolution of 1964 functionally equivalent to a declaration of war? Does the Resolution constitute congressional participation that is sufficient to sustain the President's military conduct?[69]

The prudential view of the political-question doctrine is that, although the Federal courts have jurisdiction in a case, they may, nevertheless, decline to exercise their power to decide a controversy on its substantive merits for pragmatic reasons. Judges employ the doctrine to avoid decisions that are dangerous, decisions that interfere with democratic processes and institutions, challenge popular decisions, vitiate the myth of judicial neutrality, undermine popular confidence in the judiciary's fundamental fairness and balanced judgment, weaken the judiciary's ability to protect constitutional rights, and otherwise undermine judicial power and prestige.[70] Since the political-question doctrine represents a flexible standard rather than a fixed doctrine, it resists systematic classification.[71] Therefore, the constitutional scholar cannot predict its applicability to individual cases or categories of cases. This apparent judicial inconsistency has prompted more than one scholarly wag to comment that a political question is whatever the courts say it is.

The Functional View

As a response to the empircal and normative limitations of classical and prudential theories, Fritz Scharpf offers a "functional" explanation and justification of the political-question doctrine that merits application to questions of external sovereignty. Not unlike classical and prudential theorists, Scharpf suggests that courts invoke the political question in order to screen cases and reduce their dockets. By employing the doctrine as a discretionary screening device, the judiciary restricts the adjudication of constitutional questions to appropriate cases, to ripe or mature controversies that vindicate the public's interest in constitutional government as well as the individual's constitutional rights.[72] In a judicial sytem in which constitutional review frequently is incidental to private litigation, the political question encourages a gradual development of constitutional policy.

As an empirical theory, the functional view provides verifiable criteria for explaining and predicting judical invocation of the political question in war-powers and foreign-affairs cases. According to Scharpf, the Supreme Court is likely to apply the political-question doctrine when it (1) lacks sufficient information to "correctly" determine the particular issue(s), (2) would have to question the government's position in an international dispute, or (3) would interfere with a coordinate department's specific responsibilities in an international context that exceeds the Court's reach. Although one or more of these factors are present in a case, Scharpf concedes that the Court is not likely to apply the doctrine to (1) constitutional guarantees of individual rights or (2) conflicts of competence among the Federal government's departments.[73]

While the functional theory provides empirical criteria for determining the application of the political-question category to " . . . questions of international and domestic law which immediately concern the political or military interactions of the United States with foreign states,"[74] Scharpf does not explain why the doctrine is functional to the courts or to the political and constitutional systems in which they operate. Is judicial self-restraint functional to the courts because it contributes to their survival, the optimal use of judicial resources, or their ability to protect constitutional government and the individual's constitutional rights? Is judicial abstention functional to the orderly development of public law or constitutional principles? Or, is judicial abstention from political questions functional because it permits the political departments to respond flexibly to external forces, to an international environment that is beyond the reach of judicial power and influence? Unfortunately, Scharpf's theory lacks an operational definition of functionalism.

All three approaches to the political-question doctrine incorporate empirical and normative elements that lead to substantially different conclusions regarding the conditions, desirability, and justification for applying the political-question category to questions of external sovereignty. The classical theory begins with the assumption that the courts have a constitutional duty to decide all cases that meet jurisdictional and procedural requirements. Classical theorists recognize, however, that the exclusive constitutional commitment of a question to Congress or the President removes it from judicial competence or jurisdiction.[75] Without an exclusive textual commitment, classical theory permits the courts to entertain war-powers controversies (which are a genus of boundary disputes or separation-of-powers controversies) and breaches of individual constitutional rights. In other words, the classical view severely restricts the scope and applicability of the political-question category.

The functional view assumes that, although the courts have power to decide constitutional questions, they also have discretion to screen cases, to refrain from deciding cases in which (1) the judiciary lacks information, (2) the political departments have specific responsibility to decide, (3) the courts cannot control the broader international context, or (4) judicial decisions conflicting with legislative or executive judgment would embarrass the nation's external relations or impair its vital national-security interests. Even when these factors are present in a case, the courts may, nevertheless, intervene to protect the individual's rights or decide conflicts of competence between the political departments. The purpose or function of the political-question doctrine is to protect the individual's constitutional rights and society's interest in constitutional government without impairing national security.[76] The functional theory does not restrict the scope and application of the political question as severely as the classical theory.

The prudential view assumes that, although the courts have jurisdiction in a case, they may refuse to exercise their power of constitutional review for various prudential reasons. Since judicial criteria for entertaining or abstaining from cases are pragmatic, they defy systematic classification. Therefore, one cannot confidently predict when the courts will invoke the political question to avoid constitutional review. Although the courts do not invoke the political question dogmatically, one cannot conclude that their decisions are unprincipled or merely self-serving. In the event that cases meet jurisdictional and procedural requirements, the courts may invoke the political question in order to balance other constitutional principles with the principle of democracy.[77] The prudential view expands the scope and application of the political question to a broader range of constitutional issues than either the classical or the functional theory.

Whenever the courts invoke or apply the political question, judges deny that they have jurisdiction over the issue. The courts also deny their competence to determine and evaluate the facts, their ability to develop appropriate remedies, and their power to enforce judicial decisions. In certain cases, the courts are reluctant to legitimate a questionable decision or seal a questionable legal principle with the judicial imprimatur. In practical terms, the judiciary withdraws from the field, leaving Congress or the President free to determine legal principle and to accommodate boundary disputes through political negotiation.[78]

JUDICIAL ABSTENTION: THE STATE OF THE POLITICAL-QUESTION DOCTRINE AND THE WAR POWERS

In *Baker* v. *Carr* (1961), Justice Brennan articulated the Court's criteria for invoking the political question. Like the classical theorists, Brennan began his analysis with the constitutional separation of powers. "The nonjusticiability of a political question," he remarked, "is primarily a function of the separation of powers."[79] If an issue has been textually committed to another branch of the national government and that branch has not exceeded its constitutional authority, the separation of powers requires that the Court abstain from deciding the case. However, the Court must make at least two preliminary determinations. It must decide (1) whether an exclusive textual commitment exists, and (2) the scope of such a commitment. In addition, the Court must determine whether the other branches have exceeded the scope of power that the Constitution commits to their discretion.[80] As Brennan admits, these preliminary judgments are " . . . a delicate exercise in constitutional interpretation," which is within the Supreme Court's competence "as ultimate interpreter of the Constitution."[81]

Thus far, Brennan's analysis squares with the classical theory expressed by Marshall in *Marbury* v. *Madison* and *Cohens* v. *Virginia*. The separation of powers, however, is the beginning rather than the conclusion of Brennan's analysis.[82] Brennan's five other discretionary criteria expand the political question so that it apparently conforms to Alexander Bickel's prudential theory. A case involving a political question is one in which the Court finds (1) a lack of judicially discoverable and manageable standards for resolving it, (2) the impossibility of deciding without an initial policy determination of a kind clearly for nonjudicial discretion, (3) the impossibility of a court's undertaking independent resolution without expressing lack of the respect due coordinate branches of government, (4) an unusual need for unquestioning adherence to a political decision already made, or (5) the potentiality of embarrassment from multifarious pronouncements by various departments on one question.[83]

Although the first three criteria can be inferred from the separation of powers, the fourth and fifth are discretionary and vague criteria that permit judicial avoidance of dangerous cases.[84] However, as Brennan applies these criteria to issues of external sovereignty, to foreign relations and the war powers, the political question resembles Scharpf's functional analysis. First, Brennan observes that the doctrine does not sweep the whole realm of foreign affairs. Rejecting sweeping statements

" . . . that all questions touching foreign relations are political questions," Brennan argues that the Court's decisions turn on the facts and issues in specific cases and reveal "a discriminating analysis of the political question posed."[85] "Does the case," for example, "involve the exercise of discretion demonstrably committed to the executive or the legislature?"[86] Does the Court possess the information and judgmental standards necessary to decide the case? What are the possible consequences of judicial intervention in international contexts that are beyond the reach of judicial influence?[87]

When such factors are not inextricably present in a case, however, Brennan concludes that the political question does not pose an insurmountable barrier.[88] Although the Constitution grants Congress the power to declare war and the President defensive power to resist sudden attack, the courts can develop criteria for determining whether congressional or presidential action implies the commencement or termination of war and hostilities.[89] In the absence of a declaration of war, has Congress otherwise authorized the President's conduct of offensive military operations?[90] These judicial decisions do not scan the constitutionality of congressional and presidential actions; the courts merely determine whether the political departments have taken the constitutionally prescribed action necessary to exercise the discretionary power conferred.[91] Such judicial decisions question neither the wisdom and desirability of legislative policy and executive conduct nor the constitutional authority of the political departments.

According to Brennan's analysis, cases involving the conduct of war and hostilities are less intractable than those involving the commencement or termination of war and hostilities. Since many wartime programs do not involve serious "considerations of finality" or impinge directly on foreign relations, judicial intervention does not imperil national-security interests or insinuate the courts into an international context beyond their reach.[92] Furthermore, many wartime programs are conducted under delegation statutes that are contingent on the exigencies of an emergency. Since judicial standards exist for determining the constitutionality of domestic delegation statutes, another important element of the "political question barrier falls away."[93] Enactment and enforcement of wartime price controls or domestic allocation of scarce resources required for the war effort, for example, do not require the finality and unanimity that preclude judicial review of such emergency legislation. The Emergency Price Control Act of 1942, which delegated contingent power to regulate the wages and prices of goods and services, operated as long as the exigencies upon which the law was predicated continued.[94] Although Congress and the President must initially determine the necessity for such emergency measures, in the face of a clear mistake or executive silence the courts can "'. . . inquire whether the exigency still existed upon which the continued operation of the law depended.'"[95]

Although Justice Brennan conceded the difficulty of establishing a blanket rule concerning the political question, he asserted categorically that the Court "will not stand impotent before an obvious instance of a manifestly unauthorized exercise of power."[96] Not unlike Scharpf's functional theory of the political question, Brennan implies that the Court is unlikely to apply the doctrine to cases that clearly involve (1) constitutional guarantees of individual rights or (2) conflicts of competence between the political departments. Brennan's position is that determining whether another branch has exceeded its constitutional authority is eminently a judicial responsibility.[97] Since interpreting the Constitution is a judicial function, the courts do not lack judicially discoverable and manageable standards.[98] Nor are the Court's decisions contingent on nonjudicial policy determinations.[99] Inasmuch as interpreting the Constitution is a judicial function, such decisions cannot imply disrespect for other departments.[100] In the event of conflict between Congress and the President over the allocation and exercise of the war powers, judicial abstention cannot rest on the need for unquestioned adherence to established policy or on the potential for embarrassment from multifarious pronouncements on one question.[101] By definition, conflict means the absence of a single uniform policy, i.e., the existence of multifarious pronouncements. Indeed, judicial intervention may be necessary to restore the unity and finality that dictate judicial abstention in other circumstances.[102]

Justice Brennan's analysis of the political-question doctrine is similar to the functional theory in another important respect. Both Brennan and Scharpf conclude that the political question is an instrumental category whose function is promoting constitutional government. "The political question doctrine, a tool for maintenance of governmental order," Brennan wrote, "will not be so applied as to promote only disorder."[103] In other words, the Supreme Court will employ the political question to protect the individual's constitutional rights and society's interest in constitutional government without impairing national-security interests. The Court probably will intervene to conserve constitutional principle when it believes that intervention will not seriously disrupt governmental policies and programs essential to national survival. However, the Court probably will abstain when intervention can only impair national security, i.e., the government's ability to protect the whole scheme of constitutional government. While Justice Brennan's analysis is partial

rather than exhaustive, his explanation of the political question in
Baker v. *Carr* opens rather than forecloses the possibility of judicial
intervention in questions of foreign relations and the war powers.

Speaking for a majority (with Associate Justice Potter Stewart dissenting) in *Powell* v. *McCormack*, Chief Justice Earl Warren lowered
the political-question barrier even further than Justice Brennan had in
Baker.[104] Since *Powell* deals with Congressman Adam Clayton Powell's
exclusion from the Ninetieth Congress rather than a question of external sovereignty, one should apply Warren's formulation of the political-
question doctrine cautiously to foreign relations and the war powers.
Nevertheless, Warren's formulation is consistent with other contemporaneous decisions that lowered procedural barriers to judicial review.
The Warren Court's decisions concerning standing to sue, for example,
reveal a similar propensity to decide thorny or intractable constitutional
questions on their merits.[105]

After disposing of jurisdictional questions, Warren set aside claims
that the Court lacked judicially discoverable and manageable standards
to determine Congressman Powell's constitutional claims or to fashion
judicial remedies.[106] Warren then confronted the political-question barrier. He quickly disposed of the claim that the Court's decision en-
tailed a

> "potentially embarrassing confrontation between coordinate
> branches" of the Federal Government. . . . Such a determination
> falls within the traditional role accorded courts to interpret the
> law, and does not involve a "lack of the respect due [a] coordinate
> [branch] of government," nor does it involve an "initial policy
> determination of a kind clearly for nonjudicial discretion." Our
> system of government requires that federal courts on occasion
> interpret the Constitution in a manner at variance with the con-
> struction given the document by another branch. The alleged
> conflict that such an adjudication may cause cannot justify the
> courts' avoiding their constitutional responsibility.[107]

The balance of Warren's treatment of the political-question doctrine
flows from his conception of the constitutional separation of powers. If
the Constitution commits the determination of an issue exclusively to
Congress, the Court cannot declare the law without exceeding its judicial function and impairing another branch's functions.

Despite the Court's deference to the other political-question criteria
in *Baker*, Warren rested his opinion largely, but not exclusively, on the
separation of powers and the absence of a demonstrable textual commitment of the issue to Congress.[108] Since he did not conclude that any

" . . . other formulations of the political question doctrine are 'inextric-able from the case at bar,' "[109] it is difficult, if not impossible, to determine whether *Powell* or any future case would turn exclusively on the criterion of a demonstrable textual commitment. Even if *Powell* does not rest exclusively on this criterion, Warren's opinion significantly lowers the political-question barrier. Indeed, the majority's opinion resembles but is not identical to the classical theory, which severely limits the Supreme Court's invocation of the political question in cases that require the judiciary to determine whether another department has exceeded its constitutional authority.

Arising from President Richard M. Nixon's unqualified claim of executive privilege against disclosing confidential information, *United States v. Nixon*[110] rekindled the controversy over the scope of the political-question doctrine and its applicability to foreign relations and the war powers. In *Nixon*, a unanimous Court (Associate Justice William Rehnquist did not participate) decided that the President's blanket claim of confidentiality did not pose a political question.[111] Although *Nixon* does not involve questions of external sovereignty (e.g., diplomatic, military, or national-security secrets), Chief Justice Warren Burger, speaking for a unanimous Court, provided further evidence that the Supreme Court has narrowed the scope of the political-question doctrine.[112] Its applicability to questions of foreign relations and the war powers, however, remains problematic since these issues are not present in *Nixon*.

After concluding that the Court has jurisdiction, that Special Prosecutor Leon Jaworski has standing to sue, and that the constitutional issues present a mature case or controversy, Burger confronted the political-question barrier. Not unlike Brennan (in *Baker*) and Warren (in *Powell*), Burger began his analysis by examining the constitutional separation of powers. He, too, had to determine whether the Constitution commits power exclusively to the President to decide his own claim of privilege against disclosure. If such a textual commitment exists, Burger had then to determine the scope of presidential discretion.[113]

In the absence of an *explicit* textual commitment, Burger attempted to determine whether an *implicit* commitment exists.[114] Does the President's claim to absolute privilege against disclosure flow from his constitutionally enumerated powers and duties? Is the claim of absolute privilege an incidental power that is indispensable to the performance of some power vested in the presidential office? Without further analysis, Burger concluded that

> . . . neither the doctrine of separation of powers, nor the need for confidentiality of high-level communications, without more, can

sustain an absolute, unqualified Presidential privilege of immunity from judicial process under all circumstances. . . . Absent a
claim of need to protect military, diplomatic, or sensitive national
security secrets, we find it difficult to accept the argument that
even the very important interest in confidentiality of Presidential communications is significantly diminished by production of
such material for *in camera* inspection with all the protection that
a district court will be obliged to provide.[115]

Althouth Burger accepted the need for executive privilege against
disclosure of diplomatic, military, and national-security secrets, he rejected more than the President's blanket claim of confidentiality. Burger
rejected the concept that the President has exclusive power to determine the scope of executive privilege. The Chief Justice asserted judicial power to evaluate and decide presidential claims. However, he admitted that the Court would show deference to claims of privilege
incidental to the President's performance of his constitutional duties.
Indeed, Burger recognized the Court's duty to defer to the President's
power to withhold information that could jeopardize diplomatic, military, or national-security secrets.[116] Quoting approvingly from *United
States* v. *Reynolds* (1953), Burger affirmed that the judiciary "' . . .
should not jeopardize the security which the privilege is meant to protect by insisting upon an examination of the evidence, even by the
judge alone, in chambers.'"[117]

Nixon does not involve diplomatic, military, or national-security secrets; however, the Court's opinion suggests that a presidential claim of
privilege to withhold such information would be conclusive rather than
presumptive.[118] If the information upon which the President bases his
claim is not subject to *in camera* inspection, then, the claim is not re-
buttable. The Court does not, however, explain why *in camera* inspection jeopardizes national-security secrets. After admitting that *in camera* inspection affords confidentiality in an era of legislative and
executive leaks, Burger states that *in camera* judicial inspection of intelligence information does not seem particularly threatening to national security. The Court's treatment of the political-question doctrine
invites ritualistic or talismanic claims of privilege based on "national
security." By invoking "national security," the executive can defeat judicial review of executive practices that threaten constitutional rights as
well as the delicate constitutional balance on which the separation of
powers rests.[119]

Inasmuch as *Nixon* does not involve "state secrets," Burger's comments on executive privilege against disclosing diplomatic, military, or

national-security secrets are dicta. The Court's decision affirms judicial power to entertain boundary disputes " . . . in a manner that preserves the essential functions of each branch."[120] Insofar as the President's power to withhold information flows from an exclusive textual commitment of power to the executive, the Court reaffirms *Powell* v. *McCormack*. If the President's actions breach the constitutional separation of powers by usurping power that is judicial or legislative,[121] one can infer that the political-question barrier will fall away. Similarly, if the President's conduct jeopardizes an individual's constitutional rights, he cannot hide behind the political-question barrier, since the Constitution does not commit such power to the executive.

Justice Brennan and Chief Justices Warren and Burger rest their analysis of the political question largely on the constitutional separation of powers. While Warren and Burger show some deference to the other discretionary criteria that Brennan enumerated in *Baker*, they attempt to determine whether an explicit or implicit textual commitment exists. Next, they analyze the scope of discretionary power that is constitutionally committed to Congress or to the President. Within this field, Brennan, Warren, and Burger deny the Court's jurisdiction to entertain and judicial power to decide, which leaves the "political departments" free to determine the law. If, however, presidential or congressional action exceeds their respective constitutional authority and/or endangers the individual's constitutional rights, the political-question doctrine does not pose an insurmountable barrier to judicial review. As Brennan, Warren, and Burger construe the political-question barrier, the judiciary has considerable scope to review legislative-executive boundary disputes and breaches of individual rights touching on the war-powers, foreign-affairs, national-security, and other dimensions of external sovereignty. Unless judicial intervention threatens fundamental security interests, the political-question barrier does not preclude judicial review of executive and legislative conduct.

Conclusion: Going beyond the Threshold— the Scope of Judicial Intervention

The constitutional sharing and separation of power and the absence of a clear, comprehensive, and exclusive commitment of war and foreign-affairs powers to Congress or the President creates the opportunity for judicial intervention. When Congress and the President cannot reconcile their differences through bargaining and compromise, the need for a single policy creates the occasion for judicial resolution of conflict. If the courts intervene in boundary disputes, their function is to determine whether the other departments have exceeded their constitutional competence to decide questions of war and peace. Similarly, when individuals claim that governmental action threatens their constitutional rights, the judicial function is to decide questions of constitutional authority. As long as Congress and the President act within their respective spheres of constitutional authority, the courts should not question the wisdom or desirability of legislative policy and executive conduct.

Although the constitutional separation of the congressional war powers from the office of commander in chief provides a broad standard for judicial intervention in boundary disputes,[122] further analysis is necessary to identify the scope, timing, conditions for, and consequences of judicial arbitration of government power. First, one should identify the factors that encourage judicial intervention. Are the courts likely to review governmental actions concerning the initiation, conduct, and termination of war and hostilities when (1) the President acts pursuant to an express or implied authorization of Congress; (2) the President acts in the absence of either a congressional grant or denial of authority, relying on his own independent powers; or (3) the President takes measures incompatible with the expressed or implied will of Congress?[123]

In each domain of governmental policy—the initiation, conduct, and termination of war and hostilities—one should examine the substantive nature of specific issues to explain judicial decisions to intervene and the scope of judicial intervention. Are some issues or domains more susceptible to judicial management than others? Is it easier to develop judicial standards to decide statutory or constitutional issues concerning the conduct of war than to initiate or terminate war and hostilities? Are the issues in each domain more susceptible to statutory or constitutional review? Can the Federal courts fashion judicial relief that leads to the peaceful resolution of conflict without impairing another department's performance of its essential functions?

In addition to identifying the conditions for and scope of judicial intervention in war-powers and foreign-affairs controversies, one should also attempt to determine the timing of judicial intervention. Conventional wisdom suggests that the Federal courts avoid, delay, or defer judgment in war-powers controversies during an international emergency. Once the emergency has attenuated or passed, however, the Federal courts are more likely to exercise their powers of constitutional and statutory review.[124] To what extent does "timing" or the domestic and international context affect judicial intervention?

Finally, what are the consequences or implications of judicial intervention concerning the constitutional allocation of the war powers? Is judicial intervention and/or abstention neutral with respect to congressional and presidential power? When the courts intervene in war-powers controversies do they tend to legitimate the exercise of legislative and executive power? Under what conditions do the courts attempt to limit the exercise of congressional and presidential power?

While the constitutional separation of powers does not preclude judicial review of war-powers controversies or require the absolute deference to congressional and presidential judgment that the political-question doctrine sometimes suggests, the separation of powers provides a broad standard for judicial intervention in the vast, complex, and uncertain realm of foreign affairs. When the courts intervene in boundary disputes in order to protect an individual's constitutional rights or society's interest in constitutional government, they should not impair the performance of legislative or executive functions that are essential to protecting national-security interests.[125] Although the courts do not owe Congress or the President absolute deference in defining the boundaries of legislative and executive power, the principle of comity suggests that the judiciary should search for formulas that least restrict each branch in the performance of its functions, i.e., formulas that maximize each department's independence. As Robert Nagel recommends, when the courts challenge the exercise of legislative or executive power, they should pause to examine the effect of their decisions on the other department's operation. In cases that involve conflicting claims of power, the courts should first determine how broadly and deeply their decisions cut into another department's functions before marching into the political thicket.[126]

4

The Scope of Congressional and Presidential Power to Initiate War and Hostilities

With few exceptions, during the Vietnam War (1964–1973) the Federal courts refused to decide various cases that challenged the President's authority to initiate and conduct military hostilities without a declaration of war.[1] Indeed, the Supreme Court entertained only one case challenging the President's authority to initiate or conduct military hostilities in Southeast Asia. While the lower Federal courts generally refused to decide the Vietnam cases on the merits because the petitioners lacked standing to sue or because their claims presented nonjusticiable political questions, the Supreme Court simply denied certiorari.[2] In 1968, the Court's silence prompted Justice William O. Douglas to observe that the question of the Vietnam War's constitutionality deserved more than an unexplained denial of certiorari.[3] The Federal judiciary's refusal to determine the scope of presidential authority to initiate military hostilities without a congressional declaration of war supports recent scholarly criticism that the courts are impotent in checking presidential power in foreign affairs.[4]

In his celebrated and widely accepted opinion, Justice Sutherland suggested that discretionary governmental authority to initiate war and hostilities is a plenary, extraconstitutional power that derives from the nation's existence as a sovereign state in the international political system.[5] "The powers to declare and wage war, to conclude peace, to make treaties, to maintain diplomatic relations with other sovereignties," Sutherland wrote in *Curtiss-Wright*, "if they had never been mentioned in the Constitution, would have vested in the federal government as necessary concomitants of nationality."[6] Inasmuch as governmental authority in this external realm rests on international law and practice,[7] according to Sutherland's argument, the exercise of congressional and presidential power is not subject to judicial inquiry or constitutional limitations. In this vast external realm, the separation of powers has no bearing on the exercise of the congressional war powers or the commander in chief's defensive powers. Having determined that a dispute involves questions of external sovereignty, judicial inquiry is at an end.

If such phrases as "external sovereignty" or "the war powers" are "talismanic incantations" that preclude constitutional limitations on the exercise of governmental powers,[8] as Justice Sutherland's opinion implies, the scope of judicial review of external or foreign relations is rather trivial. Sutherland's opinion also implies that governmental power can be arrayed along a continuum from exclusively domestic to exclusively external powers (see Figure 4.1). The scope of judicial inquiry varies inversely with the degree of externality. As the exercise of governmental power becomes more exclusively external, the occasion for the exercise of judicial power decreases.[9] At one end of the continuum, in domestic emergencies, congressional delegations of power are subject to judicial review and the application of judicial criteria based on the separation of powers.[10] At the other end of the continuum, in international emergencies, the congressional and presidential exercise of power is subject to few constitutional limitations.[11]

Despite broad acceptance of the doctrine of sovereign immunity in external affairs, Sutherland's theory suffers from several empirical and theoretical limitations. First is the difficulty of classifying governmental powers as either entirely domestic or external. The powers to call up the Army's reserve, to activate the National Guard, to block foreign accounts in U.S. banks, to seize enemy property, and to expel enemy aliens are domestic powers that directly affect U.S. relations with other nations. In fact, few decisions involving the exercise of the war powers are exclusively domestic or external. In classifying power according to the dimension of externality that Sutherland's opinion implies, should the courts accept congressional and presidential statements concerning the nature of a particular power as conclusive? Should the courts make

Figure 4.1 Judicial Review of Governmental Actions: The Sutherland View

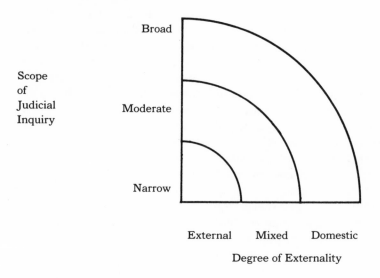

their own independent inquiry concerning the degree of externality? Sutherland's dichotomy between an external realm of sovereign power immune to judicial review and a domestic realm subject to constitutional limitations rests on a distinction that is difficult, if not impossible, to measure empirically.

In addition to these empirical problems, the theory of external sovereignty that Sutherland advanced in *Curtiss-Wright* has been seriously eroded. Justice Black's opinion in *Reid* v. *Covert* (1956)[12] vitiates the distinction between the sovereign immunity of governmental power in external affairs and constitutional limitations on governmental power in domestic affairs. In contrast to Sutherland's opinion, Black argues that all governmental power flows from the Constitution and is subject to constitutional limitations. By denying the government's inherent, sovereign, or extraconstitutional power in external affairs, Black implicitly broadens the scope of judicial inquiry into the constitutionality of congressional policy and presidential conduct in this external realm.[13] The government's invocation of "external sovereignty" or "the war powers" does not pose an impermeable barrier to judicial intervention or seriously restrict the scope of judicial inquiry. While the courts owe considerable deference to the political departments, the government cannot shield its exercise of the war powers from judicial inquiry by ritualistically incanting "national sovereignty."

THE SCOPE OF JUDICIAL INQUIRY

Although the constitutional separation of powers does not bar judicial intervention in war-powers controversies, conventional wisdom suggests that the occasions for judicial review are few, that the courts usually avoid deciding war-powers controversies, and that when the courts intervene they usually legitimate the government's actions.[14] When the courts legitimate constitutionally questionable wartime practices, as Justice Jackson observed in *Korematsu*, the wartime exception tends to become a peacetime principle.[15] Judicial attempts to limit presidential conduct as commander in chief are futile since the President is likely to ignore judicial decisions that impair military policy, as Lincoln ignored Taney's order in *Ex parte Merryman*.[16] In contrast to *Merryman*, *Youngstown Sheet and Tube Co. v. Sawyer* represents a rare victory for the Supreme Court over the President, a victory that outweighs any risk of the judgment's being ignored.

Despite judicial reluctance to decide war-powers controversies, the Federal judiciary's occasional forays into this political thicket suggest a need to explore the scope of judicial inquiry and decisionmaking. In attempting to define the scope of judicial intervention, Justice Jackson's concurring opinion in *Youngstown* is a useful starting point. However, several caveats are in order before applying Jackson's analysis to disputes involving the initiation of war and hostilities. A sometimes ignored but important point is that Jackson's opinion applies to concurrent power, i.e., the powers of war and defense that the President and Congress share. "[T]here is," as Jackson noted, "a zone of twilight in which he [the President] and Congress may have concurrent authority, or in which its distribution is uncertain."[17] Jackson's opinion has little bearing on the exercise of power that the Constitution commits exclusively to Congress or the President. Moreover, Jackson's opinion refers to the President's domestic rather than his external or international powers. Nevertheless, President Harry S Truman's seizure of the nation's steel mills was contingent on an emergency that he had created by committing U.S. armed forces to combat in Korea without a congressional declaration of war or other authorizing legislation.[18]

Insofar as Jackson's opinion is applicable to separation-of-powers controversies that involve the initiation of war and hostilities, one must first define the scope of exclusive presidential authority to deploy and commit troops to defensive hostilities and the scope of exclusive congressional authority to initiate war and hostilities. Between these two zones lies Jackson's twilight zone of concurrent authority, in which the distribution of power is uncertain. Inasmuch as Jackson's opinion does not define the boundaries of this twilight zone, one must look elsewhere in locating its perimeters.

In defining the zones of exclusive and concurrent power, two competing theories can be employed: (1) the defensive/offensive-war theory and (2) the threshold theory of congressional and presidential authority to control the initiation of war and hostilities. The defensive/offensive-war theory can be inferred from the Framers' separation of the congressional war powers from the presidential office of commander in chief. The threshold theory is of more recent parentage, a progeny of insurgency warfare and the imperial presidency. During the Vietnam War some Federal judges employed the threshold theory to determine the constitutional adequacy of congressional support for the President's military conduct. Since these two competing theories define the zones of exclusive and concurrent power differently, their assumptions and implications should be examined before attempting to apply each theory to war-powers controversies.

The Framers' defensive/offensive-war theory assumes that the President has the exclusive constitutional authority to defend U.S. citizens, territory, troops, and property against sudden attack or when the threat of attack is imminent. As long as the President's actions remain "defensive," he does not require congressional authorization to continue military operations. Once the President's conduct becomes "offensive," however, he lacks the constitutional authority to proceed further without congressional authorization through a declaration of war or other legislation. If Congress authorizes military hostilities without declaring war, such authorization should be clear, explicit, and demonstrable rather than implied or inferred from an appropriations act that merely provides funds for armed forces previously committed to hostilities.[19]

Actually, the defensive/offensive-war theory contains two dimensions: (1) the defensive-offensive character of military hostilities and (2) the duration of such hostilities (see Figure 4.2). The theory assumes that various diplomatic and military actions can be arrayed along a continuum from exclusively "defensive" to exclusively "offensive" conduct. Short of a sudden attack on the United States, however, is there a clear distinction between defensive and offensive conduct? Israel, for example, insists that its raids against Palestinian guerrilla camps in Lebanon are defensive military actions. While the United States views the

Figure 4.2 The Defensive/Offensive-War Theory: The Framers' View

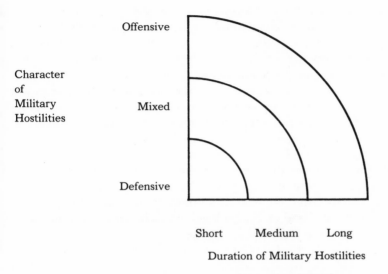

Character
of
Military
Hostilities

Offensive

Mixed

Defensive

Short   Medium   Long

Duration of Military Hostilities

deployment of neutron weapons in Western Europe as defensive, the Soviet Union perceives the same conduct as offensive. The Soviets characterize the presence of Russian combat troops in Cuba as defensive, while the U.S. perceives their presence 90 miles from the nation's shores as offensive. In addition to the difficulty of distinguishing between defensive and offensive conduct, since the ratification of the United Nations Charter no signatory nation is likely to admit that its behavior is aggressive or offensive, because to do so would be to admit violating Article 2 (Section 4) of the Charter.

Assuming that one can develop criteria for distinguishing defensive from offensive diplomatic and military conduct, how much deference should the Federal judiciary accord legislative and executive characterizations of such conduct? Should the political departments' statements be conclusive, of great weight, or subject to independent judicial inquiry? If subject to *de novo* inquiry, should the courts employ currently accepted international law and practice? Insofar as international law and practice conflict with municipal law, what is the Federal judiciary's obligation to extend the international rule of law to municipal practice?

A second assumption of the defensive/offensive-war theory is that the scope of presidential and congressional authority is a function of the duration of hostilities. As military hostilities become more prolonged, the President's military conduct is likely to become more offensive in character. If the President's defensive measures are successful, by definition military hostilities will terminate at an early stage. However, if the President's initial response is inadequate and military hostilities continue, at some point the escalation of military force transforms the character of the President's actions from defensive to offensive conduct. Prolonging military hostilities increases the probability that the President will cross the Rubicon and enter the twilight zone between the commander in chief's defensive power and the congressional war powers, which, in turn, presents the courts with an opportunity to exercise their power of judicial review.

In contrast to the Framers' defensive/offensive-war theory, the threshold theory defines the zones of exclusive and concurrent power in terms of the magnitude of military and diplomatic action.[20] The threshold theory assumes that one can array military and diplomatic actions along a continuum based on (1) the level of escalation and (2) the duration of hostilities (see Figure 4.3). At one end of the continuum (Table 4.1, categories 1–4) the President has discretionary power to initiate

Figure 4.3 The Threshold Theory: The Contemporary View

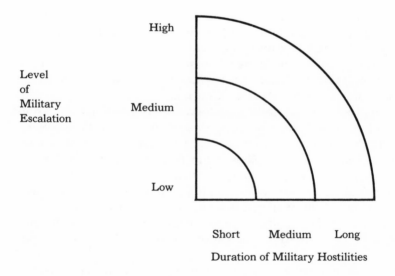

Level
of
Military
Escalation

High

Medium

Low

Short   Medium   Long

Duration of Military Hostilities

Table 4.1. An Array of Military and Diplomatic Actions in Order of Ascending Magnitude

1. Covert intelligence operations and clandestine paramilitary operations
2. Diplomatic actions that imply subsequent military operations, e.g., severing diplomatic relations
3. Deployment of armed forces in nonhostile situations, e.g., rotation of troops to meet alliance commitments
4. Mobilization of military forces, e.g., call up of army reserves
5. Deployment of armed forces in hostile situations, e.g., commitment of armed forces to combat zones
6. Limited military engagements, e.g., protection of U.S. citizens, property, and public ships, seizures, and reprisals
7. Limited military interventions, e.g., civil commotions, claims settlements, border disputes, and preemption of third-party interventions
8. Material wars, i.e., undeclared wars: the Naval War with France, the Barbary Wars, the Civil War, the Korean War, and the Vietnam War
9. Publicly declared wars: the War of 1812, the Mexican War of 1846–1848, the Spanish American War of 1898, World War One, and World War Two

limited military actions of short duration. At the other end of the continuum (category 9), at the threshold of a declaration of war, Congress has exclusive authority to initiate major actions of long duration. Between these two zones of exclusive constitutional authority lies the twilight zone of concurrent power (categories 5–8), i.e., the power to initiate limited military engagements, interventions, and material war. While one can quarrel with a particular array of military and diplomatic actions, by ordering events according to their magnitude one can develop empirical measures for determining the zones of exclusive and concurrent power. Once the boundaries of these zones have been established, Justice Jackson's criteria in *Youngstown* can be employed to determine the scope of judicial inquiry in separation-of-powers controversies.

According to Justice Jackson's analysis, once the President enters the twilight zone of concurrent constitutional power, several conditions affect judicial decisions to intervene and determine the scope of congressional and presidential authority. "When the President acts pursuant to an express or implied authorization of Congress, his authority is at its maximum, . . . "[21] and, conversely, the scope of judicial power is rather limited. While the courts have the power to review the constitutionality of legislative delegations, Congress is entitled to the presumption that its delegations are valid. Similarly, the President is entitled to the presumption that his actions have been authorized unless presidential conduct clearly exceeds a delegation statute. Unless Congress and the President manifestly exceed their powers, the judiciary should not interfere with their joint exercise of power and the performance of their constitutional functions.[22]

"When the President acts in absence of either a congressional grant or denial of authority, . . . "[23] his power rests on whatever authority the Constitution vests directly in the commander in chief. If Congress is silent the Court must determine whether the emergency warrants the President's initiative. "In this area," wrote Jackson, "any actual test of power is likely to depend on the imperatives of events and contemporary imponderables rather than on abstract theories of law."[24] Once again, Jackson raised but did not answer an important question, namely, how much weight should judges attribute to the executive's factual determinations? In a separate concurring opinion, Justice Clark also observed that " . . . the President's independent power to act depends upon the gravity of the situation confronting the nation."[25] Unfortunately, neither Clark nor Jackson provided any constitutional criteria for evaluating the gravity of an emergency.

"When the President takes measures incompatible with the expressed or implied will of Congress," Jackson argued, "his power is at its lowest ebb."[26] When the judiciary confronts a presidential claim to power opposed by a congressional denial of power, as Jackson recognized, " . . . what is at stake is the equilibrium established by our constitutional system."[27] Although he paid deference to the President's lawful role as commander in chief, Jackson acknowledged the Court's responsibility to decide controversies involving competing claims of power. Rather than relying on such tecniques of avoidance as the political question, he accepted the judiciary's responsibility to preserve limitations on governmental power as well as the equilibrium upon which the separation of powers and constitutional government rest.[28] Clear, irreconcilable conflict between Congress and the President provides the occasion for the responsible exercise of judicial power.

While Justice Jackson acknowledged the dangers implicit in theories that justify emergency power, he denied the possibility of developing *a priori* tests to evaluate the constitutionality of exercising such power. Indeed, he suggested that the courts could employ only *a posteriori* tests based on "the imperatives of events" and "contemporary imponderables" in reviewing the scope of legislative and executive power.[29] When the Federal courts review executive or legislative judgments concerning the facts of or response to a military emergency, Jackson's pragmatic approach suggests that judges should consider such factors as (1) the timing and (2) the consequences of their decisions.[30]

Justice Black's opinion in *Duncan* v. *Kahanamoku* (1945) and District Judge McLaughlin's opinion in *Ex parte White* (1944) also suggest that the timing of judicial intervention can affect the scope of judicial inquiry.[31] In the early stages of a military emergency, when the facts of the emergency are unclear to the courts as well as to the commander in chief, the judiciary has reason to exercise self-restraint and to proceed cautiously in exercising its power. As the emergency abates, however, the courts are in a better position to review legislative and executive determinations concerning the facts of a military emergency. Since there is less justification for executive privilege against disclosure after the emergency has ended than during ongoing military operations, there should be greater access to the information that the courts require in appraising the constitutionality of legislative and executive actions. Speaking for a majority in *Duncan*, Justice Black noted that the events leading to Duncan's arrest and trial by a military tribunal in Hawaii were somewhat remote by the time he was convicted.[32] As Judge McLaughlin had written in *Ex parte White* (the companion case to *Duncan*), "The highly successful Battle of Midway was over early in June, 1942. After that battle it was and is common knowledge that the danger of a land invasion of Hawaii was removed and has never since re-existed."[33] By the time the civilian courts disposed of these two cases, the emergency had abated and the judiciary did not require access to classified diplomatic or military secrets.

Jackson's pragmatic approach also recommends that the judiciary attempt to evaluate the scope of its inquiry in relation to its effect on the performance of legislative and executive functions. Jackson remarked:

> We should not use this occasion to circumscribe, much less to contract, the lawful role of the President as Commander in Chief. I should indulge the widest latitude of interpretation to sustain his exclusive function to command the instruments of national force, at least when turned against the outside world for the security of our society. But, when it is turned inward, not because of rebellion but because of a lawful economic struggle between industry and labor, it should have no such indulgence. His command power is not such an absolute as might be implied from that office in a militaristic system but is subject to limitations consistent with a constitutional Republic whose law and policy-making branch is a representative Congress.[34]

Althouth one can quarrel with Jackson's internal/external criterion for determining the scope of legislative and executive functions, one should not denigrate his search for a formula that least impairs the other branches in performing their respective constitutional roles.

In a separate concurring opinion, Justice Frankfurter clearly stated the formula that provided an otherwise fragmented majority with a common denominator and least restricted the scope of executive power:

> The issue before us can be met, and therefore should be, without attempting to define the President's powers comprehensively. . . . The judiciary may, as this case proves, have to intervene in determining where authority lies as between the democratic forces in our scheme of government. But in doing so we should be wary and humble. . . . We must therefore put to one side consideration of what powers the President would have had if there had been no legislation whatever bearing on the authority asserted by the seizure, or if the seizure had been only for a short, explicitly temporary period, to be terminated automatically unless Congressional approval were given. These and other questions, like or unlike, are not now here. I would exceed my authority were I to say anything about them.[35]

By evading the broader question of inherent power, of the President's seizure power in the absence of congressional legislation to the contrary, the Court avoided a basic decision that goes to the core of the President's military power as civilian commander in chief. In cases that involve conflict between Congress and the President, in the twilight zone of concurrent power, the Jackson-Frankfurter approach recommends that the courts decide on the narrowest grounds available, limit their conclusions to the particular factual setting, and avoid stating broad constitutional rules.[36]

THE SCOPE OF CONGRESSIONAL AND PRESIDENTIAL POWER: EARLY JUDICIAL INQUIRY

Although the Federal courts have had relatively few opportunities to decide war-powers cases, as early as 1800 the judiciary entered this political thicket to decide several controversies involving congressional and presidential power to initiate war and hostilities. Arising from the captures of the vessels *Eliza* and *Amelia* during the Naval War with France (1798–1800), in *Bas* v. *Tingy* and *Talbot* v. *Seeman* (1800),[37] the Supreme Court sustained the exercise of the congressional prize power to authorize and control the conduct of military hostilities. In *seriatim* opinions, three of the justices emphasized the congressional power to initiate offensive war, whether limited or general.[38] Their opinions support the argument that the offensive/defensive character of military action rather than the magnitude of military activities determines the zone of exclusive congressional authority. Justice Chase noted in his opinion:

> I have never entertained a doubt on the subject. Congress is empowered to declare a general war, or Congress may wage a limited war; limited in place, in objects, and in time. If a general war is declared, its extent and operations are only restricted and regulated by the *jus belli*, forming a part of the law of nations; but if a partial war is waged, its extent and operation depend on our municipal laws.[39]

In addition to commenting on the scope of congressional authority, Justice Washington observed that presidential power to conduct military operations is subject to the limitations of international and municipal law.[40] Although the Court sustained the seizure and condemnation, the justices' opinions do not reveal unusual caution in confronting congressional and presidential power to initiate and conduct military hostilities.

The justices' *seriatim* opinions also reveal a willingness to examine congressional intent in authorizing naval hostilities with France. Four of the justices examined congressional legislation to determine the character of the naval war as well as the scope of military hostilities that Congress had authorized.[41] While the Court did not question the wisdom of congressional policy, the justices did not hide behind procedural barriers to avoid deciding the legality of the seizure. Furthermore, the Court decided the two cases during rather than after the termination of the Naval War with France.

In a subsequent decision,[42] following the cessation of hostilities against France, the Supreme Court sustained the exercise of the congressional prize powers to limit executive conduct of the naval war. During the hostilities, a U.S. naval officer, Captain Little, had captured a Danish vessel, the *Flying Fish*, en route from Jeremie, a French West Indian port, to St. Thomas, a neutral Danish possession.[43] Although Captain Little apparently was acting under presidential instructions, the Supreme Court held him personally responsible since the seizure was unauthorized by congressional legislation. An act of February 9, 1799, authorized capture of ships bound *to* but not *from* French ports.[44] In his opinion, Marshall did not confront the apparent conflict between the congressional act and the President's instructions, but he recognized that such a conflict existed:

> ... the legislature seems to have prescribed that the manner in which this law shall be carried into execution, was to exclude a seizure of any vessel not bound to a French port. ... It was so obvious, that if only vessels sailing to a French port could be seized on the high seas, that the law would be very often evaded, that this act of Congress appears to have received a different construction from the executive of the United States; a construction much better calculated to give it effect.[45]

Marshall's opinion supports the view that Congress has plenary power to limit the scope of an undeclared war as well as the power to initiate such hostilities.[46] Recognizing the imperatives of military necessity, however, Marshall avoided a decision that would unnecessarily restrict the President's authority as commander in chief by formulating a rule broader than necessary under the circumstances. Rather than deciding that the President had exceeded his authority, Marshall concluded that Captain Little was answerable for damages to the vessel's owner. "I acquiesce in [the opinion] of my brethren, ... " Marshall concluded, "that the instructions cannot change the nature of the transaction, or legalize an act which, without those instructions, would have been a plain trespass."[47]

While the previous decisions sustain congressional power to control the initiation and scope of limited hostilities, in *Brown v. U.S.* (1814) the Supreme Court examined legislative power to authorize the seizure of property as incidental to a declaration of war.[48] Following the U.S. declaration of war against Great Britain on June 18, 1812, the U.S. attorney for Massachusetts brought a libel action against a cargo of timber as enemy property. The district court dismissed the libel action since Congress had not authorized the seizure.[49] However, the circuit court subsequently sustained the seizure as incidental to the congressional declaration of war. In addition to authorizing the initiation of war, the circuit court decided, a declaration of war authorizes measures that are necessary to wage war successfully and that international law permits.[50]

Although the Supreme Court decided the narrow question of the circuit court's condemnation of the cargo as a prize of war, Marshall's majority opinion raised the broader question of congressional power to control the scope of a *de jure* war subsequent to and independent from the congressional declaration. Admitting that a congressional declaration of war creates the rights and obligations of belligerency, Marshall denied that a declaration automatically effects a seizure of enemy property. Only Congress can authorize such seizures as an exercise of its auxiliary war powers.[51] War furnishes Congress the occasion to authorize measures necessary to wage war successfully, but a declaration of war does not confer the auxiliary war powers on the executive:

> That the declaration of war has only the effect of placing the two nations in a state of hostility, of producing a state of war, of giving those rights which war confers; but not of operating, by its own force, any of those results, such as a transfer of property . . . is fairly deducible from the enumeration of powers which accompanies that of declaring war.[52]

After examining various measures that Congress had authorized, including laws prohibiting trade with the enemy and governing treatment of prisoners of war, Marshall concluded that Congress had not authorized the seizure and condemnation of enemy property in the United States. According to Marshall, congressional initiation of *de jure* war neither confers auxiliary war powers on the President nor precludes subsequent legislation limiting presidential conduct of war.[53]

In a dissenting opinion, Justice Story observed that the congressional declaration of war as well as subsequent prize legislation of June 26, 1812, authorized the seizure of enemy property.[54] Besides disagreeing with Marshall's statutory construction of the declaration of war and various auxiliary war measures, Story also commented on the scope of congressional power to authorize military hostilities and the scope of presidential power to conduct such hostilities. After commenting extensively on the international law governing prizes and captures, Story observed, "[t]he next question is, whether Congress (for with them rests the sovereignty of the nation as to the right of making war, and declaring its limits and effects) have authorized the seizure of enemies' property afloat in our ports."[55] Finding that the congressional declaration of war did not limit presidential conduct, Story concluded that the President is free to employ military measures concerning captures that the law of nations permits. Although Story does not argue that a declaration of war, per se, confiscates an enemy's property, he suggests that the President has the power to employ such measures unless Congress limits his conduct as commander in chief:[56]

> If, indeed, there be a limit imposed as to the extent to which hostilities may be carried by the executive, I admit that the executive cannot lawfully transcend that limit; but if no such limit

exist, the war may be carried on according to the principles of the modern law of nations, and enforced when and where, and on what property the executive chooses.[57]

Despite their fundamental disagreement over the authority that a congressional declaration of war confers on the President, Marshall and Story concur that Congress can control the scope of *de jure* as well as an undeclared or limited war. By denying that a declaration of war confers auxiliary war powers on the President, Marshall infers that the commander in chief lacks authority to employ these powers unless Congress authorizes military, diplomatic, and other measures that contemporary international law and practice permit. By contrast, Story argues that a congressional declaration of war authorizes the President to take whatever measures international law and practice permit unless Congress specifically restricts presidential conduct. Since the declaration of war authorized the measures necessary to carry it into effect, the President's duty to faithfully execute the law confers the power to employ " . . . every incidental power which the law of nations authorizes and approves in a state of war."[58]

Although these early cases were decided before Marshall developed the political-question doctrine in *Foster* v. *Neilson* (1829),[59] the Court's decisions suggest several important propositions about the scope of congressional power to initiate war and hostilities. First, these early decisions define the zone of exclusive congressional power to initiate war and hostilities in terms of the offensive/defensive character of military conduct rather than the magnitude of hostilities. The Supreme Court recognized exclusive congressional power to initiate limited military hostilities as well as *de jure* war. Second, if Congress authorizes or proclaims limited war, it has the power to restrict the magnitude, duration, and objectives of military hostilities. Third, if Congress declares a *de jure* war, such a declaration does not automatically confer the auxiliary war powers on the President. As Marshall suggests in *Brown* v. *U.S.*, only Congress can authorize the measures necessary to wage war successfully. Marshall's opinion also suggests that such authorization must be specific, flows from the various auxiliary war powers vested exclusively in Congress, and cannot be inferred from a declaration of war. In his dissenting opinion, Story suggests that a declaration of war authorizes such measures that the international law of belligerency permits unless Congress specifically restricts the scope of executive power. Despite their disagreement concerning congressional silence on the power to seize the enemy's property, Marshall and Story sustain legislative power to initiate and control the magnitude and duration of offensive war and hostilities.

Although Congress has exclusive power to initiate war and hostilities, as early as 1806 a Federal circuit court recognized the President's power as commander in chief to defend the nation against sudden attack. Acting as circuit judge, in *United States* v. *Smith* (1806),[60] Justice Paterson emphasized the distinction between offensive and defensive war as the sole criterion for defining the zones of exclusive congressional and presidential power. Along with several other co-conspirators, a Colonel William S. Smith had organized and outfitted a military expedition of several hundred men and a converted merchant ship, the *Leander*, to liberate the Spanish province of Caraccas.[61] The expedition violated an act of June 5, 1794, which prohibited commencing military operations against nations with whom the United States is at peace.[62] In his defense, Colonel Smith claimed that the expedition had been initiated and planned with the knowledge of the President and the secretary of state.[63] Without admitting that Smith's allegations were true, Paterson argued that neither the President nor a private citizen could initiate war against a nation at peace with the United States. Even if the President had known and approved of Smith's expedition, only Congress can authorize such a military expedition since the power to make or initiate war " . . . is exclusively vested in congress. . . ."[64]

While Paterson emphasized congressional authority to initiate military hostilities, he recognized the President's defensive powers as commander in chief. Paterson also argued that the "principle of self defense" includes the power to "carry hostilities into the enemy's own country" as well as the right to resist invasion. Paterson recognized that in the "storm of battle" and the "full tide of victory" it would be difficult, if not impossible, to defeat an enemy without invading his territory. When Congress is not in session, the President has discretionary power to determine the force necessary to resist and subdue an invading enemy. According to Paterson, the President derives his authority from three sources: (1) the Constitution, (2) congressional statutes, and (3) the inherent right of self-defense.[65] In addition to the defensive powers that the Constitution vests in the commander in chief, the Militia Act of February 28, 1795, authorizes the President to call forth the militia to repel invasions.[66] Since the right to "self-preservation and defence" is a "primary law of nature" and "constitutes part of the law of nations," the President has an inherent duty to "repel an invading foe."[67]

Much of Paterson's opinion is dictum, however, since (1) Congress was in session, (2) presumably, the President was unaware and did not approve of Colonel Smith's military expedition, and (3) the expedition was offensive rather than defensive. Nevertheless, Paterson's opinion offers an early, if not authoritative, exposition of the President's defensive military powers. Although one can quarrel with Paterson's characterization of pursuing an enemy to his own territory as "defensive," he accepts the offensive/defensive character of military hostilities rather than their magnitude as the appropriate criterion for determining the zones of exclusive congressional and presidential authority.[68] By circumventing the question of whether the President actually knew and approved of Colonel Smith's expedition, Paterson avoided deciding whether the President's conduct conflicted with the express will of Congress. In dictum, Paterson emphasized the broad scope of congressional power to initiate war and hostilities and presidential power to defend the nation against sudden attack. Thus, Justice Paterson's opinion avoids interfering with the performance of either legislative or executive functions in the realm of external sovereignty.

More than fifty years later the same circuit court (the Circuit Court for the Southern District of New York) had the opportunity to rule on the President's power to dispatch naval forces abroad in order to protect U.S. citizens and their property from depredations. Responding to acts of violence against U.S. citizens, on July 13, 1854, Captain George N. Hollins, commander of the U.S. naval vessel *Cyane*, bombarded and burned Greytown (San Juan del Norte), Nicaragua. In his defense, Captain Hollins argued that he was not personally liable for damage to the community at Greytown since he had acted under lawful public orders from the President and the secretary of the Navy.[69]

Acting as circuit judge, in *Durand* v. *Hollins* (1860), Justice Nelson noted that the President's discretionary power to conduct the nation's foreign affairs includes selecting the appropriate diplomatic and military means to protect the lives and property of U.S. citizens abroad. Since neither Congress nor the President can anticipate or provide for such acts of violence, " . . . the interposition of the president abroad, for the protection of the citizen must necessarily rest in his discretion. . . ."[70] When other nations threaten the lives and property of U.S. citizens, the President must be free to take prompt and decisive action. A government that cannot protect its citizens, Nelson concluded, does not deserve their allegiance and is not worth preserving.[71]

Justice Nelson's interpretation of the Greytown incident implies that the executive's actions were defensive rather than offensive. As long as the President's military conduct is defensive, the Constitution commits exclusive discretion to the commander in chief. Within the zone of exclusive presidential authority, the courts lack jurisdiction and judicial power to intervene. When the President or his military agents exercise such discretionary power, they are responsible to the country through the political process rather than to the courts:[72]

> The question whether it was the duty of the president to interpose for the protection of the citizens at Greytown against an irresponsible and marauding community that had established itself there, was a public political question, in which the government, as well as the citizens whose interests were involved, was concerned, and which belonged to the executive to determine; and his decision is final and conclusive. . . .[73]

Although Justice Nelson concluded that the President's decision to respond militarily to threats against U.S. citizens is a political question, the Court, nevertheless, made a preliminary inquiry to determine whether the executive's conduct falls within the zone of authority that the Constitution vests exclusively in his office. In determining that the President's power is plenary, Nelson accepted implicitly the defensive/offensive-war theory that the Federal courts had employed in the earlier cases. After making these preliminary determinations, Justice Nelson concluded that the constitutional separation of powers precludes further judicial inquiry. Despite the circuit court's caution, its rationale is consistent with earlier judicial opinions, which defined the scope of presidential authority to initiate military hostilities in terms of the defensive/offensive-war theory.

THE CIVIL WAR CASES: CREATION OF A NATIONAL WAR POWER

A little more than six months after the circuit court decided *Durand* v. *Hollins*, the Civil War opened on April 12, 1861, with the bombardment of Fort Sumter. In the eleven weeks of "constitutional dictatorship"[74] that occurred between April 12 and July 4, when Congress finally convened, President Lincoln took a series of military actions that the legislature subsequently ratified. On April 15 the President called up 75,000 militiamen for ninety days' service,[75] a power that Congress had delegated in the Militia Act of 1795 and that the Supreme Court had sustained in *Martin* v. *Mott* (1827).[76] On April 19 and 27 Lincoln proclaimed a naval blockade of Confederate ports. According to Secretary of State Seward, the blockade was a defensive emergency measure aimed at suppressing the rebellion and preserving the Union.[77] On May 3 Lincoln issued a proclamation increasing the armed forces by 40,714 men and calling for 42,034 volunteers. Congress subsequently ratified the President's diplomatic and military actions on August 6, as though Lincoln had acted with the "express authority and direction" of the legislature.[78]

Less than a month after the President's proclamation of blockade, a U.S. naval frigate captured the *General Parkhill* off Charleston, South Carolina, on her voyage from Liverpool, England. In one of the first prize cases of the Civil War, on July 23, 1861, the U.S. District Court for the Eastern District of Pennsylvania sustained the seizure as a legitimate war measure sanctioned by the international law of belligerency despite the fact that the United States was not engaged in international hostilities.[79] District Judge Cadwalader's opinion deserves attention because the court decided *The Parkhill* two weeks before Congress ratified Lincoln's emergency war measures. *The Parkhill*, therefore, provides a clear test of presidential power to authorize "defensive" measures in response to armed rebellion.

After commenting on the rebellion's brief history, Judge Cadwalader confronted the important threshold issue posed by the political-question barrier. First, he observed that *The Parkhill* does not involve the treaty power or foreign relations, which the Constitution commits exclusively to the discretion of the political departments. Second, neither the President nor any other department can recognize a state's right to secede or alter the constitutional relation of the states to the Union. The Constitution simply does not vest such discretionary power in any department of the national government. Therefore, the constitutional separation of powers does not preclude judicial review of the President's decision to proclaim a blockade and seize the "enemy's" ships.[80]

While Judge Cadwalader acknowledged that civil war is categorically different from international war, he asserted that during a civil war " . . . hostilities may be prosecuted on the same footing as if those opposing the government were foreign enemies invading the land."[81] Indeed, when armed rebellion closes the civilian courts and imperils domestic order, the President has a constitutional duty to faithfully execute the law throughout the nation by armed force, if necessary. Only the President can judge the severity of the emergency when Congress is not in session. Under the circumstances, the President could employ belligerent measures, which include seizure of the enemy's property,[82] without recognizing the Confederacy's international sovereignty.

Despite the fact the Congress cannot declare war against a state, the

President has the authority to employ the law of belligerency since there is no " . . . difference as to belligerent rights in civil or foreign war."[83] According to Cadwalader,

> Any nation may be involved in a war which has not been declared, and as to which her government has not legislated. Judges of English prize courts have agreed with Bynkershoek in the opinion, which publicists no longer dispute, that the legal consequences of an actual war must be the same, whether it has or has not been formally declared.[84]

Thus, the President's authority to order defensive measures does not depend on a formal declaration of war. During a military emergency, when Congress is not in session, the President can employ such measures that military necessity requires and that municipal and international law permit.[85] When the President cannot execute the law peacefully, he has discretionary power as commander in chief to oppose force with force.

Although Judge Cadwalader conceded that only Congress can initiate offensive war measures, his opinion substantially enlarges the scope of the President's defensive powers. When the President confronts a sudden attack, he is required by the Constitution

> to "take care that the laws be faithfully executed." While other officers only swear to support the constitution, his official oath, as prescribed in it, requires him "to the best of his ability" to "preserve, protect, and defend the constitution." Therefore, when hostilities actually waged against the constitution and laws assume the dimensions of a general war, he must prosecute opposing hostilities, *offensive as well as defensive*, upon such a proportional scale as may be necessary to re-establish, or to support and maintain, the government.[86]

The President cannot initiate offensive war, but once the enemy attacks, he has discretionary power to employ whatever defensive or offensive measures "existing acts of Congress" and the "rules of public law" permit.[87] Despite Judge Cadwalader's deference to congressional authority, his opinion breaches the Framers' defensive/offensive-war theory and broadens the scope of presidential emergency powers.

The *General Parkhill* was but one of many ships that the United States Navy seized for running the President's blockade. Shortly thereafter the Navy seized four other vessels attempting to run the blockade:

The Crenshaw (May 17), *The Hiawatha* (May 20), *The Brilliante* (June 23), and *The Amy Warwick* (July 10).[88] Subsequently, Federal prize courts condemned the ships as legitimate prizes of war.[89] Although the Supreme Court sustained these condemnation proceedings after Congress had ratified Lincoln's proclamation of blockade, *The Prize Cases* (1862) raise the same issues that Judge Cadwalader had decided in *The Parkhill.*

In a 5–4 opinion that the minority strongly protested, Justice Grier sustained the President's power to initate a blockade. While he paid lip service to congressional authority to initiate war and hostilities, Grier argued that, as chief executive and commander in chief, the President has a constitutional duty to resist force with force.[90] Neither the vesting clause, nor the take-care clause, nor the commander-in-chief clause authorizes the President to initiate offensive war, but these constitutional provisions confer whatever power, in the President's judgment, he requires to suppress the rebellion. Whether the gravity of the emergency warrants the President's decision to grant the rebels belligerent status and to employ the belligerent rights of blockade, only the chief executive can judge.[91] Besides confirming Lincoln's authority to exercise power that falls within the scope of the congressional war powers, Justice Grier's opinion makes the President the sole judge of his own powers. The majority's opinion legitimized the eleven weeks of "constitutional dictatorship" between April 12 and July 4.

In a forceful dissenting opinion, Justice Nelson (speaking for Justices Catron and Clifford and Chief Justice Taney) emphasized that only Congress could initiate war and authorize lawful measures of belligerency. Until Congress acts, the President has ample defensive powers under the Constitution and the standing laws to suppress the rebellion without resorting to such measures as blockade and the seizure of enemy property, which are legislative powers.[92] When Congress convenes, it can determine whether to " . . . bring into operation the war power, and thus change the nature and character of the contest."[93] While Justice Nelson asserted congressional power to authorize future condemnations, he disputed the power to ratify or retroactively authorize condemnation proceedings in the prize courts.[94]

Both the majority's and the minority's opinions in *The Prize Cases* accept the logical distinction between offensive and defensive war on which the constitutional separation of the congressional war powers from the office of commander in chief rests. Justices Grier and Nelson agreed that only Congress can initiate war. The justices also agreed that the President has the constitutional authority to defend the nation against armed attack. While Grier argued that the President can employ whatever means, in his exclusive judgment, are necessary to suppress rebellion, Nelson argued that only Congress can authorize belligerent measures permitted by international law and practice.

Justices Grier and Nelson also disagreed on the justiciability of *The Prize Cases*. Since Grier believed that the Constitution confers discretionary power on the President, he argued that the commander in chief's military judgment is not subject to judicial inquiry. However, Nelson asserted that only when " . . . such a war is recognized or declared to exist by the war making power, but not otherwise, it is the duty of the courts to follow the decision of the political power of the government."[95] In the absence of a violation of constitutional rights, once the Court determines that the Constitution vests discretionary power in another department, judicial inquiry ceases. When the President exercises power that the Constitution confers on Congress, however, neither the separation of powers nor the political question poses a barrier to judicial review. While Justice Grier carried the majority, Justice Nelson remained faithful to the constitutional separation of powers.

Following the Civil War, the Supreme Court reaffirmed Justice Grier's opinion in *The Prize Cases*. In three separate cases involving trade with the enemy, suspension of an enemy creditor's claims, and blockade of the enemy's ports during the war, the Court sustained the position that President Lincoln's proclamation on April 19, 1861, marked the beginning of the Civil War.[96] In the absence of a congressional declaration of war, the President's proclamation is conclusive evidence of the Civil War's commencement. Chief Justice Chase commented in *The Protector*, a prize case:

> Acts of hostility by the insurgents occurred at periods so various, and of such different degrees of importance, and in parts of the country so remote from each other, . . . that it would be difficult, if not impossible, to say on what precise day it began or terminated. It is necessary, therefore, to refer to some public act of the political departments of the government to fix the dates; and, for obvious reasons, those of the executive department, which may be, and, in fact, was, at the commencement of hostilities, obliged to act during the recess of Congress, must be taken.[97]

If there was any doubt concerning the President's discretionary authority to respond to armed attack, the Supreme Court erased that doubt during its 1875 and 1877 terms. In *Matthews v. McStea* (1875) the Court reiterated its acceptance of the presidential proclamation of April 19 as " . . . conclusive evidence that a state of war existed between the people inhabiting those [named Confederate] States and the United States."[98] The President's first proclamation, however, did not interdict commercial intercourse, including business partnerships. Unless such commerce was incompatible with the blockade, it was lawful until the President issued another proclamation on August 16, which explicitly suspended most commerce with the Confederate States.[99]

Beyond affirming the President's proclamations as conclusive, Justice Strong's opinion for the Court emphasized the President's " . . . duty as well as his right to direct how [the war] should be carried on."[100] His opinion left no doubt that once hostilities had commenced, the President had discretionary power to meet the emergency with whatever force, in his judgment, was necessary to suppress the rebellion.[101] Justice Strong's opinion reaffirmed Grier's view in *The Prize Cases* that when hostilities begin during a congressional recess, in the absence of a declaration of war, the President has authority to order both defensive and offensive war measures. Not a single justice dissented in *Matthews* v. *McStea*.

During its 1877 term, the Supreme Court decided *Williams* v. *Bruffy*,[102] which denied the power of the Confederate States to sequester the credits and property of loyal U.S. citizens. Although the President's proclamations had conferred limited rights of belligerency on the Confederacy, the United States never recognized its international sovereignty. From the Court's perspective, the Confederacy was not entitled to exercise belligerent powers under international law. Moreover, the Constitution's contracts clause prohibited the Confederate States from confiscating credits and property. The President's decision to confer limited rights of lawful belligerency was an act of grace and humanity that avoided condemning the rebels as traitors under the Constitution's treason clause, but in no way conferred sovereignty on their cause. President Lincoln's proclamations merely recognized the existence of military hostilities, which he was constitutionally obliged to do without waiting for Congress to act.[103] Speaking for the Court, Justice Field noted that the President had discretionary power to " . . . determine what degree of force the crisis demanded, and whether the hostile forces were of such a character as to require him to accord to them the character of belligerents. . . ."[104] From the time the war began until Congress convened, only the President could determine the military and diplomatic actions necessary to preserve the Constitution and its government.

Although the Civil War precedents are inapplicable to international wars in the twentieth century, they demonstrate that a subtle but fundamental change had occurred in judicial opinion on the respective war powers of Congress and the President. The Federal courts denied that the President had the constitutional authority to initiate either material or *de jure* war, but argued that he had a constitutional duty and right to judge the severity of a military emergency and to take the military and diplomatic measures that, in his exclusive judgment, were necessary to confront the crisis without waiting for Congress to act. In the absence of a declaration of war, which was constitutionally impossible and politically imprudent, the President was free to employ both defensive and offensive war measures. Thus, the Court legitimated the President's exercise of war powers that the Constitution vests exclusively in Congress. In the Civil War cases, the Supreme Court acted as a midwife to the birth of constitutional dictatorship.

CONCLUSION: THE SUPREME COURT AS MIDWIFE TO CONSTITUTIONAL DICTATORSHIP

Between 1800 and 1877 the Federal courts had the opportunity to decide war-powers cases that involved the authority to defend U.S. citizens abroad, to suppress rebellion, and to initiate material and *de jure* war and hostilities. Throughout this period, the Federal courts ostensibly acknowledged the constitutional separation of the congressional power to initiate war and hostilities from the presidential office of commander in chief. The judiciary defined the zones of exclusive congressional and presidential authority in terms of the offensive or defensive character of military hostilities rather than their magnitude. The zone of exclusive congressional authority includes the power to initiate limited as well as *de jure* war. The zone of exclusive presidential authority includes the power to defend the nation and its citizens from armed attack, at home and abroad.

The Supreme Court's pre–Civil War decisions support the argument that Congress has exclusive power to determine the scope of military hostilities subsequent to a declaration of war. Congressional power to control the scope of military hostilities flows from the various auxiliary war powers that the Constitution vests exclusively in the legislature. A declaration of war, therefore, does not confer the auxiliary war powers on the President. In the absence of legislation authorizing or limiting military hostilities, how extensive are the incidental powers that the vesting, take-care, and commander-in-chief clauses confer on the President? While John Marshall favored a narrow construction of the President's incidental powers, Joseph Story believed that congressional silence gives broad scope to the President's incidental powers so that he can conduct hostilities according to international law and practice.

In this early period, the Federal courts adhered to the Framers' distinction between the offensive war powers of Congress and the defensive powers of the commander in chief. Justice Paterson, however, argued that the President's defensive powers include carrying military measures to an enemy's territory. When Congress is not in session, constitutional grants of power, congressional delegations of power, and the inherent right of self-defense make the President the sole judge of military necessity. In a later circuit-court opinion, Justice Nelson extended the concept of defensive power to include protection of citizens' lives and property abroad. These circuit-court opinions expanded the concept of defensive power but did not abandon the Framers' distinction between offensive and defensive war as the sole criterion for separating the exclusive zones of congressional and presidential authority.

During the Civil War and in the postwar era that followed, the Federal courts expanded the scope of the President's defensive powers while ostensibly deferring to congressional authority to initiate war and hostilities. In the absence of a congressional declaration of war, the courts legitimated the President's exercise of auxiliary war powers, i.e., powers that the Constitution confers exclusively on Congress. When an enemy attacks the United States, the Supreme Court concluded, the President has the constitutional duty and authority to take whatever measures are necessary to maintain or restore public order and to preserve constitutional government. During a congressional recess, the President is the sole judge of military necessity.

The Civil War cases suggest that in a military emergency, the President can exercise the powers that the Constitution vests in his office as well as the constitutional powers of Congress. If Congress disapproves of his conduct, it can restrict the President's actions retroactively. Should the President veto congressional attempts to restrict his military conduct, however, Congress must then muster a two-thirds majority to override his actions. In fact, Congress ratified Lincoln's emergency measures as though they had been taken with prior approval. Therefore, the Civil War decisions vitiate the constitutional equilibrium between Congress and the President, since the legislature is unlikely to override the commander in chief's conduct once military hostilities are in progress.

By legitimating congressional ratification of the President's conduct, the Supreme Court also undermined the separation of powers. The Court legitimated the transfer of the auxiliary war powers to the President. Unlike later delegation standards, the Court simply accepted the

President's exercise of power that is vested exclusively in Congress. The Supreme Court created a "national war power" by fusing the constitutional powers of Congress and the President. The concept of a national war power, however, is an extraconstitutional concept that is irreconcilable with the separation of the congressional war powers from the office of commander in chief. This concept differs significantly from the eighteenth-century British concept of royal prerogative, since the British constitution did not restrict the Crown's power to protect the national interest or security during a military emergency. In the American constitutional system the concept of an indivisible national war power permits the President to suspend the constitutional separation of powers as long as Congress concurs in his actions. Although the Civil War cases are remote from the legal, military, and diplomatic battlefields of Southeast Asia, the extraconstitutional concept of a national war power anchored in joint legislative-executive participation bridges the century between the Civil War and the undeclared war in Vietnam.

5

Vietnam: Entering the Twilight Zone of Concurrent Power

THE POLITICAL SETTING

Unlike the U.S. Civil War, the Vietnam War did not erupt or spring " . . . forth suddenly from the parent brain, a Minerva in the full panoply of war."[1] Almost two decades before the Gulf of Tonkin incident on August 2, 1964,[2] the Vietnam conflict began as a guerrilla war between the Vietnamese and the French who attempted to reestablish their authority in Indochina after the Second World War. For more than twenty-five years five U.S. Presidents from Harry S Truman to Richard M. Nixon committed the nation's resources to armed struggle in Indochina. In the context of a global cold war, the Korean Conflict, and a communist victory in China, Congress supported presidential initiatives by authorizing economic and military assistance programs and appropriating billions to support the President's policies.[3] American involvement in the Vietnamese conflict resulted from joint congressional-presidential action that began long before the first U.S. Army combat troops arrived in Vietnam in 1965. American decisions to engage militarily in Vietnam resulted from a foreign-policy consensus that committed the U.S. to security agreements with forty-two other nations.[4]

During the century between the Civil War and the Vietnam War numerous Presidents dispatched armed forces abroad to protect the lives and property of U.S. citizens as well as American security interests.

Usually, these military operations were limited in scope and duration, were conducted against relatively defenseless nations, and did not involve the major military powers. Thus, there was little opportunity to test the President's constitutional authority to send U.S. armed forces abroad without congressional authorization. Although the Korean War (1950–53) was a major undeclared war, it did not furnish the occasion to test President Truman's constitutional authority to initiate and conduct military operations. Inasmuch as the Second World War did not terminate until April 1952, when the Japanese peace treaty came into effect, Truman had initiated military operations under operative wartime statutes. Furthermore, as President Truman observed, his actions were pursuant to a United Nations resolution. In dispatching combat forces to Korea, the President was enforcing the United Nations Charter, a treaty that has the force of domestic law in the United States. Therefore, the Vietnam War was the first modern undeclared war that provided the occasion to test the President's constitutional authority as commander in chief.

Although U.S. concern about the French-Vietnamese guerrilla war dates to 1946, the first important decision regarding American military involvement in Vietnam occurred on May 1, 1950, when President Truman " . . . approved the allocation of $10 million to the Department of Defense to cover the early shipment of urgently needed military assistance items to Indochina. . . ."[5] By July 1954 the United States had delivered $2.6 billion in aid to the French and Vietnamese forces fighting the Vietminh. During this early period a small group of U.S. military advisors provided supply support to the French authorities.[6] Until 1954, however, the French had virtually exclusive responsibility for conducting the war against the Vietnamese guerrillas.

In the two years that followed the signing of the Geneva Accords on July 21, 1954, the United States broadened its military advisory role in South Vietnam. As French armed forces withdrew from Vietnam, the United States increased its military assistance. In August 1954 Congress amended the Mutual Security Act to provide for direct aid to Vietnam.[7] Shortly thereafter, on September 8, the U.S. signed the Southeast Asia Collective Defense Treaty (SEATO), to which the Senate consented on February 1, 1955 (82–1).[8] Although South Vietnam was not a party to the treaty, a protocol extended protection against aggression to Laos, Cambodia, and South Vietnam. Even before the SEATO treaty went into effect, on February 12, 1955, a U.S. Military Assistance Advisory Group (MAAG) under Lieutenant General John W. O'Daniel assumed direct responsibility for organizing and training the South Vietnamese army.[9]

According to *The Pentagon Papers*, between 1954 and 1960 the United States concentrated its efforts on creating, organizing, and training an effective South Vietnamese military establishment. More than 80 percent of $2 billion in American aid that flowed into South Vietnam between 1955 and 1960 " . . . went toward providing security for the Government of Vietnam." Despite these efforts, in 1960, the U.S. Joint Chiefs of Staff (JCS) concluded that the South Vietnamese armed forces were inadequately trained and organized to counter the " . . . 'communist military-political-economic campaign' aimed at overturning the Government of Vietnam." The U.S. military aid program simply failed to create an effective counterinsurgency force capable of dealing with a flexible and versatile enemy.[10]

As the ineffectiveness of the South Vietnamese government and its armed forces became apparent, the American military role in Vietnam changed. In May 1959 the U.S. Commander-in-Chief of the Pacific (CINCPAC) directed that military " . . . advisors be provided to infantry regiment, artillery, armored, and separate Marine batallion level."[11] A year later, in May 1960, the United States increased its MAAG from 327 to 685 men,[12] bringing the total of authorized military personnel in South Vietnam to approximately 900. As the "military-political-economic" situation deteriorated over the next four years, the United States gradually increased its military personnel in Vietnam: 3,200 in 1961, 11,300 in 1962, 16,300 in 1963, and 23,300 in 1964.[13] The litany of military escalation and the deployment of U.S. armed forces at the corps, divisional, regimental, batallion, and provincial levels reflect the U.S. government's growing entanglement in the Vietnamese armed struggle.

Following the first Gulf of Tonkin incident on August 2, 1964, the Vietnam War entered a new phase in which the United States assumed an active combat role. Early in 1965 the first U.S. combat forces were deployed in South Vietnam. On February 9 the U.S. deployed a Marine Corps Hawk air-defense missile batallion at Danang. In March the first U.S. Army batallion (the 716th MP Bn) arrived in South Vietnam, followed in May by the 173rd Airborne Brigade. By June, military authorities confirmed that more than 50,000 American military personnel were in Vietnam (Army, 21,500; Marine Corps, 16,500; Air Force, 9,500; and Navy, 3,500).[14] The counterinsurgency war that began in Saigon in 1946 became an international war in the 1960s. Indeed, the Vietnam War would become the longest, if undeclared, war in U.S. history.

After two naval engagements in the Gulf of Tonkin on August 2 and 4, 1964, at President Lyndon Johnson's request Congress quickly approved the Southeast Asia Resolution. With only six hours of debate on August 6 and 7, the Senate passed the resolution 88–2, Senators Wayne Morse (D-Oregon) and Ernest Gruening (D-Alaska) voting against the measure. Morse argued that the resolution was an open-ended declaration of war, represented an unconstitutional delegation of power to the President, and violated the constitutional separation of powers. The Chairman of the Senate Foreign Relations Committee, J. William Fulbright (D-Arkansas), however, commended President Johnson's response to the armed attack and urged the Senate to support the President's actions. Although six members of the House of Representatives opposed the Southeast Asia Resolution, the House adopted the measure after only 40 minutes of debate by a vote of 416–0.[15]

Since 1964 considerable controversy has surrounded congressional adoption of the Southeast Asia Resolution. Did Congress authorize hostile measures short of a declaration of war? Was the Gulf of Tonkin Resolution the "functional equivalent" of a declaration of limited war or hostilities? Did Congress merely intend to give the President moral support? Was the resolution intended as a warning to the Chinese and North Vietnamese to restrain their intervention in the south? Was Congress deliberately or inadvertently misinformed about the naval engagements that had occurred in the Gulf of Tonkin? Did President Johnson deceive Congress about his intention to conduct a major land war in Southeast Asia?[16]

However one answers these questions about congressional and presidential intent in August 1964, there remains the inescapably broad language of the resolution itself:

> . . . the Congress approves and supports the determination of the President, as Commander in Chief, to take all necessary measures to repel any armed attack against the forces of the United States and to prevent further aggression. . . . Consonant with the Constitution of the United States and the Charter of the United Nations and in accordance with its obligations under the Southeast Asia Collective Defense Treaty, *the United States is, therefore, prepared, as the President determines, to take all necessary steps, including the use of armed force*, to assist any member or protocol state of the Southeast Asia Collective Defense Treaty requesting assistance in defense of its freedom.[17]

The Southeast Asia Resolution *authorized* the President to take whatever action, including armed force, which in his exclusive judgment was necessary to promote American security interests as well as the national security of SEATO's members and the protocol states (Laos, Cambodia, and South Vietnam). Not unlike the Formosa Resolution of 1955 and the Middle East Resolution of 1957, the Gulf of Tonkin Resolution placed few, if any, restraints on the exercise of presidential power to make war.[18]

As the *Congressional Record* indicates, some senators realized that the Gulf of Tonkin Resolution authorized the President to take whatever actions were necessary to restrain the Chinese and North Vietnamese from intervening, short of a declaration of war. Although Senator Fulbright later claimed that he did not believe that President Johnson would expand the scope or intensity of the conflict, he admitted clearly that the resolution's language gave the President discretionary authority to resist aggression in South Vietnam. "The resolution," Fulbright stated, "further expresses *the approval and support of the Congress for the determination of the President to take such action as may be necessary, now and in the future, to restrain or repel Communist aggression in southeast Asia.*"[19]

Whether the Gulf of Tonkin Resolution was tantamount to a predated, unconstitutional declaration of war, as Senator Morse argued,[20] or the "functional equivalent" of a declaration of war, as Undersecretary of State Nicholas deB. Katzenbach later claimed,[21] the resolution was an *indicium* of joint congressional-presidential participation in the Vietnamese armed struggle. Following the President's decision to commit combat forces to Vietnam in 1965, until 1969, Congress continued its unqualified support of the President's decisions. Despite growing congressional restiveness and popular unrest following the Viet Cong's Tet Offensive in January–February 1968, between August 1964 and December 1969 Congress enacted at least twenty-four public laws that supported the President's conduct of the war: foreign-aid authorization and appropriations acts, defense authorization and appropriations acts, military construction acts, defense procurement acts, the Military Selective Service Act of 1967, and the Veterans Pension and Readjustment Assistance Act of 1967. Although one can argue that Congress had no choice but to support the President's decisions once he had committed the nation's armed forces to battle, congressional enactment of restrictions on presidential power beginning in 1969 belies the argument. Between 1969 and 1973 Congress enacted no less than ten public laws that limited or restricted presidential authority to conduct military operations in Laos, Cambodia, and South Vietnam. For more than a decade (1954–1969) Congress supported the President's escalation of U.S. military activity in Indochina.

In 1969 the Vietnam War entered a new phase in which the United

States disengaged from active combat. While the war continued (between 1969 and 1973), the United States and North Vietnam negotiated a peace agreement in Paris. Five days after President Nixon's inauguration, the first substantive peace talks began in Paris on January 25, 1969.[22] Almost four years later, on January 23, 1973, President Nixon announced that Secretary of State Henry Kissinger and Le Duc Tho, the North Vietnamese special advisor, had concluded an agreement ending the war in Vietnam. This agreement did not, however, terminate U.S. military action in Cambodia, which ended on August 15, 1973.[23]

During this phase (1969–1973) the United States unilaterally withdrew its combat forces from South Vietnam. Between December 31, 1969, and December 31, 1972, the U.S. decreased its armed forces in Vietnam from 474,400 to 24,000.[24] As the United States withdrew its ground forces and transferred combat responsibilities to South Vietnamese armed forces, it placed greater emphasis on the use of air and naval power against North Vietnam, in the demilitarized zone (DMZ) between the north and the south, and against North Vietnamese, Pathet Lao, and Khmer Rouge forces in Laos and Cambodia. On May 2, 1970, for example, the United States announced that it had conducted heavy bombing raids in the DMZ, the first major bombing raids against North Vietnam since November 1968. A day later, on May 3, the Pentagon confirmed that the U.S. had bombed targets forty-five miles above the DMZ.[25] More than a year later, in August 1971, the U.S. acknowledged that it had conducted B-52 raids in the southern DMZ and that a Seventh-Fleet task force had struck the DMZ. In December 1971 Army and naval aircraft conducted heavy bombing raids against North Vietnam. The U.S. continued its bombing in April 1972, striking targets in the DMZ, around Haiphong, and in Hanoi, the North Vietnamese capital.[26] On May 8, President Nixon announced that Haiphong harbor would be mined and that air and naval strikes against military targets in North Vietnam would continue.[27] Between January 27 and April 30, 1973, the U.S. dropped 82,837 tons of bombs on Cambodia and 63,082 tons of bombs on Laos.[28] Apparently, "Vietnamization" of the war and disengagement of U.S. ground forces necessitated expanding the scope and intensity of the air and naval war against the North Vietnamese, Pathet Lao, and Khmer Rouge.

Both Congress and the nation reacted negatively to intensification of air and navel hostilities in Indochina. As popular consensus evaporated, congressional support for the war also waned. For the first time, in 1969, Congress enacted a $2.5 billion ceiling on support for South Vietnamese and other allied forces in Vietnam. Congress also approved a defense-appropriations bill that prohibited the introduction of U.S. combat troops in Laos or Thailand.[29] In 1970 Congress repealed the Gulf of Tonkin Resolution although the Nixon Administration argued that the President's authority to continue military operations did not depend on the resolution.[30] Congress also passed a revised version of the "Cooper-Church Amendment," which prohibited the use of funds to introduce U.S. combat troops in Cambodia or to provide U.S. advisors to the Cambodian armed forces. In a related measure, Congress prohibited the use of U.S. funds by Vietnamese and other allied forces to support the Cambodian or Laotian governments.[31]

During 1971, as *Congressional Quarterly* observes, " . . . five major bills were vehicles for efforts to limit U.S. participation in the Indochina War."[32] After a month-long stalemate, Congress enacted the Military Selective Service Act Extension (September 21, 1971), which contained a mild version of the Mansfield Amendment providing that the U.S. should end military operations in Indochina "at the earliest practicable date" and should establish a "date certain" for troop withdrawal. On November 11 Congress approved a defense procurement bill, which contained a second Mansfield Amendment and limited U.S. expenditures in Laos to $350 million. In any event, President Nixon rejected the Mansfield Amendment as neither legally binding nor reflecting his Administration's policies.[33]

Although Congress enacted a $375-million ceiling on aid to Laos, the war's opponents could not mobilize congressional support to enact binding "end-the-war" legislation in 1972. However, the Senate adopted an "end-the-war amendment" offered by Senator Edward Brooke (R-Massachusetts), which Senate and House conferees later dropped from the defense-appropriations bill.[34] As U.S. participation in the Indochinese conflict drew to a close in 1973, Congress adopted several measures prohibiting U.S. military operations in Indochina after August 15. After President Nixon vetoed a second supplemental appropriations bill (H.R. 7447) that prohibited the use of all funds to support combat in or over Laos and Cambodia, Congress and the executive agreed to an August 15 cutoff compromise measure averting a direct confrontation between the two branches.[35]

During the final phase of American participation in the Indochinese War, the United States continued to negotiate in Paris while withdrawing its ground combat forces from Vietnam and escalating air and naval hostilities in Indochina. As public fatigue and frustration with the war intensified, congressional support for the war ebbed. Although the war's critics were able to mobilize support for tempered limitations on and criticisms of the Nixon Administration's policies, they were unable to mobilize the congressional votes necessary to pass binding "end-the-war" legislation. Even if the congressional doves had secured the passage of such legislation, the Administration probably would have vetoed their measures. Confronted with a presidential veto, it is rather doubtful that the doves could have secured the two-thirds vote necessary to override the President's action. Despite doubt that the doves could override a presidential veto, passage of the second supplemental appropriations bill (H.R. 7447), President Nixon's veto of the bill, and the subsequent enactment of a compromise measure (H.R. 9055) indicate the intensity of legislative-executive conflict that existed as the longest war in the nation's history drew to a close on August 15, 1973.

The history of U.S. involvement in the Vietnam War suggests that Congress and the President were acting in a constitutional twilight zone " . . . in which he and Congress may have concurrent authority, or in which its distribution is uncertain."[36] At various phases in the war, the pattern of congressional legislation and presidential conduct suggests the applicability of all three criteria that Justice Jackson articulated in *Youngstown Sheet and Tube Co.* v. *Sawyer.* Until 1969 the President acted " . . . pursuant to an express or implied authorization of Congress. . . ."[37] Congress explicitly authorized the President " . . . to take all necessary steps, including the use of armed force, . . . " to prevent aggression against South Vietnam.[38] Between August 1964 and November 1969 Congress enacted the Gulf of Tonkin Resolution and at least twenty-three other laws that authorized the conduct of military operations in South Vietnam. The pattern of legislation indicates that presidential conduct in this period fulfilled the first of Jackson's criteria.

Between November 1969 and August 1973 the pattern of congressional legislation and presidential conduct suggests that, at times, the President was acting either (1) "upon his own independent powers" or (2) in conflict with "the expressed or implied will of Congress."[39] There is considerable disagreement, for example, concerning the source of the President's constitutional authority to invade Cambodia (April 29 to June 29, 1970). The Nixon Administration maintained that the invasion was neither a new war nor an escalation of the existing war. The invasion's purpose was to protect the security of U.S. armed forces (in South Vietnam) whose eventual departure depended on the success of the President's Vietnamization program. Therefore, President Nixon's actions were defensive rather than offensive in character. The President's decision to invade Viet Cong and North Vietnamese sanctuaries in Cambodia was merely a tactial decision within the commander in chief's zone of exclusive discretionary constitutional authority.[40]

In contrast to the Administration's justifications of the Cambodian invasion, critics argued that the invasion was a new or wider war than had previously existed. The invasion's purpose was neither to protect the security of U.S. armed forces in South Vietnam nor to secure their orderly withdrawal from Vietnam. Rather, President Nixon ordered the invasion to bolster the South Vietnamese regime following U.S. disengagement from ground combat in Vietnam. Thus, President Nixon's Cambodian invasion was offensive rather than defensive in character. The President was exercising power within the zone of exclusive congressional authority.[41]

Following congressional repeal of the Gulf of Tonkin Resolution (December 31, 1970), President Nixon's critics argued that whatever authority Congress had delegated to the President no longer existed. Although Congress continued to enact defense-procurement legislation, defense authorization and appropriations bills, military and foreign-aid authorization and appropriations bills, foreign military sales legislation, and military selective-service extension legislation, these measures neither explicitly nor implicitly authorized the President to conduct military operations in Indochina. Inasmuch as Congress had no choice but to support the armed forces engaged in combat, one cannot infer authorization from such legislation. Moreover, congressional limitations on the President's authority indicate or imply disapproval of his military conduct. The only possible justification for the President's military conduct is a broad construction of the authority that Article 2 vests in his office or the incidental powers that are necessary to perform his constitutional functions. However, Article 2 does not authorize the President to initiate or conduct war and hostilities without a declaration of war or other explicit legislative authorization. Therefore, repeal of the Gulf of Tonkin Resolution left the President without constitutional authority to continue military operations in Indochina.[42]

Responding to its critics, the Nixon Administration argued that the resolution's repeal could not alter or interfere with the independent authority that the Constitution vests exclusively in the President. Since the purpose of the President's policy was to disengage American combat troops from Vietnam, President Nixon was acting within the zone of authority that the Constitution confers exclusively on the commander in chief. While pursuing a policy of Vietnamization and withdrawal, the commander in chief has a constitutional duty to protect American armed forces under attack. As long as the President's military conduct was defensive rather than offensive, Congress could not interfere with his constitutional duty and authority to protect the security of American combat troops in Vietnam.[43]

President Nixon's decision to continue bombing Cambodia after the

Vietnamese cease-fire (January 27, 1973) generated another controversy concerning the President's power to conduct military hostilities. Within twenty-four hours after Congress approved H.R. 7447, which cut off funds for combat activities in or over Laos and Cambodia, President Nixon vetoed the measure. Although the President opposed the restriction on his authority, he signed a compromise bill (H.R. 9055), which delayed the cutoff until August 15.[44] If the President's veto of H.R. 7447 reflected conflict between the two branches, did the President's acceptance of H.R. 9055 signal agreement between Congress and the executive? In other words, was President Nixon acting pursuant to or in conflict with the expressed or implied will of Congress?

THE JUDICIAL RESPONSE

For the first time since the Civil War, during the Vietnam War various litigants, including citizens, taxpayers, servicemen, members of Congress, and the Commonwealth of Massachusetts, challenged the President's authority to initiate and conduct military hostilities without a congressional declaration of war. The Vietnam War was the first modern international war to test the concurrent congressional and presidential power to initiate and conduct military hostilities without declaring war. Although President Truman dispatched U.S. combat forces to Korea without prior congressional authorization, he initiated the Korean War prior to the termination of the Second World War. The existence of a state of *de jure* war and the continuing operation of wartime emergency statutes, therefore, mooted most attempts to test the scope of presidential authority to inititate war and hostilities during peacetime.[45] Unlike the Korean War, the Vietnam War occurred during "peacetime."

Despite numerous cases challenging the President's authority to initiate and conduct the Vietnam War, the Federal courts exhibited extreme caution in entering this twilight zone of constitutional power. The federal judiciary's reluctance to decide war-powers controversies reveals a respect for the constitutional separation of powers, an appreciation of the respective constitutional functions of Congress and the President in external affairs, and a sense of judicial self-restraint. Although most Federal courts exercised self-restraint, several courts scaled such procedural barriers as jurisdiction, standing to sue, sovereign immunity, and the political question to address the scope of congressional and presidential power to initiate war and military hostilities without a declaration of war. The latter decisions reveal an appreciation of the constitutional equilibrium upon which the separation of powers and the rule of law rest. Despite judicial caution, several Federal courts entered the political thicket in order to restore the constitutional balance between Congress and the President.[46] Toward the end of the war in Indochina, judicial concern for the rule of law recommended intervention rather than self-restraint.

Despite their factual variations, the Vietnam cases can be classified into four broad categories according to the Federal courts' invocation of the political-question doctrine. Such decisions as *Luftig* v. *McNamara* (1966) and *Mora* v. *McNamara* (1967) constitute the first category.[47] In *Luftig* the court asserted categorically that the complaint raised a political question that was beyond the court's jurisdiction and judicial competence.[48] Such cases as *Velvel* v. *Johnson* (1968), *United States* v. *Sisson* (1968), *Davi* v. *Laird* (1970), *Meyers* v. *Nixon* (1972), *Atlee* v. *Laird* (1972), and *Drinan* v. *Nixon* (1973) belong to a second category.[49] Although the Federal courts asserted that the President's authority to conduct military activities without a declaration of war posed a nonjusticiable political question, they proceeded to determine whether the President had acted on his own authority, pursuant to or in conflict with either the expressed or implied will of Congress. Federal judicial decisions in *Berk* v. *Laird* (1971), *Orlando* v. *Laird* (1971), *DaCosta* v. *Laird* (1971), and *Massachusetts* v. *Laird* (1971) constitute a third category.[50] In these cases, the Federal courts decided that the political-question doctrine does not foreclose judicial inquiry into the existence and constitutional sufficiency of joint congressional-presidential participation in prosecuting the war. A fourth category includes *Mottola* v. *Nixon* (1970) and *Holtzman* v. *Schlesinger* (1973), in which the district courts decided the cases on their merits.[51] As legislative-executive conflict over the war's conduct became more evident, the Federal courts marched further into this political thicket.

Luftig v. McNamara

In one of the earliest Vietnam cases, *Luftig* v. *McNamara* (1966), District Judge Alexander Holtzoff dismissed Private Robert Luftig's suit to enjoin military authorities from ordering him to Vietnam.[52] Judge Holtzoff concluded that the question of presidential power to conduct war or hostilities and to transfer members of the armed forces to a particular geographic area " . . . is obviously a political question that is outside of the judicial function."[53] In sustaining the district court's dismissal, the court of appeals (D.C. Cir.) asserted categorically that the complaint raised political questions that were beyond its jurisdiction and judicial competence.[54] This proposition was so clear to the court that it required " . . . no discussion or citation of authority."[55] Not unlike Judge Holtzoff, the court of appeals concluded that Luftig had raised questions of foreign and military policy that the Constitution commits exclusively to presidential and congressional discretion. The court left little doubt that the constitutional separation of powers removes such questions from judicial competence.[56]

Velvel v. Johnson

Despite the court of appeals' categoric dismissal of *Luftig*, Lawrence Velvel, professor of law at the University of Kansas, brought a class action against President Johnson and the secretaries of state and defense for conducting the Vietnam War illegally, i.e., without a congressional declaration of war.[57] Although District Judge George Templar dismissed *Velvel v. Johnson* (1968) on procedural grounds, he addressed the political-question doctrine, which barred consideration of the case on its merits. According to Judge Templar, Velvel was asking the courts to determine questions of foreign and military policy that the Constitution commits exclusively to the political departments. As commander in chief, the President has discretionary power to protect " . . . the interests of the country and to carry on such activities in managing our concerns with foreign nations."[58] In exercising such discretionary power, the President is responsible to the country and his own conscience rather than to the judiciary. Since the courts lack the information as well as the competence to evaluate the data upon which the President decides military policy, judges should refrain from subjecting presidential judgment to judicial scrutiny. If the courts are powerless to influence the international environment, they should avoid embarrassing " . . . the government in conducting its international affairs."[59]

Turning specifically to the constitutionality of waging military hostilities without declaring war, Judge Templar emphasized:

> That the executive or legislative branches of the government have seen fit to carry on a limited military action without a formal declaration of war by the legislative branch is a matter resting solely within the discretion of those duly elected representatives of the people. There may be sound reason for not making a formal declaration of war. Such a declaration might bring on an international conflagration which our political leaders are carefully seeking to avoid. This Court has neither the information necessary nor the power required to question the wisdom of the manner in which the military activity of our country is being conducted.[60]

In the absence of congressional legislation limiting the President's conduct, the court declined to determine (1) the legality, wisdom or propriety of dispatching American armed forces to South Vietnam, (2) whether a state of war existed between the United States and North Vietnam, or (3) whether Congress had authorized the President's military actions or any other question that the Constitution commits exclusively to the political departments.[61]

U.S. v. Sisson

In *United States* v. *Sisson* (1968), District Judge Charles Wyzanski also asserted that the President's authority to conduct the Vietnam War without a congressional declaration of war posed a nonjusticiable political question.[62] John H. Sisson, Jr. had refused to comply with his draft board's order to submit to induction into the armed forces because " . . . there is under the Constitution of the United States no authority to conscript him to serve in a war not declared by Congress."[63] Since there was a "strong probability" that Sisson would be required to serve in Vietnam and since there would be "no clear right" to challenge the order following induction, Judge Wyzanski conceded that Sisson had standing to raise the constitutional issue. However, Wyzanski denied that the court had jurisdiction to consider the constitutional issue since it posed a nonjusticiable political question.[64]

Although Judge Wyzanski asserted that Sisson's claim presented a political question, he nonetheless proceeded to determine whether there had been joint legislative-executive action in the absence of a congressional declaration of war. As Judge Wyzanski framed the question, Sisson had asked the court to decide whether the government could compel his military service in " . . . a war carried on for a long time without a declaration of war but as a result of combined legislative and executive action. . . ."[65] Moreover, the court inferred such joint participation in the war's prosecution from the Gulf of Tonkin Resolution, the Selective Service Act extension of 1967, and various military appropriations acts. While Judge Templar had refused to determine the war's constitutionality without congressional legislation limiting the President's military actions, Judge Wyzanski refused to decide the political question because the legislature and the executive had acted jointly.[66]

Despite Wyzanski's refusal to decide *Sisson* on its merits, he marched further into the twilight zone than Templar had in *Velvel*. In *Sisson*, the court determined that (1) Congress had authorized or supported military hostilities without declaring war, (2) Congress had discretionary authority to declare a *de jure* war or authorize limited war and hostilities, and (3) the judiciary lacked the evidence and competence to evaluate the policy considerations that motivated congressional military decisions. After making these preliminary determinations, Judge Wyzanski concluded that "[i]t is not an act of abdication when a court says that political questions of this sort are not within its jurisdiction."[67]

Davi v. Laird

In a similar vein, District Judge H. Emory Widener, Jr. concluded in *Davi* v. *Laird* (1970) that the plaintiffs' claim involved " . . . precisely that inquiry into principles and policy considerations which the Constitution has committed to the political branches, and with which the judiciary is ill-suited to cope."[68] As taxpayers and guardians of an eighteen-year-old brother subject to induction into the armed forces, Phillip and Betty Davi filed a complaint against Melvin Laird, secretary of defense, challenging the constitutionality of U.S. military activities in Southeast Asia. The Davis sought a declaratory judgment and injunction against Secretary Laird for conducting military hostilities without a declaration of war. They argued that the secretary's conduct violated Article 1, Section 8 (Cl. 11) of the Constitution, which grants Congress the power to declare war.

After reviewing the Davis' claims, Judge Widener proceeded to make " . . . a threshold inquiry into whether the issue involves a nonjusticiable political question" since the complaint raised " . . . the gravest questions regarding the relationship between the judiciary and the coordinate branches of government."[69] Citing *Baker* v. *Carr*, but omitting *Powell* v. *McCormack*,[70] Judge Widener rested his views of the political question and the judicial function on a mistaken conception of the separation of powers. In *Powell*, the Supreme Court narrowed the political question substantially to "a textually demonstrable commitment of the issue to a coordinate political department."[71] In the absence of such an exclusive commitment, neither the separation of powers nor the political-question doctrine requires judicial abstention.[72] If a case meets other jurisdictional and procedural requirements, the claim that Congress and the President have exceeded their respective constitutional powers presents a judicially cognizable issue. However, Judge Widener apparently believed that the political-question doctrine poses a barrier to judicial intervention in cases in which the Constitution commits concurrent powers to Congress and the President.[73]

"The power to commit American military forces under various sets of circumstances," argued Widener, "is shared by Congress and the Executive."[74] Within this zone of concurrent power, Congress has the constitutional authority to restrain presidential initiative as well as the power to declare war. Below the threshold of a declaration of war, Congress can employ the auxiliary war powers to check executive conduct of foreign policy and warmaking.[75] Whether Congress chooses to declare war, authorize hostilities short of war, or restrain executive warmaking, the Constitution confers exclusive discretion on the legislature. The Constitution " . . . provides Congress with an array of powers which it may exercise to sanction or restrain executive action."[76] In this twilight zone of concurrent power, only Congress can decide whether to employ its auxiliary war powers to support or restrict the President's military conduct.[77]

Although Judge Widener's logic suggests limiting judicial inquiry to determining whether the conduct of military operations falls within this twilight zone, he also determined whether Congress actually had authorized or restricted presidential action. Widener concluded "[t]hat Congress has participated actively with respect to the military effort in Vietnam . . . " through enactment of the Selective Service Act and various military-appropriations acts.[78] While Widener acknowledged various legislative efforts to reassert congressional authority, he did not conclude that Congress had, in fact, restricted the President's military conduct. Aware of its responsibility and constitutional authority, only Congress can determine whether the executive has usurped legislative power.[79]

After claiming that Congress and the President share the power to commit American armed forces to hostilities, in a volte-face, Widener implied that only Congress can authorize military hostilities.[80] If Congress has exclusive power or prerogative to authorize military hostilities, whether Congress actually has authorized the President's military actions hardly poses a nonjusticiable political question. Similarly, absent congressional authorization, the presidential exercise of power that falls within the zone of exclusive legislative authority does not pose a political question. In a second volte-face, Judge Widener returned to his original argument, noting that "[t]o the extent that the present sharing of responsibility for the Vietnam conflict may be characterized as a struggle, it is clearly a result of the separation of powers, and is not subject to judicial interference."[81] These internal contradictions aside, Judge Widener marched cautiously into the political thicket despite his apparent refusal to decide *Davi* on the merits.

Meyers v. *Nixon*

More than a year later, in *Meyers* v. *Nixon* (1972), District Judge Dudley Bonzal also concluded that the legality of the Vietnam War was a political question for which the Federal courts lacked judicially manageable standards. William Meyers had filed a class action as a taxpayer and citizen against President Nixon and Defense Secretary Laird for conducting the Vietnam War in violation of the U.S. Constitution (the declaration-of-war clause, the supremacy clause, and the Fifth and Ninth Amendments) as well as various international conventions. In dismissing the motion for a declaratory judgment and injunctive relief, Judge Bonzal ruled that Meyers lacked standing as a taxpayer and that the complaint raised nonjusticiable political questions.[82] Not unlike his judicial brethren in *Davi*, *Sisson*, and *Velvel*, Bonzal also examined the adequacy of congressional participation in prosecuting the Vietnam War.

Although there had been " . . . no formal declaration of war," Judge Bonzal wrote, "the evidence of congressional action through appropriations and extensions of the Military Selective Service Act . . . is sufficient to imply authorization or ratification of the military activity in question and to satisfy the requirements of the declaration-of-war clause."[83] In contrast to the *Davi* opinion, Judge Bonzal's opinion is internally consistent insofar as he argues that only Congress can initiate or authorize military hostilities. Since the court's preliminary inquiry indicated that Congress had authorized or ratified the President's military actions, Bonzal refused to adjudicate political questions for which there were no judicially discoverable or manageable standards. In other words, he refused to decide the constitutionality of the means that Congress had selected to ratify the President's conduct. However, Judge Bonzal already had expressed the opinion that congressional legislation satisfied the declaration-of-war clause.[84] In reality, Bonzal ventured an opinion without deciding the case on its merits.

Atlee v. Laird

Several months after *Meyers*, in *Atlee v. Laird* (1972), a three-judge district court provided the most explicit and extensive analysis, to date, for refusing to decide the Vietnam cases on their merits. Speaking for the majority, Circuit Judge Arlin Adams concluded that (1) whether U.S. military action in Southeast Asia is a "war," (2) whether Congress had taken constitutionally sufficient action to satisfy the declaration-of-war clause, and (3) whether the President had the authority to maintain American armed forces in Southeast Asia constituted political questions that courts should not adjudicate. Although the court alluded to such other issues as standing, sovereign immunity, and the plaintiff's failure to state a claim upon which relief could be granted, the court decided *Atlee* exclusively on the issue of justiciability.[85]

While the Federal courts have long recognized the political-question doctrine, Judge Adams acknowledged that the Constitution's judiciary article (Art. 3, Sect. 2) fails to mention " . . . that certain disputes otherwise subject to the judicial power should not be adjudicated."[86] The courts have inferred this discretionary authority from the constitutional separation of powers, which commits various discretionary powers exclusively to Congress or the President.[87] Before turning specifically to questions of foreign affairs and the war powers, virtually every judicial precedent that Adams cited rests on the assumption that the government's policy decisions " . . . are wholly confided by our Constitution to the political departments of the government, Executive and Legislative."[88] Since *Atlee* falls within the twilight zone of concurrent authority, as Adams admits, the classical view of the political-question doctrine does not support the case for judicial abstention. Therefore, Adams turns to the pragmatic and functional views, which emphasize the President's special role in foreign affairs, the lack of information and judicial expertise, the consequences of judicial intervention, and a keen sense of judicial self-preservation.[89]

"[W]hen the conduct of the foreign relations of the country is at stake," Adams remarked, "courts will be more hesitant to consider certain issues on the merits than when internal operations are involved."[90] Casting a wide judicial net, Adams claimed that various Supreme Court decisions teach that " . . . the federal judiciary should not adjudicate questions of foreign policy."[91] While the judicial precedents cited suggest that certain subjects of foreign policy are beyond judicial competence, they hardly demonstrate conclusively that every question touching on the administration of U.S. foreign policy is outside the judiciary's power and jurisdiction.[92] At the most, these decisions " . . . demonstrate the need for federal courts to move with extreme caution in the sensitive area of foreign policy"[93] rather than the need for total abstention.

After examining the genesis and development of the political-question doctrine, Adams attempted to apply *Baker* v. *Carr* and *Powell* v. *McCormack* to questions of foreign and military policy. Although *Powell* narrowed the political-question criteria substantially, Adams professed that *Powell* " . . . affirmed the validity of the six-point *Baker* test, at least so far as domestic problems are concerned. . . ."[94] Despite his profession of fidelity to the *Baker* test, Adams observed:

> Whereas in *Powell*, a case concerning domestic affairs, the primary thrust of the political-question discussion naturally centered on the textual commitment test, our examination of the authorities leads to the conclusion that, when dealing with a foreign policy case, the court should focus its attention primarily on

the other factors discussed above and crucially important in the foreign affairs area.[95]

Adams' admission that *Powell* rested primarily on the "textual commitment test" exposed the difficulty of applying the decision to the twilight zone of concurrent power. Therefore, Adams shifted to other factors in foreign affairs, to the pragmatic and functional rationale for declining to decide *Atlee* on the merits.[96]

However, these rationales are less than an extraordinary category of political questions removed from judicial competence by a demonstrable textual commitment to either Congress or the President. According to Adams, the courts lack the information necessary to decide foreign-policy cases. Since the judiciary does not control the sources of information, " . . . the parties might not assemble all the data" that the courts require. "In certain instances, . . . the information necessary to a reasoned judgment should remain confidential."[97] Under these circumstances, the courts could not perform their judicial function without impairing the President's performance of his legitimate constitutional role.

In addition to these factors, several other pragmatic considerations suggest judicial self-restraint. First, the courts cannot " . . . predict the international consequences flowing from a decision on the merits."[98] Second, the judiciary is powerless to control the international consequences flowing from such a decision. Courts simply do not possess the diplomatic and military instruments necessary to influence the international system. Third, the judiciary lacks standards to evaluate foreign-policy judgments or decisions.[99] Such decisions involve the application of political criteria that are unfamiliar to judges. Finally, in foreign-policy cases courts must review initial policy determinations " . . . made by the political branches, individually or in concert, and committed by the Constitution to those branches for resolution."[100]

Like the author of the *Davi* opinion, Judge Adams defines a political question as one that the Constitution commits to the political branches, "individually or in concert." He notes that

> . . . the Constitution commits the entire foreign policy power of this country to the executive and legislative branches. Because the Constitution does not itemize all possible prerogatives in this field it is a difficult task of interpretation to state categorically that the authority to perform a particular act resides solely in either the executive or the legislature.[101]

To the extent that *Atlee* falls within this twilight zone, Adams concludes

" . . . that the questions presented are collectively political within the textual commitment test of *Baker* v. *Carr*."[102] Aside from misinterpreting the textual commitment test, which means an exclusive commitment to either Congress or the President, Adams's view would exclude all but a patently obvious exercise of legislative power by the President.

Since he admits that "Congress is, of course, the only branch of government with the power to declare war," one might wonder why presidential initiation of war without such a declaration is a political question. Adams's position is even more curious, since he adds, "Implicit in this constitutional provision may be congressional authority to take steps short of a formal declaration of war, equivalent to an authorization."[103] If Congress has the exclusive power to declare either a *de jure* war or limited war and hostilities, the court's ordinary skills of statutory and constitutional interpretation should be adequate to determine whether the legislature has authorized the President's military actions. Although *Atlee* raised complex, delicate, and far-reaching questions, the court did not require oracular wisdom to determine whether the President had exceeded his constitutional authority. *Atlee* posed questions of constitutional power or authority rather than " . . . the wise use of executive authority," as Judge Adams claimed.[104]

In contrast to the majority's opinion, Chief District Judge Joseph Lord concluded that the issue was justiciable, that the plaintiffs had fulfilled Federal jurisdictional requirements, and that they had " . . . a right to a federal forum to adjudicate their claims on the merits."[105] Absent a demonstrable textual commitment of the issue to either Congress or the President, Lord reasoned that when another " . . . branch exceeds its constitutional authority in its actions our system of separation of powers with its checks and balances dictates that a court proceed to the merits of a controversy."[106] While most questions of foreign relations are committed to either the executive or legislature, when a case falls within the twilight zone of concurrent power the judiciary has a duty to proceed on the merits. Only when the courts find a clear commitment does the separation of powers foreclose further judicial inquiry.[107]

As for *Atlee*'s claims, Lord concluded that the hostilities in Southeast Asia constituted war in the constitutional sense (of Art. 1, Sect. 8, Cl. 11). "When nations contend with force under the authority of their respective governments with the scope of troop commitment and casualties involved here," emphasized Lord, "the conflict must be considered war or the word has lost all meaning."[108] Inasmuch as the Constitution confers the power to initiate war (declared or undeclared) on Congress rather than the President, the declaration-of-war clause is a limitation on the commander in chief's power. Therefore, whether the legislature has authorized the commander in chief's military actions presents a justiciable question.[109]

According to Lord's analysis, *Atlee* raised " . . . a constitutional question concerning the division of power within our system, involving a determination of whether the executive branch has exceeded the scope of its constitutional power."[110] The questions that *Atlee* posed require only conventional judicial skills of statutory interpretation rather than a diviner's rod. Should the court find that the President's conduct exceeds his constitutional authority, Lord expressed confidence that it could " . . . prescribe appropriate steps to put an end to an unlawful enterprise without creating ridiculous and unmanageable situations."[111] While Judge Lord recognized the difficulty of fashioning relief that would not impair the President's constitutional role, he stressed that protection of the individual's rights and the people's right to constitutional government sometimes requires the judiciary to perform its traditional duty to interpret the law and the Constitution "' . . . in a manner at variance with the construction given the document by another branch.'"[112]

The differences between Judge Adams's majority opinion and Judge Lord's dissenting opinion reflect a fundamental conflict concerning the Federal judiciary's role in American society that goes far beyond the Vietnam cases or war-powers controversies. Judge Adams's opinion echoed a familiar refrain of " . . . legal thought discernible from Thayer through Holmes, from Brandeis through Frankfurter . . . that courts serve democracy best by leaving the principal issues confronting the citizenry for decision to the political branches of the government."[113] Since the Constitution commits such policy decisions to the political departments, the citizenry should turn to Congress in order to restrain the " . . . usurpation of power by the President."[114] Only Congress possesses the power necessary to limit presidential conduct. Judicial intervention in such controversies is imprudent since it can only impair the judiciary's powers and violates the democratic principle of popular sovereignty.[115]

Judge Lord's opinion echoed another, but no less familiar refrain of legal thought discernible from Hamilton and Marshall through Warren and Wechsler that the Federal judiciary is responsible for enforcing a hierarchy of law in which the Constitution is supreme and all legislative and executive action must conform to its commands. If a controversy meets jurisdictional and procedural requirements, the judiciary cannot decline to decide a case simply because it involves political issues. "The judiciary cannot, as the legislature may," Marshall wrote in *Cohens* v. *Virginia*, "avoid a measure because it approaches the confines of the constitution. We cannot pass it by because it is doubtful."[116] In the American political system, the judiciary has a special responsibility to limit each branch to the exercise of its constitutional authority.[117]

Drinan v. Nixon

The conflict over the judiciary's relationship to the legislature and executive also is apparent in *Drinan* v. *Nixon* (1973), decided in the waning days of the war in Southeast Asia. In *Drinan*, District Judge Joseph Tauro ruled that President Nixon's authority to continue bombing Cambodia until August 15, 1973, presented political questions that were beyond the Federal judiciary's jurisdiction and judicial power.[118] Nevertheless, Judge Tauro proceeded to determine whether the President was acting pursuant to or in conflict with the expressed or implied will of Congress. After Congress passed two compromise measures on June 29 terminating the expenditure of all funds for military hostilities in or over Laos, Cambodia, and North and South Vietnam (effective August 15), Congressman Robert Drinan (D-Massachusetts), three other representatives, and an airman in the U.S. Air Force challenged the government's authority to continue the bombing until August 15. Seeking a declaratory judgment, the plaintiffs claimed that the government's actions were in conflict with the congressional intent to cease all military hostilities in Southeast Asia.[119]

Although Judge Tauro admitted that " . . . not all issues involving foreign relations are political questions," he accepted the familiar pragmatic and functional arguments (inadequate information, the need for secrecy, lack of judicial expertise and standards, and the international consequences) that counsel judicial self-restraint.[120] Like Judge Adams, Judge Tauro argued that the political-question doctrine applies to decisions that the Constitution commits to the exclusive discretion of Congress and the President, "individually or in concert."[121] While the "textual commitment test" of *Baker* and *Powell* obviously applies to all decisions committed solely to Congress or the President, Judge Tauro articulated a different test for abstaining from issues that fall within the twilight zone of concurrent authority. In this zone,

> . . . should it be apparent that *the political branches themselves are clearly and resolutely* in opposition as to the military policy to be followed by the United States, such a conflict could no longer be regarded as a political question, but would rise to the posture of a serious constitutional issue requiring resolution by the judicial branch.[122]

Judge Tauro's opinion suggests a three-stage test for determining the justiciability of cases in the twilight zone. First, the court must decide whether the Constitution commits power concurrently to Congress and the President. Second, the court must determine whether a conflict actually exists between actions that the legislative and executive branches have taken. Third, the court must conclude that the conflict is " . . . clear and at least apparently incapable of resolution, absent judicial intervention."[123] However, if the legislature and the executive have acted jointly, there is no need to decide the boundaries of their respective authority unless their concerted action violates an individual's constitutional rights.[124]

After establishing these threshold criteria, Judge Tauro made a preliminary finding " . . . that Congress does not have the exclusive right to determine whether or not the United States will engage in war."[125] Since the power to wage war and hostilities is concurrent, when presidential action goes beyond emergency defense Congress can authorize or ratify the commander in chief's conduct. Although Congress has exclusive discretion to decide the form and manner of such approval, the judiciary has the power to determine whether Congress has given its express or implied consent. The court cannot and should not evaluate the wisdom or propriety of the form that congressional approval takes, because the Constitution confers plenary power on Congress and because congressional policy judgments are beyond judicial competence. In other words, Congress can satisfy the requirements of the declaration-of-war clause in one of several ways, which include military and foreign-aid authorization and appropriations bills that either authorize or ratify the President's military actions.[126]

Despite congressional revocation of the Gulf of Tonkin Resolution, the record reveals that Congress continued to authorize and appropriate funds for military hostilities in Cambodia. However, Congressman Drinan contended that, after the U.S. withdrew its armed forces from South Vietnam and the Viet Cong and North Vietnamese returned American prisoners of war, the factual situation had changed appreciably. Since April 1, 1973, the record reveals continuing legislative-executive conflict over the bombing of Cambodia. Indeed, President Nixon's veto of H.R. 7447 on June 27 measures the depth and intensity of legislative-executive conflict.[127]

While Judge Tauro acknowledged that between April 1 and June 30 Congress and the President had disagreed concerning military policy, he denied that the conflict " . . . went beyond the boundaries of traditional dispute and disagreement, which are the prerogatives of these two independent branches, so as to reach the point of clear and resolute

conflict that would warrant judicial intervention."[128] Despite their disagreement, enactment of the compromise measure terminating hostilities on August 15 " . . . clearly evidences that the branches, themselves,
were able to resolve the serious and emotion-charged differences that
had occupied them. . . ."[129] Enactment of the Supplemental Appropriations Act for Fiscal 1973 and the Continuing Appropriations Resolution
for Fiscal 1974 effected a legally binding compromise, averted a constitutional crisis, and ratified the bombing of Cambodia until August 15.[130]
The language of the statutes and the *Congressional Record* reveal that
Congress had exercised its free will and independent judgment " . . . so
as to avoid resolute conflict."[131] Since Congress had resolved the political question, Judge Tauro concluded, there was no justiciable issue before the court.[132]

Despite his refusal to decide the political question, Judge Tauro
marched further into the political thicket than had any other Federal
judge who concluded that the President's power to wage war and hostilities without a congressional declaration of war presented a nonjusticiable question. In order to avoid deciding *Drinan* on its merits, Judge
Tauro extended the political-question doctrine into the twilight zone of
concurrent power. Since the Constitution confers concurrent power and
discretion on the political departments, the courts should not interfere
with legislative and executive functions as long as the two branches act
in concord. When clear and resolute conflict develops, the rationale for
abstention evaporates. A judicial excursion into the external realm does
not risk embarrassment arising from *multifarious pronouncements on
one question*, since such conflict already exists.[133] Indeed, the need to
restore order and unity recommends judicial intervention rather than
abstention. Moreover, the existence of legislative-executive conflict
probably reduces the risks to judicial power that such intervention entails. Although *Drinan* could not surmount Judge Tauro's three-stage
test, the existence of a clear and resolute conflict in the future would
create the conditions for judicial intervention in warpowers controversies.

CONCLUSION: SELF-RESTRAINT PREVAILS

The Vietnam decisions examined thus far rest largely on pragmatic and
functional theories of judicial self-restraint. These decisions reflect the
conventional wisdom that judges should refrain from deciding questions
of military and foreign policy. In the complex and uncertain realm of

external sovereignty, the judiciary lacks the competence, training, information, and mature judgment to consider questions that the Framers wisely committed to the people's representatives. Pragmatism, the separation of powers, and democratic principle (i.e., the principle of popular sovereignty) converge to recommend that the Federal courts exercise self-restraint and abstain from deciding questions that affect the government's conduct of war and foreign affairs.

Such opinions as *Luftig* v. *McNamara* and *Velvel* v. *Johnson* implicitly reject the classical argument for judicial review, which assumes that judges have an obligation to decide constitutional questions insofar as it is necessary to dispose of the case at bar. According to the classical view, the judiciary does not have discretionary authority to refrain from deciding "political questions" in cases that otherwise meet a court's jurisdictional requirements. The only exception to this rule arises from a textually demonstrable constitutional commitment of an issue to congressional or presidential discretion. Having decided that the Constitution confers the power to declare war exclusively on Congress or the power to wage military hostilities exclusively on the President, judicial inquiry should cease. Further inquiry would go beyond the judiciary's jurisdiction, might impair another branch in performing its constitutional function, and could vitiate the constitutional separation of powers.

If the rationale for judicial self-restraint rests on the separation of powers (i.e., the textual commitment argument), extension of the political-question doctrine into areas of concurrent constitutional authority represents judicial abdication rather than prudent self-restraint. To the extent that the Federal courts classify the Vietnam War in the twilight zone of concurrent constitutional authority and extend the political-question doctrine into this zone, they minimize the occasions for exercising judicial power and reduce the scope of judicial inquiry. According to the judicial opinions in *Davi* v. *Laird* and *Atlee* v. *Laird*, in this twilight zone of concurrent authority, the only justification for exercising judicial power is the existence of resolute legislative-executive conflict. Nothing less than prolonged, irreconcilable conflict should serve as an invitation to judicial intervention in war-powers controversies.

Absent such conflict within the twilight zone of concurrent authority, the political departments are the indisputable arbiters of the separation of powers as well as the boundaries of legislative and executive power. Below the threshold of a declaration of war, for example, Congress and the President can fuse their separate constitutional authority to initiate and conduct military hostilities into a virtually unlimited national war power whose only standard is military necessity and success. More precisely, the President is free to present Congress with a military *fait ac-compli* by initiating hostilities whose continuation Congress has no choice but to approve. As long as the political departments act jointly or do not engage in resolute conflict, the courts are powerless to vindicate constitutional government. When Congress and the President engage in protracted conflict, however, the courts are more likely to enter the political thicket and to decide war-powers controversies on their merits. As Congress attempted to limit President Nixon's military conduct in Southeast Asia after 1969, several Federal courts entertained and decided cases involving the scope of the President's authority to conduct undeclared war.

6

Vietnam: Exploring the Twilight Zone of Concurrent Power

With few exceptions, the Federal courts refused to approach or decide the Vietnam cases on their merits prior to 1970. However, in 1969–1970 several important events occurred that may explain the willingness of several Federal judges to approach the merits of war-powers controversies. On June 16, 1969, the Supreme Court decided *Powell v. McCormack*.[1] Although *Powell* deals with the congressional power to exclude a member from the House of Representatives, some judges subsequently applied the Supreme Court's criteria for invoking the political question to the congressional war powers.[2] If the Constitution commits the determination of an issue exclusively to either Congress or the President, as *Powell* implies, the courts cannot declare the law without exceeding their judicial function or interfering with legislative and executive functions. However, if such an exclusive commitment does not exist, when there is conflict between the legislative and executive branches, the political-question doctrine does not preclude judicial intervention to resolve such a controversy.[3]

In addition to these changes in judicial doctrine, after 1969, there was evidence of growing, if not resolute, conflict between Congress and President Nixon regarding the conduct of the Vietnam War. Between November 1969 and August 1973 Congress enacted at least ten major laws limiting the President's power to conduct military operations in Indochina. President Nixon's opposition to congressional interference with his military authority also provided evidence of legislative-executive conflict over the Vietnam War.[4] By July 1973 even a doubting Thomas would have recognized the existence of prolonged and, perhaps, irreconcilable conflict between Congress and President Nixon. In the absence of a congressional declaration of war and in the face of legislative-executive conflict, several Federal judges read *Powell* as an invitation to examine or decide war-powers cases on their merits. As an analysis of these Vietnam cases will reveal, in the twilight zone of concurrent constitutional authority, the existence of legislative-executive conflict created the opportunity for judicial intervention and the limited exercise of judicial power.

MITCHELL V. *LAIRD*: WHAT EVERY SCHOOLBOY KNOWS

In one of the most curious opinions of the Vietnam era, *Mitchell* v. *Laird* (1973), the Court of Appeals for the District of Columbia concluded that under certain circumstances the President has authority to initiate war, but lacks authority to continue a war of "considerable duration and magnitude" indefinitely without congressional approval. The court also concluded that following congressional repeal of the Gulf of Tonkin Resolution (December 31, 1970) the President lacked authority to continue the war except to withdraw U.S. armed forces in safety. However, the court refused to decide whether President Nixon's military actions exceeded his constitutional authority as commander in chief to defend remaining U.S. armed forces in Indochina.[5]

On April 7, 1971, Congressman Parren Mitchell and 12 other representatives filed a complaint in the district court against the President, the secretaries of state and defense, other Defense Department officials, and the United States of America, alleging that for seven years the government had been conducting an illegal war without "explicit, intentional and discrete" congressional authorization. The congressmen's counsel, Lawrence Velvel, also claimed that the government had impaired his plaintiffs' right (under Art. 1, Sec. 8, Cl. 11) to " . . . decide whether the United States should fight a war." Mitchell *et al.* sought a declaratory judgment and injunctive relief against the Government " . . . from prosecuting the war in Indochina unless, within 60 days from the date of such order, the Congress shall have explicitly, intentionally and discretely authorized a continuation of the war. . . ." The district court dismissed the complaint.[6]

Although the court of appeals sustained the dismissal, Judge Wyzanski asserted that presidential power to continue the war indefinitely is a justiciable question.[7] Despite the court of appeals' contrary decision in *Luftig* v. *McNamara*, Wyzanski asserted judicial power, in some cases, to determine whether military activities in Indochina constitute war and whether Congress had approved the President's military actions. In determining whether the Indochina conflict was a war in the constitutional sense, Judge Wyzanski employed the now familiar threshold theory. Given the duration and magnitude (i.e., the scope and intensity) of military activities, he saw no " . . . difficulty in a court facing up to the question as to whether because of the war's duration and magnitude the President is or was without power to continue the war without Congressional approval."[8]

Like Judge Tauro, Wyzanski observed that Congress has discretion to " . . . decide in which form, if any, it will give its consent to the continuation of a war already begun by a President acting alone."[9] Since the Constitution vests such discretionary power in the legislature, Congress can employ any form that is "constitutionally permissible." Without deciding whether the Gulf of Tonkin Resolution constituted congressional consent, Judge Wyzanski simply noted that the resolution " . . . cannot serve as justification for the *indefinite* continuance of the war since it was repealed by subsequent Congressional action. . . ." While the government conceded that the resolution no longer provided authority for continuing the war, it argued that military authorization and appropriations acts and the Selective Service and Training Act provided such authority. Despite the "overwhelming weight" of judicial precedent, including his own opinion in *United States* v. *Sisson*, Judge Wyzanski and Chief Circuit Judge David Bazelon concluded that the earlier body of judicial authority was unsound.[10]

"This court," Wyzanski emphasized, "cannot be unmindful of what every schoolboy knows:"

> that in voting to appropriate money or to draft men a Congressman is not necessarily approving of the continuation of a war no matter how specifically the appropriation or draft act refers to that war. A Congressman wholly opposed to the war's commencement and continuation might vote for the military appropriations and for the draft measures because he was unwilling to abandon without support men already fighting. An honorable, decent, compassionate act of aiding those already in peril is no proof of consent to the actions that placed and continued them in that dangerous posture. We should not construe votes cast in pity and piety as though they were votes freely given to express con-

sent. *Hence Chief Judge Bazelon and I believe that none of the legislation drawn to the court's attention may serve as a valid assent to the Vietnam war.*[11]

The third member of the panel, Circuit Judge Edward Tamm, adhered to the line of judicial precedent that inferred congressional approval from selective-service extension, military authorization and appropriations, and foreign-aid authorization and appropriations acts, and therefore he, too, voted to dismiss the complaint.[12]

After asserting judicial power to determine (1) whether a war existed and (2) whether Congress had authorized presidential military action, the court-of-appeals panel refused to decide whether President Nixon had abused his constitutional authority. Even if Nixon's predecessors had exceeded their authority, Wyzanski claimed that the court could not procure the evidence necessary to determine whether the President's actions were defensive or offensive, i.e., within the zone of authority that the Constitution allocates to the President or Congress. Even if the court could obtain such evidence, argued Wyzanski, the judiciary should not substitute its judgment for the executive's. Unless the President's conduct represents a " . . . case of clear abuse amounting to bad faith," the judiciary should not interfere with the executive's constitutional role in foreign affairs.[13] In the final analysis, the circuit court exercised prudence and self-restraint while issuing a clear warning to the President.

In contrast to the line of judicial precedent from *Velvel* through *Drinan*, in which various Federal courts ruled that the issues presented political questions, *Mitchell* held that the issue of presidential power to wage a war of indefinite duration and great magnitude is justiciable. Unlike the lines of precedent that include *Orlando* v. *Laird*, *Mottola* v. *Nixon*, and *Holtzman* v. *Schlesinger*, the circuit court refused to determine whether President Nixon's military actions were defensive and, therefore, within the scope of his authority as commander in chief.[14] In *Mitchell*, Judge Wyzanski backed away from a direct confrontation with the executive by claiming that he did not have the requisite information to decide the case on its merits. The *Mitchell* decision remains a curious anomaly falling somewhere between *Drinan* and *Orlando*.

FROM *BERK* TO *MASSACHUSETTS*: DID CONGRESS SUPPORT THE WAR?

In a series of decisions that includes *Berk* v. *Laird*, *Orlando* v. *Laird*, *DaCosta* v. *Laird*, and *Massachusetts* v. *Laird*, several district and circuit courts decided that the political-question doctrine does not fore-close judicial inquiry into the existence of joint congressional-presiden-tial participation in the prosecution of the war. Since the congressional power to declare war " . . . was intended as an explicit restriction upon the power of the Executive to initiate war on his own prerogative . . . ," the existence of congressional authorization poses a justiciable ques-tion.[15] Speaking for the Second Circuit Court of Appeals, Judge Robert Anderson concluded that congressional action was constitutionally suf-ficient to authorize or ratify the President's military conduct. The courts did not, however, determine the wisdom or propriety of the means that Congress had selected to authorize presidential conduct. The courts concluded that " . . . the constitutional propriety of the means which Congress has chosen to ratify and approve the protracted military op-erations in Southeast Asia is a political question."[16] Inasmuch as the Constitution does not prescribe the means that Congress must employ to authorize or ratify military hostilities, the legislature has discretion to employ any form that is constitutionally acceptable.

Berk v. Laird

In *Berk* v. *Laird*, Judge Anderson denied Private Malcolm Berk's mo-tion for a preliminary injunction against Secretary Laird and other De-fense Department officials. Berk claimed that his military superiors lacked authority to order him to Vietnam or Cambodia because they were waging "war" without the explicit congressional authorization that the Constitution requires. Since the Defense Department had not yet ordered Private Berk to report to Vietnam or Cambodia, the court could have dismissed the motion for a preliminary injunction without com-menting on the congressional power to authorize military hostilities in the absence of a declaration of war.[17] Nevertheless, Judge Anderson proceeded to evaluate the merits of Berk's claim.

First, Judge Anderson concluded that Berk's claim presents justicia-ble issues inasmuch as " . . . the power to commit American military forces under various sets of circumstances is shared by Congress and the executive."[18] Although the Constitution assigns the powers to de-clare war and defend the nation against sudden attack exclusively to Congress or the President, the Vietnam War falls within the zone of concurrent constitutional power. Therefore, the separation of powers does not preclude judicial determination of the existence of joint congressional-presidential participation in the war's prosecution. In this twilight zone of concurrent power, there may be a judicial duty to de-termine whether Congress and the President have acted jointly to au-thorize military hostilities in Vietnam and Cambodia.

While Judge Anderson acknowledged judicial competence to determine whether mutual participation existed, he observed that *Berk* might, nevertheless, present a political question for which the court lacked judicially discoverable and manageable standards. If the President had waged the Vietnam War without congressional participation, the court " . . . might be able to determine that this extreme step violated a discoverable standard calling for *some* mutual participation by Congress in accordance with Article 1, section 8."[19] However, Congress had authorized military hostilities expressly through the Gulf of Tonkin Resolution and, by implication, through various appropriations acts. In reality, Berk was challenging the constitutional adequacy or sufficiency of the legislation that Congress had enacted rather than the mere existence of such legislation. Were these legislative enactments sufficiently explicit to satisfy the constitutional requirements of the declaration-of-war clause?[20] Without concluding that Berk's claim posed a political question, Judge Anderson invited Berk to fashion standards that would allow the district court, on remand, to " . . . escape the liklihood that his particular claim about this war at this time is a political question."[21]

In remanding the case to the district court for a hearing on Berk's motion for a permanent injunction, Judge Anderson suggested the standards requisite for a decision on the merits. Before a court could proceed to the merits, Berk had to specify the joint legislative-executive action sufficient to authorize military hostilities in Vietnam. Even if Private Berk could demonstrate that the President had exceeded the scope of defensive authority that the Constitution confers on the commander in chief, he had to show that the Gulf of Tonkin Resolution and other congressional action over six years did not provide "explicit approval" to conduct military hostilities in Vietnam and Cambodia.[22] Despite the difficulty of scaling these procedural obstacles, Judge Anderson did not foreclose the possibility that Berk could "escape the political question doctrine" and establish his claim in a hearing on a permanent injunction.

On remand, District Judge Orrin Judd dismissed the complaint against the government. Judd noted that Congress (1) has the power to authorize partial or limited war, (2) had "authorized military hostilities in Vietnam in a manner sufficiently explicit to satisfy constitutional requirements," and (3) has plenary power to decide whether a declaration of war or other modes of authorization are desirable.[23] While the first two issues are within the court's jurisdiction, the third calls for a policy judgment that only Congress can make. Congress has exclusive authority and competence to weigh the risks, costs, benefits, and consequences, and to decide the wisdom of waging limited or general war.[24]

According to Berk's contention, which Judd apparently accepted, the sufficiency of congressional authorization varies directly with the magnitude rather than the defensive/offensive character of military hostilities.[25] At one end of the scale are emergency actions,

> . . . such as repelling an attack on the United States or protecting American citizens from attack, which the President may take without any action by Congress. In the second category are placed other acts of war against organized states, and aid in protecting any other nation from armed attack; plaintiff says these acts may be authorized or ratified by any explicit Congressional action, but not by appropriations acts, unless such acts "explicitly and by their own terms authorize, sanction and/or direct military action."

> The third category is described as "hostilities of the highest magnitude," as measured by numbers of men involved, amounts of equipment, and use of the most powerful weapons. Such action, plaintiff says, cannot be initiated without *prior* explicit Congressional authority.[26]

Even if the Vietnam conflict began as an emergency action within the scope of exclusive presidential authority, Berk argued, it had since escalated into a war "of the highest magnitude," requiring prior congressional authority " . . . through a declaration of general war or limited war or treaty, law or resolution explicitly authorizing the use of military force."[27]

Conceding that the Vietnam conflict was a major war, Judd did not accept the requirement of prior explicit congressional authorization. After reviewing the Vietnam War's long and complicated history, Judd examined congressional powers to authorize partial or limited war. As judicial precedent and the historical record indicate, Congress had authorized limited war and hostilities against France (1798), Tripoli (1802), Algiers (1815), and Mexico (1914) without declaring war. More recently, Congress had authorized the use of armed forces to protect Formosa (1955), in the Middle East (1957), to prevent Cuban subversion in the western hemisphere (1962), and to secure access to Berlin (1962).[28] Measured against earlier congressional authorizations, Judd concluded that the Gulf of Tonkin Resolution gave the President broad authority to resist aggression in Southeast Asia. "This court," he remarked, "cannot say that the present conflict is 'wider' than was authorized by the Joint Resolution and the subsequent acts of Congress."[29]

Judge Judd rejected Berk's contention that neither the Gulf of Tonkin Resolution nor the various military-appropriations acts cited authorized the President's military actions, since " . . . Congress was always presented with a *fait accompli* which it was compelled to ratify." "The course of events," Judd observed, " . . . is more consistent with Congress and the President moving in concert."[30] Despite congressional opposition to the war, Congress continued to enact legislation recognizing that the United States was engaged in a partial or limited war in Vietnam and Cambodia. The various appropriations and authorization acts cited reveal that Congress knowingly approved the President's military conduct in Vietnam.[31] If Congress can authorize military hostilities prospectively without formally declaring war, Judd observed, judicial precedent permits Congress to ratify any executive act "that could have been authorized." "The entire course of legislation shows," according to Judd, "that Congress knew what it was doing, and that it intended to have American troops fight in Vietnam."[32]

Insofar as Berk asked the court to determine the propriety of waging war without a formal declaration, Judd argued that only Congress could decide whether the United States should wage a partial or a general war. Only Congress has the constitutional authority to determine the consequences that might result from a declaration of war. Such a declaration could trigger responses from allies, neutrals, and enemies that no court could anticipate or influence. Prudence, respect for congressional judgment and the legislative function, and the separation of powers suggest that courts should not interfere with such policy decisions. In this twilight zone of concurrent power, the existence of joint legislative-executive action precludes judicial intervention. Having found that mutual action is constitutionally sufficient, " . . . the court should respect the authorization which Congress has given to the President."[33] To proceed any further would raise a nonjusticiable political question that is demonstrably committed to the political departments.

Orlando v. Laird

Almost two weeks after the circuit court remanded *Berk*, the district court denied a similar motion for a preliminary injunction in *Orlando* v. *Laird*. In accordance with Judge Anderson's opinion in *Berk*, District Judge John Dooling ruled that a court could determine whether valid authorization to conduct hostilities existed without raising a political question. Judge Dooling evaluated the constitutional sufficiency of congressional authorization but refused to determine the wisdom or propriety of the mode that Congress had selected to authorize or ratify the President's military conduct.[34] Since the Constitution grants Congress exclusive power to decide whether the U.S. should wage partial or general war, the courts cannot develop judicial standards to determine whether congressional policy is wise.[35] As Judge Dooling framed the issues, *Orlando* posed traditional questions of statutory and constitutional interpretation.

Not unlike Judges Judd and Anderson, Dooling began his opinion by delineating the congressional power to initiate war from the presidential power to take emergency defensive measures:

> The language of the Constitution makes the war power a legislative power. . . . Nothing relevant flows from the designation of the president as commander-in-chief of the armed forces except to confirm that his executive power includes the power to "conduct" wars declared by legislative act . . . , to deny autonomy to the military, and to locate the fountainhead of necessary emergency combat initiatives when the straitness of the exigency denies the Congress the time to act.[36]

Initially, Dooling distinguishes the zones of exclusive congressional and presidential power according to the Framers' defensive/offensive-war theory. As a species of twentieth-century insurgency warfare, however, the Vietnam War resists the Framers' classification. Therefore, Dooling turns to the threshold theory in order to classify the Vietnam War and to determine the authorization necessary to wage hostilities.[37] As measured by the war's magnitude (scope and intensity) and duration, does U.S. military conduct fall within a zone of exclusive or concurrent authority? If it falls within the latter zone, is there sufficient mutual legislative-executive participation in the war's prosecution to pass constitutional muster?

Without explicitly reviewing the history of military escalation, Judge Dooling noted that the Vietnam War had long ago attained a "magnitude in size and duration" requiring "affirmative and systematic legislative support." The volume of annual appropriations, the language of specific military authorization and appropriations acts, and repeated extensions of military conscription demonstrate that Congress supported the war freely and knowingly. Whatever may have motivated individual congressmen to vote for or against such legislation, the very existence of steady and continuing legislative authorization satisfies the constitutional requirement of mutual participation.[38] The court did not consider the wisdom or desirability of waging military hostilities without declaring war, a policy judgment that only Congress can make.

Thrice bloodied but unbowed, Berk appealed the district court's summary judgment while Orlando appealed the denial of a preliminary injunction. Speaking for the court of appeals in *Orlando* v. *Laird*, Judge Anderson affirmed the district court's decisions. The court-of-appeals panel held that (1) the political-question doctrine does not preclude judicial determination of either the existence or constitutional sufficiency of congressional authorization, (2) Congress has discretionary power to select means other than a declaration of war, and (3) the judiciary lacks competence to determine the wisdom or propriety of the means that Congress chooses to authorize hostilities.[39] Judge Anderson concluded that " . . . Congress and the Executive have taken mutual and joint action in the prosecution and support of military operations in Southeast Asia from the beginning of these operations." The legislative record satisfied the court's test of "sufficient" mutual and joint action to authorize the government's military conduct.[40]

Neither the language of the Constitution nor the record of the Federal Convention suggests that the Framers intended to restrict congressional discretion in authorizing or ratifying military hostilities. Since the Constitution neither prescribes nor proscribes a particular form for authorizing or ratifying hostilities, the court concluded that "[t]he framers' intent to vest the war power in Congress is in no way defeated by permitting an inference of authorization from legislative action furnishing the manpower and materials of war. . . ."[41] Judge Anderson acknowledged the flexibility and exclusive authority that the Constitution confers on Congress and the President in dealing with other nations. "The making of a policy decision of that kind," he wrote, "is clearly within the constitutional domain of those two branches and is just as clearly not within the competency or power of the judiciary."[42] In other words, the Constitution does not straitjacket Congress and the President by forcing them to choose between emergency defensive measures or an explicit declaration of war.[43]

DaCosta v. Laird

Following repeal of the Gulf of Tonkin Resolution, the court of appeals reached a similar decision in *DaCosta* v. *Laird*. Sustaining its previous decision in *Orlando*, the court rejected Ernest DaCosta's claim that the government was without authority to order him to Vietnam " . . . because Congress had never declared war against North Vietnam."[44] The court specifically dismissed DaCosta's contention that repeal of the Gulf of Tonkin Resolution withdrew congressional authorization to continue military operations in Vietnam. Even without the resolution, by continuing appropriations for military operations and extending the Selective Service Act, Congress ratified and approved the President's military decisions. Although Congress urged a prompt and orderly withdrawal of U.S. armed forces through a nonbinding sense-of-congress amendment to the Selective Service Act, it did not fix a date for removing American troops.[45] Inasmuch as the court had previously inferred congressional support for continuing the war from military authorization and appropriations acts, surely, Congress and the President could " . . . achieve an orderly deceleration and termination of the conflict" through similar joint action. Consistent with its *Orlando* opinion, the court sustained the constitutional sufficiency but refused to determine the propriety of legislation ratifying hostilities without a formal declaration of war.[46]

Massachusetts v. Laird

In another case decided after Congress had repealed the Gulf of Tonkin Resolution, *Massachusetts v. Laird* (1971), District Judge Wyzanski adhered to the Second Circuit's opinion in *Orlando*. Wyzanski dismissed the complaint either because it was nonjusticiable or because legislation that Congress had enacted " . . . in connection with the Vietnam war was sufficient to justify a judicial inference that Congress had in fact authorized the Vietnam war."[47] Since Congress had "repeatedly authorized" the President's conduct in Vietnam, Wyzanski could not find any rationale to ignore the *Berk* and *Orlando* decisions. Apparently, Wyzanski believed that repeal of the Gulf of Tonkin Resolution did not restrict the President's authority so long as Congress authorized military operations and appropriated funds for the war's prosecution. If Congress wanted to limit presidential power to wage war, it had ample power and the means to vindicate its constitutional authority.[48]

On appeal, the First Circuit Court of Appeals affirmed Judge Wyzanski's dismissal of the complaint against Secretary Laird.[49] Speaking for the court, Circuit Judge Frank Coffin first disposed of such threshold issues as jurisdiction and standing to sue. Having overcome these threshold barriers, Coffin turned to the barrier posed by the political-question doctrine. While he acknowledged the pragmatic difficulties of developing workable standards, finding the facts, and conflicting with decisions of inferior courts, Coffin asserted a judicial duty to decide the constitutional issue "if at all possible." In his desire to avoid the appearance as well as the reality of judicial abdication, Judge Coffin sidestepped the political question by sustaining the constitutional sufficiency of joint legislative-executive action. Despite his caution, Judge Coffin attempted to "identify the scope of the power which has been committed to a coordinate branch in this case."[50]

"[T]he war power of this country," he remarks, "is an amalgam of powers, some distinct and others less sharply limned."[51] While Congress has exclusive power to declare or initiate war, the President has independent authority to repel sudden attacks.[52] In defining the zones of exclusive congressional and presidential authority, obviously, Coffin accepted the Framers' distinction between offensive and defensive war and hostilities. Beyond these exclusive zones, he continued, "the Constitutional scheme envisages the joint participation of the Congress and the executive in determining the scale and duration of hostilities." In this zone of concurrent power, "[t]he Constitution does not contain an explicit provision to indicate whether these interdependent [legislative and executive] powers can properly be employed to sustain hostilities in the absence of a Congressional declaration of war."[53]

Neither the language of the Constitution nor the debates of the Framers, according to Coffin, casts light on the scope of independent legislative and executive power in the twilight zone of undeclared war and hostilities. While the Framers were familiar with undeclared war, they did not specify the form of joint action necessary to sustain such hostilities. In the absence of a demonstrable textual commitment of the power to wage undeclared war, Judge Coffin asserted judicial "license to construe the sense of the Constitutional framework," i.e., license to construct a theory of joint participation from the Constitution's logic and structure. Carefully avoiding the doctrine of "implied powers inherent in sovereignty," Coffin inferred the power to wage undeclared war from the various auxiliary war powers that the Constitution vests in Congress.[54]

Turning to the Vietnam War, Coffin accepted the view that the war was the product of joint congressional-presidential action. However, he declined to determine whether congressional action amounted to the functional equivalent of a declaration of war or constituted either the expressed or implied will of Congress. Relying on the plaintiffs' complaint, Coffin casually noted that there had been " . . . a prolonged period of Congressional support of executive activities." Under the circumstances, there was no need to comment on the President's acting on his own authority or in conflict with Congress. The court simply avoided the constitutional issues that would flow from conflicting claims of presidential and congressional authority. Judge Coffin merely held that " . . . in a situation of prolonged but undeclared hostilities, where the executive continues to act not only in the absence of any conflicting Congressional claim of authority but with steady Congressional support, the Constitution has not been breached."[55]

In the line of judicial precedent from *Berk* v. *Laird* to *Massachusetts* v. *Laird*, the Federal courts asserted a judicial duty to inquire into the existence and constitutional sufficiency of congressional legislation authorizing or ratifying military hostilities, but they refused to determine either the wisdom or propriety of authorizing undeclared war and hostilities. Since the courts concluded that joint participation was sufficient, there was no need to determine the boundaries between Congress and the President in this twilight zone. However, the courts did not foreclose the possibility of intervening in the event that conflict developed between the legislative and executive branches. Beyond determining the existence and sufficiency of congressional authorization, the political-question doctrine precludes further judicial intervention, since the Constitution confers discretionary power on Congress to decide whether to wage a limited or a general war.

The Federal courts adhered to the Framers' distinction between offensive and defensive war and hostilities in defining the zones of exclusive congressional and presidential authority. Since the Vietnam War falls into a twilight zone of concurrent power, the Federal courts abandoned the Framers' theory in order to determine the authorization necessary to sustain the war's prosecution. In this twilight zone, the courts measured the adequacy of joint participation according to the threshold theory. As the scope, intensity, and duration of an undeclared war or hostilities approach "the highest magnitude," the government requires affirmative and systematic legislative support to continue military operations. However, the Constitution does not require a declaration of war or other explicit authorization or ratification. In the absence of explicit approval, the courts can infer approval of the President's military actions from appropriations, military-authorization, selective-service, and other public acts supporting military operations.

MOTTOLA AND *HOLTZMAN*: DECISIONS ON THE MERITS

In contrast to their brethren, District Judges Orrin Judd and William Sweigert asserted a judicial duty to determine the constitutionality of the President's power to wage war without a congressional declaration of war or other explicit authorization.[56] In *Mottola* v. *Nixon* (1970), *Holtzman* v. *Richardson* (1973), and *Holtzman* v. *Schlesinger* (1973), Judd and Sweigert marched further into the political thicket than had their judicial brethren to determine whether: (1) Congress had authorized or ratified the President's military actions, (2) the means that Congress had chosen to authorize or ratify presidential conduct were constitutionally acceptable, (3) the President's actions conflicted with the will of Congress, or (4) the President's actions exceeded the scope of his independent constitutional authority.

Mottola v. Nixon

In *Mottola*, Judge Sweigert set aside the government's now-familiar contention that the plaintiff's claim presented a nonjusticiable political question. Relying on *Youngstown*, *Baker*, and *Powell*, he concluded " . . . that none of the formulations of the political-question doctrine, as stated in *Baker* v. *Carr*, barred adjudication of the issue."[57] Since the Constitution vests the power to declare war exclusively in Congress rather than the President, the separation of powers does not bar judicial determination of presidential authority to initiate and conduct war without explicit congressional authorization. *Mottola* raised familiar questions of constitutional and statutory interpretation that a court can decide without expressing disrespect for or producing embarrassing confrontation with a coordinate department. Insofar as the court merely asserted a traditional duty to interpret the Constitution, according to Sweigert, there was little risk of making nonjudicial policy determinations, deciding questions that lack judicially manageable standards, or various coordinate departments issuing multifarious pronouncements on the same question.[58] As Judge Sweigert framed the issues, the court was simply determining the President's authority to wage military hostilities without a congressional declaration of war or other explicit authorizing legislation. Judge Sweigert merely asserted a traditional judicial duty to determine " . . . whether the kind and degree of congressional action in the Vietnam situation has or has not been sufficient to amount to the cooperative joint congressional action required . . . " to commit the nation to an undeclared war.[59]

Having surmounted the political-question barrier, Judge Sweigert reserved judgment until the government had an opportunity to file responsive pleadings on the merits of the central issue.[60] Nevertheless, in dictum, Sweigert commented on the President's authority to initiate and conduct hostilities without explicit congressional authorization. Although he acknowledged that *Orlando* was "entitled to respect and careful consideration," Sweigert leaned toward the argument that the Constitution requires nothing less than a congressional declaration of war or "an equally explicit congressional expression, either general or limited," of intent to initiate or continue military hostilities. Anything less than such explicit authorization would represent either " . . . a usurpation by the President or an abdication by the Congress—or, perhaps, both."[61]

Apparently, Judge Sweigert did not accept the argument that the courts could infer congressional ratification of the President's military conduct from military authorization and appropriations bills. Joint participation was a euphemism for either the President's unconstitutional exercise of power or the unconstitutional delegation of power that is vested exclusively in Congress. In either event, joint participation vitiates the separation of powers and deprives the American people " . . . of an opportunity to reliably judge the Congress, the President, or both, in terms of the constitutionality of their conduct."[62] Under the circumstances, the judiciary has a responsibility to enforce the separation of powers and to hold Congress and the President constitutionally accountable.[63]

In defining the scope of presidential and congressional authority, Judge Sweigert's analysis of the arguments for circumventing the Constitution (Art. 1, Sec. 8, Cl. 11) reveals a fidelity to the Framers' defensive/offensive-war theory. While he recognized the President's power to repel sudden attacks against the United States and its citizens and armed forces, the Vietnam War was no longer a defensive action within the zone of exclusive presidential authority. The Vietnam War involved " . . . not only defensive, but also offensive military operations of great magnitude, and . . . has continued over a period more than sufficiently long to permit and to require exercise by the Congress of its power and responsibility under Article 1, Section 8 (11)."[64] According to Sweigert, the Vietnam War falls within the zone of exclusive congressional authority.

Judge Sweigert was even less charitable to the argument that historic precedent supported the President's power to initiate and conduct military hostilities without explicit congressional authorization. If the Vietnam War had not been constitutionally authorized, the repeated evasion of the constitutional process during the Civil War, the Korean War, and lesser military hostilities could not provide legal rationale for continuing the usurpation of power. Similarly, Sweigert rejected the argument that the Southeast Asia Collective Defense Treaty had transferred the congressional power to initiate war to the President. Indeed, the treaty specifically provides that each party is subject to its own domestic constitutional processes, which recognizes that the power to initiate war rests with Congress rather than the President.[65] In conducting foreign affairs, the President necessarily has broad incidental powers but the congressional power to declare war limits his authority to employ military means. However outmoded declarations of war may be in international law and practice, both Congress and the President have an obligation to satisfy the constitutional requirements of Article 1, Section 8 (Cl. 11).[66]

In the absence of a congressional declaration of war, Judge Sweigert's opinion suggests that nothing less than explicit congressional authorization can satisfy the constitutional requirements of Article 1, Section 8 (Cl. 11).[67] Therefore, neither the President nor the judiciary can infer congressional authorization for a prolonged, undeclared war from such legislation as military authorization and appropriations acts or the Gulf of Tonkin Resolution. Since the President had confronted Congress with a military *fait accompli*, authorization and appropriations acts merely provide material support for armed forces in combat rather than approval or ratification of the President's military policies. Ignoring the language of specific authorization and appropriations acts, Sweigert apparently accepted the argument that such legislation did not " . . . constitute the explicit ratification necessary to validate otherwise unauthorized executive action. . . ."[68]

Although Sweigert acknowledged that the language of the Gulf of Tonkin Resolution apparently authorized the President to resist aggression with military force, if necessary, he questioned whether the resolution authorized an undeclared war or amounted to the functional equivalent of a congressional declaration of war.[69] Within the context of the legislative debate, "the circumstances of its enactment," and President Johnson's ostensible determination to avoid a major war, the ambiguous Gulf of Tonkin Resolution merely supported the President's decision to repel an attack on U.S. naval forces.[70] If the resolution amounted to an undated, open-ended declaration of war that conferred plenary power on the President to choose the time, place, and enemy, as Senator Morse claimed, then it would be a "flagrantly invalid delegation" of a power that the Constitution vests exclusively in Congress. While Congress can delegate broad powers to the President in foreign affairs, it cannot delegate " . . . the power to declare, initiate or continue a war—since the power to declare war *does* require an act of Congress—a declaration of war—under the express provisions of Article 1, Section 8 (11)."[71]

Despite his failure to dispose of *Mottola* on its merits, Judge Sweigert's opinion leaves little doubt that he did not regard the Gulf of Tonkin Resolution or other legislation as providing the explicit authority that the Constitution requires to wage war. His opinion rests on the assumption that the Vietnam conflict was an offensive rather than a defensive military engagement. Therefore, the decision to continue military hostilities falls within the zone of exclusive congressional authority rather than the zones of concurrent power or exclusive presidential authority. In this context, nothing less than explicit congressional authorization would satisfy the Constitution's requirements.[72]

Holtzman v. Richardson; Holtzman v. Schlesinger

Two months before the termination of U.S. combat activities in Laos and Cambodia, District Judge Orrin Judd concluded that the President's authority to continue bombing Cambodia after the Vietnamese cease-fire agreement did not pose a political question.[73] After examining the legislative record, Judd decided that Congress had not authorized the President to continue bombing Cambodia following the withdrawal of American armed forces from South Vietnam and the release of prisoners of war. In the absence of such congressional authorization, Judd enjoined U.S. military authorities from continuing the bombing and other military activities in Cambodia.[74] Although he was subsequently overruled,[75] during the Indochinese War no Federal judge marched further into the political thicket than Orrin G. Judd.

In *Holtzman v. Richardson*, Judd ruled that (1) Congresswoman Elizabeth Holtzman had standing to challenge the government's combat operations in Cambodia, (2) the district court had subject-matter jurisdiction, and (3) the political-question doctrine did not justify dismissing the complaint without examining its merits.[76] Taking his cues from the Supreme Court's decisions in *Baker*, *Powell*, and *Youngstown* and the Second Circuit's decisions in *Berk*, *Orlando*, and *DaCosta*, Judd reasoned that "the question of the balance of constitutional authority to declare war, as between the executive and legislative branches, is not a political question."[77] Although the Supreme Court had summarily affirmed *Atlee v. Laird*, in which the district court refused to decide whether Congress had authority to approve military hostilities through appropriations bills, Judd distinguished *Holtzman* from *Atlee*.[78] In *Holtzman* the issue was whether Congress had, in fact, authorized the Cambodian operation rather than the wisdom or propriety of the mode that Congress had employed. Since the substantive issues in *Holtzman* were different from and narrower than *Atlee*, according to Judd, the Supreme Court's summary affirmation of *Atlee* did not necessarily preclude a review of the merits.[79]

After the government had withdrawn U.S. troops from Vietnam and the North Vietnamese and the Viet Cong had repatriated American prisoners of war, prudence no longer required judicial abstention. "Reluctance to jeopardize the safety of American soldiers or prisoners," Judd argued, "is no longer a barrier to judicial determination of the constitutionality of a phase of war activity."[80] If the Vietnam War had ended, there was little danger of embarrassing the government during an authorized military operation. Therefore, Judd concluded that the political-question doctrine did not justify dismissing the complaint without examining its merits. Despite his refusal to dismiss the complaint, Judd held Miss Holtzman's motion for a summary judgment in abeyance until the government could submit additional documents.[81]

On July 25, 1973, Judd decided that the judiciary could determine whether Congress had authorized the Cambodian operation without posing a nonjusticiable political question. In *Holtzman v. Schlesinger*, Judd also concluded that Congress had not authorized continuing combat operations in Cambodia after termination of the Vietnam War. Although he recognized that Congress could authorize military operations through appropriations bills, Judd denied that either the Joint Resolution Continuing Appropriations for Fiscal 1974 or the Second Supplemental Appropriations Act, 1973, which contained provisions cutting off funds for Cambodian military operations after August 15, authorized continuing the bombing until that date. Therefore, Judd granted Miss Holtzman's motion for a summary judgment enjoining the President and his military subordinates from continuing the bombing, but postponed the effective date of the injunction, pending the government's application for a stay in the circuit court, which the Second Circuit granted on July 27.[82]

Despite congressional failure to deny the President's authority to continue military operations until August 15, Judd refused to infer such authorization from legislative inaction. After examining the legislative record between 1970 and 1973 Judd concluded that Congress had never authorized expanding the war to Cambodia except insofar as it was necessary to ensure the safety of U.S. armed forces in South Vietnam and secure the release of American prisoners of war. Once the Administration had accomplished these objectives and terminated the war, the authority and rationale for the Cambodian operation no longer existed. Although the Nixon Administration considered the bombing as essential to enforcing Article 20 of the Paris Agreement of January 27, 1973, which prohibited the signatories from using Cambodia militarily, Congress had not authorized such actions.[83]

Beginning in October 1970, Congress had limited military support to Cambodia. The War Forces Military Procurement Act of 1971 (approved October 7, 1970), the Defense Appropriations Act of 1972 (approved December 18, 1971), and subsequent military authorization and appropriations acts restricted the use of funds to aid the Cambodian government or Vietnamese and other free-world forces assisting Cambodia except for " . . . support of actions required to ensure the safe and orderly withdrawal or disengagement of U.S. Forces from Southeast Asia, or to aid in the release of Americans held as prisoners of war."[84] The Special Foreign Assistance Act of 1971 also provided that " . . .

none of the funds authorized or appropriated pursuant to this or any other Act may be used to finance the introduction of United States ground combat troops into Cambodia, or to provide United States advisors to or for Cambodian military forces in Cambodia."[85] Both the Special Foreign Assistance Act of 1971 (approved January 1, 1971) and the Foreign Assistance Act of 1971 (approved February 7, 1972) denied that the United States was committed to defend Cambodia.[86] Despite the Nixon Administration's claim that the Indochinese War was "of one piece," according to Judd the legislative record indicated that the Cambodian operation was related to the extrication of U.S. troops and prisoners of war. Subsequent to the war's termination, the President would require congressional authorization to continue military operations in Cambodia.[87]

After the cease-fire agreement, on May 10, the House of Representatives refused to approve a Defense Department request to transfer approximately $175 million from other accounts to be earmarked for Cambodian bombing operations. Then, on June 26, Congress adopted H.R. 7447, which provided for the immediate cutoff of funds for bombing Cambodia.[88] Following the President's veto of H.R. 7447, Congress adopted two compromise measures on June 29 and 30 providing for an August 15 cutoff, which President Nixon approved on July 1.[89] Although a congressional majority voted to override the President's veto, the Administration's opponents could not muster the two-thirds necessary to overturn the veto.[90] Faced with the urgent need to provide funds for governmental operations and the President's threat to veto any bill that included amendments to cut off aid to Cambodia, Congress accepted the compromise measure.[91] Thus, Congress ended a legislative impasse and averted a constitutional confrontation with the President.

According to Judd, Congress had never authorized the bombing of Cambodia through an explicit declaration of war or any other legislative action. If the Cambodian operation were an integral part of the Vietnam War, however, the President would not require explicit congressional authorization for a tactical decision that falls within the scope of the commander in chief's authority to conduct military operations. Since Congress had not acquiesced to the Administration's view that the Indochina War was "all of one piece," as a congressional agent the President could not venture beyond the limited legislative mandate to bomb Cambodia insofar as necessary to protect U.S. troops in South Vietnam and secure the release of American prisoners of war. Once these objectives had been achieved and the war had ended, the President would require explicit legislative authorization to continue the bombing.[92]

Although President Nixon continued bombing Cambodia despite the

Vietnam War's termination, Judd refused to equate congressional failure to disavow Nixon's actions with "an implied grant of power." "While Congress can exercise its war-making power through measures other than an express declaration of war," he noted, "courts should not easily infer the exercise of such a grave responsibility." If, for example, Judd had inferred such authorization from congressional failure to override President Nixon's veto of H.R. 7447, the President would require " . . . a vote of only one-third plus one of either House in order to conduct a war. . . ." Conversely, " . . . Congress must override a Presidential veto in order to terminate hostilities which it has not authorized."[93]

Implicit in Judd's analysis of the respective powers of Congress and the President to wage military hostilities is the Framers' distinction between offensive and defensive war. If the Cambodian bombing had been a tactical operation designed to protect U.S. troops and prisoners of war, it would have been a defensive measure within the zone of exclusive presidential authority. However, if the Cambodian operation were a distinct military engagement, it would be an offensive measure within the zone of exclusive congressional authority. Although Judd did not conclude that the bombing was a distinct military adventure, he argued that the President could not continue military operations without usurping congressional authority.[94] In the absence of congressional authorization, the constitutional separation of powers recommends judicial intervention rather than abstention. The Federal courts have a duty to employ their powers of statutory and constitutional review in order to limit each branch of the national government to exercise of its constitutional powers.

On July 27 the Second Circuit granted the government's request for a stay and set oral argument on the motion for August 13.[95] In the interim, the American Civil Liberties Union, representing Miss Holtzman and the other plaintiffs, applied to Justice Thurgood Marshall, in his capacity as a circuit justice, to vacate the court of appeals' stay of the district court's injunction.[96] While he denied the motion, Justice Marshall acknowledged that Miss Holtzman's claims were "far from frivolous," that a growing and respectable body of judicial opinion held such war-powers controversies justiciable, and that the President cannot wage war without congressional authorization, "except, perhaps, in the case of a pressing emergency or when the President is in the process of extricating himself from a war which Congress once authorized."[97] Furthermore, Marshall apparently sympathized with the view that Congress had never approved the Cambodian operation except insofar as necessary to "extricate" U.S. troops and prisoners of war from Vietnam.

Subsequent to the Paris Peace Accords, noted Marshall, the Court could easily conclude that the bombing was no longer justifiable.[98]

Acting as a surrogate for the Court, which was not in session, Marshall denied Congresswoman Holtzman's motion despite his personal convictions. As a surrogate, Marshall declined to anticipate his brethren's views on the complex questions " . . . of standing, judicial competence, and substantive constitutional law which go to the roots of the division of power in a constitutional democracy."[99] Without consulting his brethren, Marshall was not prepared to conclude that the circuit court had abused its discretion in granting the stay. Since he could not exclude the possibility that the government would prevail on the merits, Marshall apparently concluded that the equities lay in the government's favor. In denying the application to vacate the stay, Marshall apparently questioned the war's wisdom and legality, but acknowledged the Court's limited powers and the need for judicial self-restraint in a constitutional democracy.[100]

Casting judicial self-restraint aside, on August 3, Justice Douglas vacated the court of appeals' stay and reinstated the district court's order. Treating *Holtzman* as a capital case in which some unknown person—a Cambodian peasant or a U.S. airman—was about to die, Douglas vacated the stay in order to preserve the status quo pending a hearing on the merits. Since death is irrevocable, he reasoned, there was no need to balance the equities and consider the damage to U.S. foreign policy resulting from the injunction. If the President had exceeded his constitutional authority by waging war without the requisite congressional authorization, his action would amount to a taking of life without due process.[101]

Consistent with his earlier dissents in *Holmes* v. *U.S.* and *Massachusetts* v. *Laird*,[102] Douglas was disposed to hear *Holtzman* on the merits. Relying on *Flast* v. *Cohen*, Douglas asserted that the petitioners had sufficient standing as taxpayers to challenge the President's authority to wage war without a congressional declaration of war. Similarly, Douglas argued that *Holtzman* posed a justiciable rather than a political question beyond the Court's judicial competence. Inasmuch as Douglas did not perceive serious procedural obstacles to judicial resolution of an important constitutional question, namely, the respective authority of Congress and the President to initiate and wage war, he granted the stay that Marshall had denied on August 1.[103]

Outmaneuvered, but undaunted, the solicitor general applied to the Court on August 4 to reinstate the stay pending action by the court of appeals. After telephoning his colleagues, Justice Marshall announced on the same day that the Court had granted the solicitor general's request pending a hearing on the merits, which the court of appeals had advanced from August 13 to August 8.[104] Overruled by his colleagues, Douglas dissented from the Court's order, arguing that the Supreme Court can act only when six members are present. Telephonic communications, he commented, are not an acceptable substitute for the give and take of the conference.[105] Justice Douglas's objections to the contrary notwithstanding, *Holtzman* was back in the hands of the court of appeals.

Following this brief skirmish in the Supreme Court, on August 8 the court of appeals heard and decided *Holtzman* v. *Schlesinger*.[106] Speaking for the majority, Circuit Judge William Mulligan reversed the district court's order and remanded the case to Judge Judd with instructions to dismiss the complaint. In dismissing the injunction, Judge Mulligan argued that the legality of bombing Cambodia subsequent to the withdrawal of U.S. armed forces and the release of American prisoners of war was a political rather than a justiciable question. While Mulligan admitted that the court had the power to determine whether Congress had authorized the Cambodian military operation, he denied that the judiciary could determine the political wisdom or the constitutional propriety of the means that Congress had chosen to approve and ratify such military operations. Moreover, the judiciary possesses neither the data nor the competence to evaluate whether the President's military actions were defensive or offensive. In other words, the court could not decide whether the Cambodian operation was a tactical decision within the zone of presidential authority or a "new war" within the zone of congressional authority.[107]

Nevertheless, the court of appeals proceeded to determine whether Congress had authorized the President's military activity in Cambodia. Unable to resist commenting on the legislative record, Mulligan noted that the Joint Resolution Continuing Appropriations for Fiscal 1974 clearly authorized continuing the bombing until August 15.[108] Since the statute was unambiguous, it was neither permissable nor necessary to resort to the legislative history and other legislative materials in construing congressional intent. However, a "fair reading" of the record reveals that Congress had approved the Cambodian operation until August 15. Indeed, Representative Holtzman had voted against the joint resolution precisely because it would authorize President Nixon's military conduct. Frustrated by her political impotence, Miss Holtzman turned to the courts because she could not override a presidential veto.[109]

Dissenting from the majority's opinion, Circuit Judge James Oakes argued that the issue was justiciable. The central issue was the existence rather than the propriety of the means that Congress had selected to authorize or ratify Cambodian operations following termination of the Vietnam War. Although he recognized that Congress could authorize or ratify the bombing through appropriations and authorization acts, Judge Oakes denied that Congress had, at any time, provided the explicit authorization that the Constitution requires. Prior to the Vietnam War's end, Congress had authorized Cambodian operations only insofar as necessary to extricate the U.S. from Southeast Asia. Subsequent to the war's end, Congress had never conceded the executive's authority to bomb Cambodia.[110] "I fail to see, . . . " Oakes concluded his opinion, "where the Congress ever authorized the continuation of bombing in Cambodia after the cease-fire in Vietnam, the withdrawal of our forces there, and the return of our prisoners of war to our shores."[111]

Despite serious disagreements concerning standing, justiciability, the military purpose of the Cambodian operation, and the existence of congressional authorization, Circuit Judges Oakes, Mulligan, and Timbers accepted the Framers' distinction between offensive and defensive war in determining the respective powers of Congress and the President.[112] If the Cambodian action had been a tactical defensive measure designed to protect U.S. armed forces engaged in an authorized war in South Vietnam, the President would not require congressional authorization to conduct such military operations. However, if the Cambodian operation were a "new war," the President would lack the constitutional authority to commit U.S. troops without prior congressional authorization, "absent a 'belligerent attack' or 'a grave emergency.'"[113] Without access to military intelligence or the ability to evaluate military information, judges far removed from the battlefield cannot determine whether a specific military action is an escalation or merely a tactical maneuver in an existing war.[114] Confronted with such intractable problems, the circuit court declined the opportunity to second-guess the President's military judgment.

In the waning days of the Indochinese War, the Court of Appeals for the Second Circuit sought haven in the techniques of judicial self-restraint. By invoking the political question, Judge Mulligan avoided deciding issues that, in his judgment, the Constitution commits exclusively to the political departments. Although Congress and the President had been locked in protracted conflict over extricating U.S. armed forces from the Indochinese War, in a constitutional democracy the courts are powerless to decide questions of war and peace, which are committed to the people's representatives. As Judge Mulligan recalled from *Proverbs*, " . . . wars are to be managed by governments"[115] rather than Platonic guardians in black robes.

CONCLUSION: MOVING INTO THE POLITICAL THICKET

Despite judicial reluctance to entertain or decide war-powers controversies, during the Vietnam War the Federal courts moved cautiously into this political thicket. As the conflict between Congress and President Nixon over the scope and duration of the war intensified, several Federal courts approached the substantive merits of the Vietnam cases. Between 1970 and 1973, these Federal courts raised delicate statutory and constitutional questions involving the separation of powers, the scope and boundaries of legislative, executive, and judicial authority, and the appropriate relationship among Congress, the President, and the Federal courts. Throughout this period the lower Federal courts exercised their powers of statutory interpretation and constitutional review without guidance from the Supreme Court, which denied certiorari almost invariably without comment.

During the last phase of the Vietnam War (1969–1973), the Federal courts surmounted the procedural barriers of standing to sue, sovereign immunity, and the political-question doctrine to determine such delicate issues as the presidential power to initiate and wage war and military hostilities without a congressional declaration of war. While the judicial doctrines of standing and sovereign immunity did not pose serious obstacles, until 1969 the political-question doctrine presented a seemingly insurmountable obstacle to judicial review of war-powers controversies. Following *Powell* v. *McCormack* (1969), several Federal courts read the Supreme Court's opinion as an invitation to entertain challenges to the President's warmaking authority. In the absence of an exclusive commitment of all the powers of war and defense to Congress or the President, according to Judges Judd, Lord, Sweigert, and Wyzanski, the constitutional separation of powers does not preclude judicial inquiry into the respective powers of the political departments to initiate and wage war and hostilities.

Inasmuch as the Vietnam War occupied a twilight zone of concurrent power, some courts asserted their jurisdiction to determine whether Congress had actually authorized the President's military actions in Vietnam and Cambodia. Absent a congressional declaration of war, the Federal courts inferred congressional authorization from military and foreign-aid appropriations and authorization acts. Only two district courts, in *Mottola* v. *Nixon* (1970) and *Holtzman* v. *Schlesinger* (1973), denied that Congress had authorized or ratified the President's military actions in Indochina. Federal District Judges Orrin Judd and William Sweigert refused to infer legislative authorization or ratification from laws that Congress had enacted under "duress," when confronted with a military *fait accompli* by the President.

While the courts adhered to the Framers' distinction between offensive and defensive war in determining the boundaries of exclusive congressional and presidential authority, the judiciary also employed the threshold theory in determining the scope of legislative and executive power within the twilight zone of concurrent constitutional authority. In this zone, as the magnitude (i.e., the scope and intensity) and duration of the Vietnam War increased, the courts required evidence of joint legislative-executive participation in the conduct of military hostilities. Furthermore, they inferred such joint participation from the congressional exercise of various auxiliary war powers, as expressed in selective service, veterans benefits, military appropriations, defense authorization, and related foreign-aid legislation. Below the threshold of a declaration of *de jure* war, Congress has discretionary power to select various means to approve, endorse, authorize or ratify the President's military actions. Although the courts have jurisdiction to determine the existence and constitutional sufficiency of the means that Congress has chosen to wage war, the judiciary lacks the power and competence to evaluate the wisdom or propriety of the congressional decision to wage an undeclared war.

During the last phase of the Vietnam War the Federal judiciary asserted its authority to decide war-powers controversies while limiting the scope of judicial intervention. Except for *Mottola* and *Holtzman*, the courts sustained presidential power to wage hostilities without a congressional declaration of war. As long as Congress and the President acted in concert or ostensibly reconciled their political differences, the courts legitimated the joint exercise of legislative and executive power. When Congress and President Nixon reached an apparent impasse, only one Federal judge, Orrin Judd, entered the breach in order to restrain the President from exercising authority that, in Judd's opinion, the Constitution confers exclusively on Congress.

Below the threshold of a declared or *de jure* war, judicial opinion continues to promote the development of a virtually unlimited national war power. By amalgamating the constitutionally distinct congressional war powers with the presidential office of commander in chief, the courts have acted as a midwife to the birth of constitutional dictatorship in the United States. Although the courts continue to articulate the rhetoric of constitutional limitations, the commander in chief recognizes few restrictions on his military powers other than necessity and success on the battlefield. Unless Congress exercises it constitutional authority to restrain executive power, opponents of constitutional dictatorship should not await a judicial David to slay an executive Goliath.

7

Constitutional Government: The Congressional War Powers, the Commander in Chief, and the Federal Courts

During the twentieth century the American President has become an international military-political leader whose constitutional authority parallels the royal prerogatives of the British Crown. In response to international military crises, the President has expanded his defensive powers into a prerogative to commit the nation to war and hostilities without a congressional declaration of war. Until the late 1960s Congress responded pliantly to presidential initiative by authorizing, approving or ratifying the President's decisions to commit the nation to military action without declaring war. Almost without exception, the Federal courts have sustained or legitimated presidential initiative and congressional abdication of decisions to wage undeclared war. Below the threshold of a declaration of war, the Federal courts have encouraged the fusion of the congressional war powers with the President's office of commander in chief. All three branches of the national government have vitiated the Framers' separation of the war powers from the constitutional office of commander in chief through presidential initiative, congressional indulgence, and judicial blessing.

While the Framers could not have anticipated the changes in the art, science, and technology of warfare that have occurred in the nineteenth and twentieth centuries, they were familiar with revolution and limited, undeclared war and hostilities. Despite their familiarity with such threats to national security, the Constitution's authors refused to create either a king-general or a supreme parliament that would possess the prerogatives of war and peace. Apparently, they believed that the nation's security and the citizens' liberty could be served best by separating the power to initiate limited as well as general war from command and superintendence of the armed forces. At the same time, the Framers recognized that military success requires congressional concurrence in committing the nation to war. By separating and sharing the powers to initiate war and hostilities, command the armed forces, and defend the nation against sudden attack, the Framers hoped to achieve an optimum of liberty, constitutional government, domestic order, and international security.

CONGRESS V. THE COMMANDER IN CHIEF

By sharing and separating powers of war, defense, and foreign affairs, the Framers created zones of exclusive legislative and executive authority as well as a zone of concurrent constitutional authority whose boundaries are imprecise. A lack of precision and dynamic changes in the art and science of warfare create the potential for conflict over the scope of congressional and presidential authority to initiate and sustain military hostilities. Since the boundaries between Congress and the President are unclear, some jurists and commentators advocate judicial intervention to resolve irreconcilable conflict between the political departments rather than judicial abstention from such controversy.[1] At times, maintenance of constitutional equilibrium and the separation of powers require judicial intervention to prevent Congress and the President from exercising one another's respective powers. When the occasion for the exercise of judicial power occurs, however, the Federal courts should avoid exceeding their constitutional authority or interfering with the legitimate exercise of congressional and presidential authority. The principle of comity recommends that the courts attempt to determine whether the exercise of judicial power will impair the legislature and executive from performing their functions in such sensitive areas as war and foreign affairs.

Although the zones of exclusive legislative and executive authority cannot be defined precisely, the Federal judiciary has employed the Framers' distinction between defensive and offensive war in differentiating presidential from congressional power to wage military hostilities. Article 1, Section 8 (Cl. 11) of the Constitution vests exclusive power in Congress to declare war or authorize undeclared war and military hostilities. Only Congress has the constitutional authority to initiate war and military hostilities; only Congress can change the nation's condition from peace to war. Absent a declaration of war or other explicit authorizing legislation, the President has constitutional authority to defend the nation, its armed forces, and its citizens and their property against armed attack or when the threat of such an attack is imminent. Without congressional authorization, Article 2 does not confer independent constitutional authority on the President to initiate hostilities or to transform defensive military actions into offensive wars.

Whether Congress declares war or authorizes limited military hostilities, the legislature has ample constitutional authority to restrict presidential warmaking. Although one can question the wisdom or desirability of restricting the President's power to initiate military hostilities, Congress can employ its auxiliary war powers to limit presidential initiative. Congress can use its fiscal powers (to tax and spend) to regulate the size and composition of the armed forces available to the President. Congress can control military organization and the command structure through its power to make rules for the government and regulation of the land and naval forces. Congress has the authority to limit the President's power to dispatch U.S. troops abroad by enacting conscription laws that geographically restrict military service. Congress can employ its militia powers to limit the commander in chief's authority to call up the National Guard for foreign military service. Since the Constitution confers the auxiliary war powers exclusively on Congress, only the legislature can decide the wisdom or propriety of limiting the President's power to initiate war and military hostilities.

In addition to exercising its auxiliary war powers, some commentators suggest that Congress could employ the necessary-and-proper clause to restrict presidential warmaking. If Congress can delegate power to the executive to wage war, it can also deny such power through the necessary-and-proper clause. By emphasizing the horizontal effect of the sweeping clause (Art. 1, Sec. 8, Cl. 18) and by interpreting presidential power narrowly, as William Van Alstyne implies, Congress could employ its authority to limit the commander in chief's power to initiate military hostilities without congressional authorization. However attractive the necessary-and-proper clause appears to advocates of congressional power, there is no conclusive evidence to suggest that the Framers intended the sweeping clause as an unqualified grant of power that Congress could manipulate to reduce the executive to a mere ministerial agency.[2]

Once war begins, Congress has the constitutional authority to control the magnitude, i.e., scope, and duration of military hostilities. Congress can employ its auxiliary war powers to restrict or terminate military actions that exceed the President's defensive authority. During the Vietnam War, for example, Congress enacted no less than ten major bills between 1969 and 1973 that restricted presidential power to conduct military hostilities in Laos, Cambodia, and Vietnam. Indeed, Congress enacted legislation terminating U.S. military action in Laos and Cambodia on August 15, 1973.

Although Congress may fail to delegate its auxiliary war powers to the President, congressional silence does not confer power on the President that the Constitution otherwise denies his office. Even if Congress declares war or authorizes limited military hostilities, such a declaration or authorization does not automatically confer the auxiliary war powers on the President. As John Marshall argued in *Brown v. U.S.* (1814), only Congress can authorize the measures necessary to wage war successfully. Such authorization must be specific, and cannot be inferred from a declaration of limited or general war.

While Article 1 of the Constitution confers the power to declare war and various auxiliary war powers on Congress, Article 2 confers defensive powers on the President. In fact, the President takes an oath to "preserve, protect and defend the Constitution," which implies an obligation to defend the people and their government against sudden attack or when the threat of such attack is imminent. The record of the Federal Convention also indicates that the Framers intended the President to exercise defensive powers. In changing the language of Article 1, Section 8 (Cl. 11) from "make" to "declare" war, the Framers implied a grant of defensive power to the President.[3] However, neither the presidential oath of office nor the record of the Federal Convention illuminates the scope or boundaries of the defensive power that the Constitution vests in the President.

In addition to vesting defensive powers in the executive, the Constitution confers the office of commander in chief on the President. However, the office of commander in chief does not represent an independent affirmative grant of power to the President to initiate military hostilities. Whatever authority the President exercises as commander in chief flows from the Constitution's affirmative grants of power.[4] The executive article's vesting, take-care, appointments, treaty, and recognition clauses delegate to the President the authority and imply the incidental power necessary to defend the nation's security and conduct its foreign affairs. Furthermore, Congress can delegate authority to the executive to defend national security in peacetime, prepare the nation for war, mobilize its human and material resources in wartime, and promote an orderly transition from war to peace.

Although the Constitution does not confer authority on the President to initiate military hostilities, the commander-in-chief clause grants him supreme command of the armed forces that Congress provides. By conferring the office of commander in chief on the President, the Framers provided for civilian control of the military. They made the uniformed military services directly accountable to the President, who is responsible for superintending their conduct in times of war and peace. During times of undeclared military hostilities as well as de jure war, the President is accountable to the American people for the higher direction of war (i.e., command decisions) within the limits that Congress can constitutionally impose on his conduct.[5]

By conferring defensive powers on the President as commander in chief, the Framers created a zone of exclusive constitutional authority. Within this zone of exclusive authority, the President's power is plenary. While Congress has broad power to curb presidential warmaking, the legislature can not constitutionally limit the President's defensive power. In the event of an attack when Congress is not in session, the President has plenary power to challenge an enemy without waiting for Congress to convene, ratify his past actions, and authorize his future conduct. Even if Congress is in session, the President need not necessarily wait for congressional blessing before responding to the enemy's challenge. As long as the President's actions are defensive, his conduct falls within the zone of exclusive authority that the Constitution confers on his office.

Despite the Framers' attempt to distinguish between the congressional power to initiate military hostilities and the President's defensive power, they failed to define the scope and boundaries of the offensive and defensive powers conferred on the legislature and the executive. At what exact point-does a defensive military action become an offensive war? Should one measure the defensive/offensive nature of military operations according to the international actors' intentions (whether manifest or latent), the duration of hostilities, or the scope and intensity of the violence employed? Even if one employs the Framers' defensive/offensive-war theory to define the exclusive zones of congressional and presidential authority, some military actions fall into a gray area, a twilight zone, of concurrent power in which the exact distribution of authority is unclear.

In the twentieth century, this twilight zone has expanded rapidly as recent changes in the international system have vitiated the Framers' distinction between defensive and offensive warfare. Periods of global conflict such as the cold war and regional conflicts such as the Vietnam War resist the Framers' eighteenth-century classification. The increasing frequency of international terrorism, guerrilla and insurgency warfare, and wars of national liberation has virtually erased the boundary between defensive and offensive war. In addition to the empirical difficulty of distinguishing between defensive and offensive international behavior, the United Nations' signatories are not likely to admit that their military conduct is aggressive behavior that violates the Charter's provisions.

Since the Second World War the United States has responded to changes in the international system and the Soviet military-political-economic challenge by creating mutual-security agreements with at least forty-two other nations. These agreements create national commitments—political, economic, military, and diplomatic obligations—that integrate American security with the security requirements of its allies. Although such mutual-security agreements as the North Atlantic Treaty cannot alter their signatories' domestic constitutional processes for initiating or declaring war, the stationing of U.S. armed forces in Western Europe creates the continuing threat that an attack on an ally, in fact, will constitute an attack on the United States.[6] By stationing "hostage armies" abroad, Congress and the President have expanded presidential power into the twilight zone to include protecting the security and territorial integrity of the nation's allies. These security agreements transform the President's power to defend the nation against a sudden attack into a power to defend its allies' diverse security interests.

Both jurists and commentators have attempted to accommodate the constitutional separation of powers to twentieth-century military and diplomatic conditions by developing a theory of joint or mutual participation. In the twilight zone of concurrent power, the initiation of undeclared war and military hostilities requires joint legislative-executive participation. The form and extent of such participation varies according to the scope and duration of military action. At one end of the continuum are military, political, economic, and diplomatic measures that are largely, if not exclusively, defensive. Because such actions are of low magnitude, the President can act largely on his own without supporting legislation that either authorizes or ratifies his conduct. At the other end of the continuum are actions of a magnitude that requires either explicit prior authorization or subsequent ratification by Congress.[7]

While the Framers' defensive/offensive-war theory has virtually collapsed, the threshold theory presents serious problems for the future of constitutional government. If joint participation is no more than a euphemism for presidential initiative and congressional ratification, the theory justifies continuing the practice of presidential military *fait accompli* that began with the Civil War. If joint participation permits Congress to transfer its power to initiate military hostilities to the President, the theory also serves to justify the unconstitutional delegation of the war power, which is vested exclusively in Congress. As Senator Wayne Morse argued during the debate on the Gulf of Tonkin Resolution, Congress cannot delegate its war power *in futuro*.[8] Since the Constitution vests the war power exclusively in Congress, the legislature cannot ratify, post hoc, presidential decisions to initiate war or military hostilities. Congress cannot prospectively or retroactively authorize the President to choose the enemy, the time, and the place of military hostilities.[9]

If the Federal courts employ the theory of joint participation to avoid deciding war-powers controversies on their merits, they will allow Congress and the President to determine the scope and boundaries of their respective powers in an important twilight zone. By permitting Congress and the President to decide separation-of-powers questions to the exclusion of the courts, the judiciary has encouraged the legislature and the executive to fuse their separate powers of war and defense into a national war power whose only standard is the extraconstitutional one of success on the battlefield. As the theater of battle expands to absorb the domestic society, excessive judicial self-restraint will endanger the citizens' liberty as well as constitutional government.[10]

THE FEDERAL COURTS AND CONSTITUTIONAL GOVERNMENT

Conventional wisdom suggests that the Federal courts should refrain from deciding war-powers controversies because the Constitution commits such issues as initiating war and hostilities to the people's elected representatives. If the President exceeds his authority, only Congress can limit his usurpation of constitutional power. Until Congress acts to limit presidential warmaking, the separation of powers precludes judicial intervention in war-powers controversies. Even if Congress attempts to limit presidential warmaking, the courts should refrain from deciding such cases since they raise nonjusticiable political questions, i.e., questions that are beyond the judicial function and competence. Moreover, judges lack the information, training, standards, and remedies to resolve war-powers controversies. Finally, judicial intervention is likely to produce confrontations with Congress and the President that will impair the judiciary's ability to protect individual liberty and constitutional government.

In a constitutional system that commits decisions of war and peace to popularly elected public officials and their administrative agents, judicial interference with legislative and executive policymaking requires special justification. Judicial intervention in war-powers controversies raises important normative and empirical questions. When should the courts intervene in war-powers cases? When are the courts likely to entertain and decide such cases? What are the consequences of judicial intervention for the courts and the political system? The answers to these questions depend partially on the legitimacy of and occasion for judicial review.

The classical (Marshall-Hamilton-Warren-Wechsler) argument for judicial review suggests that the courts have a special obligation to limit the legislative and executive branches to the exercise of their respective constitutional powers. Only when the Constitution commits a decision to the exclusive discretion of either Congress or the President should the judiciary defer to legislative or executive judgment. At the very least, the judiciary has an obligation to determine whether such a demonstrable commitment exists and to determine the scope of the power that the Constitution commits to Congress or the President. In contrast to the classical view, the prudential (Thayer-Holmes-Brandeis-Frankfurter-Bickel) argument is that pragmatism as well as the principle of popular sovereignty recommends judicial self-restraint. Since the courts cannot develop principled solutions to war-powers controversies, they should abstain rather than interfere with democratic institutions or legitimate popular decisions that vitiate individual liberty and constitutional government. Lying somewhere between the classical and prudential views, the functional (Scharpf) argument is that the courts should protect the individual's liberty and the citizen's right to constitutional government without impairing the legislature or the executive from protecting the national security. Before deciding war-powers cases on their merits, the courts have an obligation to determine the effects of their decisions on foreign and military policy.

Since 1798, the Federal courts have decided relatively few cases involving competing claims of power to initiate military hostilities. Despite the paucity of precedent, existing judicial opinion warrants several conclusions. Between 1798 and 1814 the Supreme Court sustained congressional power to initiate undeclared war as well as *de jure* war and to control the magnitude and duration of subsequent military hostilities. These early opinions reflect a broad construction of the congressional war powers and the presidential power to defend the nation against sudden attack. At the same time, the Supreme Court asserted its jurisdiction and judicial power to construe the scope and boundaries of legislative and executive power. Prior to *Foster* v. *Neilson* (1829) the Court did not employ the political-question doctrine or other techniques of judicial self-restraint to avoid deciding issues of external sovereignty.

While the Federal courts accepted the Framers' distinction between defensive and offensive conduct, as early as 1806 Justice Paterson argued that the President has discretionary power to determine the force necessary to resist and defeat an invading enemy.[11] Until the Civil War the Federal courts ostensibly adhered to the theory that as long as the President's actions were defensive, he had plenary power to determine the measures necessary to protect the lives and property of U.S. citizens. With the Civil War, the courts expanded the scope of the President's defensive powers to include all measures that domestic and international law permit. Once an enemy attacks, the President can employ whatever defensive or offensive measures, in his exclusive judgment, are necessary to defeat the opponent. When Congress is not in session, the Civil War cases leave no doubt that the President is the sole judge of military necessity.

Although the Civil War cases do not legitimate executive prerogative to initiate war and hostilities, they virtually erase the Framers' distinction between defensive and offensive military conduct. In addition to justifying the President's exercise of emergency powers, the Civil War cases legitimate the fusion of legislative and executive power. Between 1861 and 1877 the Supreme Court sustained congressional ratification of the President's emergency actions and the transfer of the auxiliary war powers to the President. By legitimating the pattern of presidential military *fait accompli* and congressional ratification as "joint participation," the Court abdicated its responsibility to construe and enforce the separation of powers. During the Civil War, the President became the virtually undisputed arbiter of his own power.

In the American constitutional system the concept of an indivisible national war power permits the President to suspend the separation of powers as long as Congress concurs in his decisions. If Congress loses confidence in the President's military policies, it must mobilize a two-thirds majority to override the commander in chief's actions. Unlike the British constitutional system, Congress cannot curb the executive's conduct by bringing the government down with a simple-majority vote of "no confidence." If Congress fails to override a presidential veto, the only remedy available is the rather cumbersome and traumatic process of impeachment and removal. In contrast to the British Constitution, the American system does not limit executive prerogative through parliamentary accountability.

Although the Civil War precedents are remote from the legal, military, political, and diplomatic battlefields of Vietnam, the extraconstitutional concept of a national war power or presidential prerogative anchored in legislative ratification bridges the century between the Civil War and the Vietnam War. In the intervening century, advocates of presidential power transformed the constitutional power to respond to a sudden attack into an extraconstitutional prerogative to initiate military hostilities. According to the argument for prerogative, as commander in chief the President has the authority to dispatch American armed forces around the globe and commit them to combat. While President Truman claimed such authority during the Korean War,[12] the Vietnam War provided the first occasion in the twentieth century to test the theory of presidential prerogative to wage undeclared war.

During the Vietnam War various litigants challenged presidential authority to wage a prolonged war without a congressional declaration of war. In contrast to the Civil War cases, most Federal courts refused to determine the President's authority to conduct an undeclared war. Citing such obstacles as jurisdiction, sovereign immunity, standing to sue, and the political-question doctrine, most Federal courts declined to dispose of the Vietnam cases on their substantive merits. Almost without exception, the Supreme Court refused to grant certiorari and resolve conflicts among the Federal courts. The Court's silence denies an authoritative decision on the scope and boundaries of legislative and executive power in an important twilight zone of constitutional authority. The Court's silence also casts doubt on the judiciary's effectiveness as an arbiter of the separation of powers.

Despite the Supreme Court's reluctance to decide war-powers controversies, the federal judiciary can play a positive, if limited, role as an arbiter between Congress and the President. Although the Federal courts cannot decide the wisdom, propriety, or desirability of waging war or military hostilities, they can determine whether the President's military actions are within the scope of defensive authority that the Constitution vests in his office. If the judiciary decides that the President's conduct passes constitutional muster, there is little danger of a direct confrontation with the executive. Even if the courts decide that presidential action falls within the twilight zone of concurrent power, they can determine whether Congress has authorized military hostilities. Should the judiciary conclude that congressional authorization exists, the probability of confrontation with either Congress or the President is remote.

Only when the judiciary decides that (1) congressional authorization does not exist, (2) such authorization is not constitutionally sufficient, or (3) presidential conduct conflicts with either the express or implied will of Congress is there real danger of serious confrontation with the executive or the legislature. Should the courts decide that Congress has not authorized hostilities, the legislature can provide the authorization necessary to continue military hostilities or, conversely, under the War Powers Act of 1973, require that the commander in chief disengage U.S. armed forces from combat.[13] Moreover, the courts can fashion such relief as a declaratory judgment without jeopardizing military actions in progress or endangering the lives of combat personnel. The courts can delay the timing or release of such orders to minimize their impact on sensitive diplomatic negotiations. Insofar as such judicial opinions and orders support congressional authority, the courts run the danger of conflict only with the President rather than the combined animus of the legislative and executive branches.

Both prudence and principle recommend that the Federal courts exercise caution before concluding that congressional authorization is not constitutionally sufficient to sustain the President's military conduct. When the courts find that legislative authorization is insufficient, the danger exists that both Congress and the President will rebuke the judiciary. Before the courts conclude that legislative authorization is inadequate, they should develop judicial standards to determine the degree of specificity that the Constitution requires. Absent a declaration of war, can Congress satisfy the requirements of Article 1, Section 8 (Cl. 11) by explicitly authorizing, approving, or ratifying hostilities through defense-appropriations and authorization bills or other legislation? Without explicit legislative authorization, can the courts reasonably infer authority from the standing law? Since the Federal courts failed to articulate judicial standards for determining the constitutional sufficiency of authorizing legislation during the Vietnam War, they confined their opinions to determining the mere existence of such authorization.

A substantially different problem occurs if the courts find that the President's military conduct conflicts with the express or implied will of Congress. The courts must then decide whether congressional legislation interferes with the independent authority that the Constitution confers on the President or can be inferred from the executive article's affirmative grants of power. Either way the courts decide, they risk serious confrontation with the other branches of the national government. During the Vietnam War, District Judge Joseph Tauro attempted to avoid both Scylla and Charybdis by denying that Congress and the President were locked in resolute conflict, i.e., irreconcilable conflict that required judicial arbitration. Since Judge Tauro concluded that Congress and the President had acted jointly to wage undeclared war, there was little justification for determining the scope or boundaries of legislative and executive power.[14]

While the courts have the jurisdiction to determine the scope of power that the Constitution assigns to Congress and the President, they lack the authority to decide the wisdom of declaring war or waging an undeclared war. Since the Constitution confers such policy choices exclusively on Congress, the judiciary cannot decide whether to wage a *de jure* or an undeclared war without exceeding its jurisdiction and judicial function. The American constitutional system reserves the foregoing policy choices to the people's representatives rather than " a bevy of Platonic Guardians." Therefore, respect for the democratic principle of popular sovereignty and the constitutional principle of the separation of powers requires that the judiciary abstain from making legislative policy judgments.

Prudence as well as principle recommends self-restraint. Judges do not possess the military information necessary to determine whether the nation should wage partial or general war. The judiciary also lacks the training, experience, and standards necessary to evaluate the military, political, economic, or other consequences of waging a general or a limited war. Moreover, judges do not control the military or other instruments necessary to influence the international system. The judiciary is powerless to influence the international consequences of its decisions. These pragmatic factors suggest that courts should not decide military policy.

JUDICIAL INTERVENTION: THE OCCASIONS FOR AND CONSEQUENCES

Since the early nineteenth century, the Federal courts have been reluctant to challenge presidential warmaking. Usually, the courts have refused to entertain such challenges because the litigants presented claims that are beyond judicial competence, i.e., claims that present nonjusticiable political questions. Unless the President clearly abuses his power and/or acts in conflict with Congress, the courts are unlikely to decide war-powers cases even when the private litigant alleges a personal deprivation of a constitutional right. Not even a public official, such as a member of Congress, or a state that alleges that the President's conduct interferes with an official duty or power is likely to find a receptive judicial ear. One can only wonder how the courts would respond if Congress were to authorize its presiding officers to challenge an act of presidential warmaking in derogation of the War Powers Act of 1973. Would the courts decide the case on its substantive merits or find some procedural rationale for abdicating their responsibility to decide competing claims of power?

If the courts intervene to restrain the executive or legislature, they are likely to do so only after the emergency has abated or passed. With the exception of Chief Justice Roger Taney's opinion in *Ex parte Merryman* (1861), the Federal courts sustained President Lincoln's exercise of extraconstitutional power.[15] Indeed, in *Ex parte Vallandigham* (1864) the Court avoided a confrontation with the President by denying its jurisdiction to review or reverse the findings of a military commission.[16] Only after the Civil War had ended, in *Ex parte Milligan* (1866), did the Supreme Court challenge the President's authority to suspend the privilege to the writ of habeas corpus and to substitute a military commission for a civilian court outside the actual theater of military operations.[17]

In the twentieth century the Federal courts have continued to defer to Congress and the President until the emergency has abated or passed. Early in the Second World War the Federal courts sustained the states' restrictions of religious freedom in the Jehovah's Witnesses flag-salute case. Following the Battle of Midway (June 1942), which removed the threat of a Japanese invasion, the Supreme Court became less charitable toward emergency measures that restricted the individual's religious liberty.[18] However, throughout most of the Second World War the Supreme Court sustained the exercise of national power in the Japanese curfew and detention cases. Only at the war's end did the Court strike a new balance between national security and individual liberty that was favorable to Japanese Americans.[19]

With one notable exception, *Youngstown Sheet and Tube Co.* v. *Sawyer* (1952), the courts have sustained presidential warmaking and congressional ratification of the President's military actions since the Second World War. In *Youngstown*, a divided Court overturned President Harry Truman's seizure of the nation's steel mills. Inasmuch as Congress had opposed such seizures to settle labor disputes, there was no danger of confrontation with both the legislative and executive branches. Moreover, the President's action invaded an area of congressional policymaking far removed from the battlefield. Although the Supreme Court decided *Youngstown* during the Korean War, there was no immediate threat to U.S. armed forces engaged in combat, since Congress had provided other means to settle the impasse between the steel companies and their striking employees.

In the early phases of the Vietnam War the Federal courts refused to decide claims that the President had exceeded his defensive power by waging war without congressional authorization. As the war escalated, the courts inferred the requisite authorization from congressional legislation but refused to dispose of the cases on their merits. After 1969, however, several Federal courts took judicial notice of growing legislative-executive conflict but continued to sustain U.S. military actions in Southeast Asia. Only in the waning days of the war did a Federal court deny that Congress had authorized President Nixon's military conduct.

Although one can question judicial deference to constitutionally doubtful legislative policy and the executive action once an emergency has attenuated, there are some persuasive rationales for judicial self-restraint in the early stages of war and military hostilities. Neither the judiciary nor the government possesses the information necessary to evaluate the severity of an emergency in its earliest phases. During a wartime emergency there is a need to withhold information in order to protect the security of combat troops and assure the success of ongoing military operations. In the heat of battle secrecy is also necessary to avoid sending the nation's allies and enemies the wrong cues. As long as the battle rages, some justification exists for judicial deference to congressional policy and executive judgment. Once the emergency has attenuated, however, the rationales for judicial deference become less persuasive.

As Justice Robert H. Jackson argued in *Korematsu* v. *United States* (1944), when the courts cannot reconcile military necessity with constitutional principle, judicial self-restraint is preferable to sanctioning the government's constitutionally questionable behavior.[20] By exercising the passive virtues, noted Alexander Bickel, the courts decline either to check or to legitimate congressional policy or presidential action.[21] Although the government's behavior might threaten constitutionalism and individual liberty during an emergency, the judicial imprimatur would validate military necessity long after the emergency had ended. Unable to render a principled judgment, the courts should simply defer to the principle of popular sovereignty.

During the Vietnam War some Federal courts ignored the prudential maxim of self-restraint in order to sustain the President's military conduct. By arguing that, under certain circumstances, Congress and the President share the powers to initiate and continue military hostilities, these Federal courts legitimated the fusion of legislative and executive authority and eroded the separation of powers. Such decisions as *Da Costa v. Laird* (1973) sanction the continuing practice of executive *fait accompli* and congressional ratification of presidential warmaking. Before invoking the Federal judiciary's assistance, opponents of presidential warmaking should recall that the judiciary is likely either to tolerate or to support the exercise of executive power. In the future, opponents of presidential warmaking should focus their opposition on Congress rather than the Federal courts.

A long history of undeclared war and military hostilities should also demonstrate that the constitutional questions raised during the Vietnam War are inherent in the American constitutional system. In an era of insurgency, revolution, guerrilla warfare, and wars of national liberation the conflict inherent in the separation of the congressional war powers from the office of commander in chief underscores the political necessity for consensus between Congress and the President in initiating undeclared war. Fidel Castro's revolutionary ambitions, Colonel Muammar el-Qaddafi's terrorism, the Ayatollah Ruhollah Khomeini's religious fanaticism and nationalism, and Yasir Arafat's aspiration to establish a Palestinian state will confront President Reagan and his successors with dangerous decisions, with demands and opportunities to intervene militarily in order to protect U.S. national security and the security interests of the nation's allies. Before yielding to the temptation of intervening militarily, future presidents should recall one of the Vietnam War's most important lessons—the nation should not wage a long, protracted, undeclared war without fundamental prior agreement between Congress and the President and broad, sustained public support for the government's decision to send the nation's sons and daughters off to war.

Notes

INTRODUCTION (PAGES 1 TO 8)

1. For a comprehensive list of presidential exercises of power as commander in chief, see Dorothy Schaffter and Dorothy Matthews, *The Powers of the President as Commander in Chief of the Army and Navy of the United States*, U.S. Congress, House of Representatives, Doc. No. 443, 84th Congress, 2nd Session, 6–7 and 9–10 (1953): hereinafter cited as Schaffter, *Powers of the President*; see also *U.S. Congress, House of Representatives, Committee on Foreign Affairs*, Background Information on the Use of United States Armed Forces in Foreign Countries, 1970 Revision, 91st Congress, 2nd Session, 1970 (Washington, D.C.: Government Print. Off., 1970), 44, 45, 46, and 59: hereinafter cited as *House of Representatives, Comm. on For. Aff.*, U.S. Armed Forces in Foreign Countries, 1970 Rev; *U.S. Congress, House of Representatives, Committee on International Relations*, Background Information on The Use of U.S. Armed Forces in Foreign Countries, 1975 Revision, 94th Congress, 1st Session, 1975 (Washington, D.C.: Government Print. Off., 1975): hereinafter cited as *House of Representatives, Comm. on Int'l. Rel.*, U.S. Armed Forces in Foreign Countries, 1975 Rev; *New York Times*, 26 April 1980, 1.

2. *U.S. Congress, Senate*, Report Number 797, 90th Congress. 1st Session, 1967, 17 (1967).

3. Leonard C. Meeker, Legal Advisor, U.S. Department of State, "The Legality of United States Participation in the Defense of Viet-Nam," *The Department of State Bulletin* 54 (March 28, 1966): 474–489, 484: hereinafter cited as Meeker, 54 *Dep't of State Bulletin*. Mr. Meeker also argued that the President's duties include:

> the power to deploy American forces abroad and commit them to military operations when the President deems such action necessary to maintain the security and defense of the United States.

4. See, for example, William H. Rehnquist, Assistant Attorney General, Office of Legal Counsel, U.S. Department of Justice, "The President's Constitutional Authority to Order the Attack on the Cambodian Sanctuaries," May 28, 1970, in *U.S. Congress, House of Representatives, Committee on Foreign Affairs, Congress, The President, and The War Powers*, Hearings Before the Subcommittee on National Security Policy and Scientific Developments, June, July, and August 1970, 91st Congress, 2nd Session, 1970 (Washington, D.C.: Government Print. Off., 1970), 539–549: hereinafter cited as *House of Representatives, Comm. on For. Aff.*, Congress, The President, and The War Powers.

5. See Richard H. Cox, *Locke on War and Peace* (London: Oxford, 1960), 128: hereinafter cited as Cox, *On War*; John Locke, *Treatise of Civil Government*, ed. Charles L. Sherman (New York: Appleton-Century-Crofts, 1965), secs. 166 and 210, 112 and 140–141: hereinafter cited as Locke, *Treatise*; Sir William Blackstone, *Commentaries on the Laws of England*, ed. George Sharswood (Philadelphia: J.B. Lippincott Co., 1859), Vol. 1, 253–258: hereinafter cited as Blackstone, *Commentaries*; Max Farrand, ed., *The Records of the Federal Convention* (New Haven, Conn.: Vols. 1–3, 1911; Vol. 4, 1937), Vol. 2, 143, 145, 182, 313–314, and 318: hereinafter cited as Farrand, *Federal Convention*.

6. Farrand, *Federal Convention*, Vol. 1, 64–66 and 292, Vol. 2, 157, 185, 341, 343, and 540–541; Jonathan Elliot, ed., *Debates in the Several State Conventions on the Adoption of the Federal Constitution, etc.*, 2nd ed., 5 Vols. (Philadelphia: J.B. Lippincott Co., 1836), Vol. 3, 58–60 and 160–161: hereinafter cited as Elliot, *Debates in the State Conventions*; Frances D. Wormuth, "The Nixon Theory of the War Powers: A Critique," *California Law Review* 60 (May 1972): 623–703, 631 and 643–645: hereinafter cited as Wormuth, 60 *California L. Rev.*; Ernest R. May, ed., *The Ultimate Decision: The President as Commander-in-Chief* (New York: George Braziller, 1960), 14–15: hereinafter cited as May, *Ultimate Decision*.

7. Farrand, *Federal Convention*, Vol. 2, 318–319.

8. See W. Taylor Reveley, III, "Presidential War-Making: Constitutional Prerogative or Usurpation," *Virginia Law Review* 55 (November 1969): 1243–1305: hereinafter cited as Reveley, 55 *Va. L. Rev.*

9. On the difficulty of applying eighteenth-century conceptions of warfare to twentieth-century military conflicts, see Donald E. King and Arthur B. Leavens, "Curbing the Dog of War," *Harvard International Law Journal* 18 (Winter 1977): 59–96: hereinafter cited as King, 18 *Harvard Int'l. L. J.*

10. Reveley, 55 *Va. L. Rev.*, 76–95.

11. See Robert A. Dahl, *Congress and Foreign Policy* (New York: W.W. Norton & Co., 1950), 105–106: hereinafter cited as Dahl, *Congress and Foreign Policy*.

12. *Ibid.*, 205–220.

13. See Justice Robert H. Jackson's concurring opinion in *Youngstown Sheet & Tube Co. v. Sawyer*, 343 U.S. 579, 637 (1952).

14. 63 Stat. 2241 (1949); T.I.A.S. No. 1964.

15. 97 *Cong. Rec.* A1714–A1715 (1951).

16. See, for example, District Judge Charles Wyzanski's opinion in *Mitchell v. Laird*, 488 F. 2d 611 (D.C. Cir. 1973).

17. See, for example, District Judge Joseph Tauro's opinion in *Drinan v. Nixon*,

364 F. Supp. 854 (D. Mass. 1973). Although Judge Tauro refused to decide *Drinan* on the merits, in the event that resolute conflict developed, he left the door to judicial intervention open, at 858.

18. See Alexander M. Bickel, *The Least Dangerous Branch* (Indianapolis, Ind.: Bobbs-Merrill Co., 1962): hereinafter cited as Bickel, *Least Dangerous Branch.*

19. See *United States* v. *Sisson*, 294 F. Supp. 511 (D. Mass. 1968) (*Sisson* 1); *Davi* v. *Laird*, 318 F. Supp. 478 (W.D. Va. 1970); *Meyers* v. *Nixon*, 339 F. Supp. 1388 (S.D. N.Y. 1972); *Atlee* v. *Laird*, 347 F. Supp. 689 (E.D. Pa. 1972).

20. See Bickel, *Least Dangerous Branch*, 184; Also see Justice Felix Frankfurter's opinion in *Colegrove* v. *Green*, 328 U.S. 549, 552–556 (1946).

21. See Chief District Judge Joseph Lord's dissenting opinion in *Atlee* v. *Laird*, 347 F. Supp. 689 (E.D. Pa. 1972).

22. See District Judge William Sweigert's opinion in *Mottola* v. *Nixon*, 318 F. Supp. 538, 550–552 (N.D. Calif. 1970), and District Judge Orrin Judd's opinion in *Holtzman* v. *Richardson*, 361 F. Supp. 544, 550–552 (E.D. N.Y. 1973).

23. See Fritz W. Scharpf, "Judicial Review and the Political Question: A Functional Analysis," *Yale Law Journal* 75 (March 1966): 517–597: hereinafter cited as Scharpf, 75 *Yale L. J.*; Robert F. Nagel, "Separation of Powers and the Scope of Federal Equitable Remedies," *Stanford Law Review* 30 (April 1978): 661–724: hereinafter cited as Nagel, 30 *Stanford L. Rev.*

24. *Mottola* v. *Nixon*, 318 F. Supp. 538 (N.D. Calif. 1970); *Holtzman* v. *Schlesinger*, 361 F. Supp. 553 (E.D. N.Y. 1973).

25. *Mottola* v. *Nixon*, 464 F. 2d 178 (9th Cir. 1972); *Holtzman* v. *Schlesinger*, 484 F. 2d 1307 (2nd Cir. 1973).

26. In a memorandum opinion, the Supreme Court affirmed *Atlee* v. *Laird*, 347 F. Supp. 689 (E.D. Pa. 1972), *aff'd sub nom. Atlee* v. *Richardson*, 411 U.S. 911 (1973).

CHAPTER 1 (PAGES 9 TO 30)

1. Locke, *Treatise*, sec. 131, 85; Cox, *On War*, 110–111, 117.

2. Cox, *On War*, 124.

3. Locke, *Treatise*, sec. 146, 98; Cox, *On War*, 124, 125.

4. Cox, *On War*, 126–127, 129.

5. Locke, *Treatise*, sec. 145, 98; Cox, *On War*, 124–125.

6. Locke, *Treatise*, secs. 147, 156, and 157, 98–99, 104–105, 105–106. Locke argues that the federative power " . . . must necessarily be left to the prudence and wisdom of those whose hands it is in to be managed for the public good." Locke, *Treatise*, sec. 147, 99; Cox, *On War*, 126–127.

7. Cox, *On War*, 126–127.

8. *Ibid.*, 128; Locke, *Treatise*, secs. 166 and 210, 112, 140–141.

9. Locke, *Treatise*, sec. 166, 112.

10. On April 19, 1861 Lincoln ordered a naval blockade of southern ports. On May 3, the President increased the regular Army by 22,714 and the Navy by 18,000 men, and called for an additional 42,034 volunteers for three years. See:

Wilfred E. Binkley, *President and Congress*, 3rd rev. ed. (New York: Vintage Books, 1962), 136, 138: hereinafter cited as Binkley, *President and Congress*; Wilfred E. Binkley, *Powers of The President: Problems of American Democracy* (Garden City, N.Y.: Doubleday, Doran and Co., 1937), 115–116: hereinafter cited as Binkley, *Powers*; Emory Upton, *The Military Policy of the United States* (Washington, D.C.: Government Print. Off., 1904), 229: hereinafter cited as Upton, *Military Policy*.

In a book reminiscent of Locke's view on emergency power, William Whiting, Solicitor of the War Department, wrote, "The sovereign and almost dictatorial military powers existing only in actual war . . . are, while they last, as constitutional, as sacred, as the administration of justice by judicial courts in time of peace." Quoted in George F. Milton, *The Use of Presidential Power 1789–1943* (Boston: Little, Brown & Co., 1944), 111: hereinafter cited as Milton, *Presidential Power*.

11. Cox, *On War*, 128.

12. Locke, *Treatise*, sec. 168, 113.

13. *Ibid.*, 113–114; Cox, *On War*, 129.

14. Arthur T. Vanderbilt, *The Doctrine of The Separation of Powers* (Lincoln, Neb.: Univ. of Neb. Press, 1953), 37: hereinafter cited as Vanderbilt, *Separation of Powers*.

15. Francis Wormuth, *The Origins of Modern Constitutionalism* (New York: Harper & Brothers, Publishers, 1949), 19–23: hereinafter cited as Wormuth, *Origins*. M.J.C. Vile, *Constitutionalism and The Separation of Powers* (Oxford, England: Clarenden Press, Oxford Univ. Press, 1967), 22–23, 25: hereinafter cited as Vile, *Constitutionalism*.

16. Gordon S. Wood, *The Creation of The American Republic, 1776–1787* (Chapel Hill, N.C.: Univ. of North Carolina Press, 1969), 199–200, 201; hereinafter cited as Wood, *Creation*; Vile, *Constitutionalism*, 37, 38.

17. Vile, *Constitutionalism*, 3, 38; Max Raden, "The Doctrine of The Separation of Powers in Seventeenth-Century Controversies," *University of Pennsylvania Law Review*, 86 (June 1938): 842–866, 848–849, 850, 851: hereinafter cited as Raden, 86 *Pennsylvania L. Rev.*

18. Wormuth, *Origins*, 165.

19. Vile, *Constitutionalism*, 3.

20. Wormuth, *Origins*, 63, 69–70, 136–137, 163–164, 165; William B. Gwyn, *The Meaning of The Separation of Powers* (New Orleans: Tulane Univ. Press, 1965), 37, 38, 40, 41–42: hereinafter cited as Gwyn, *Meaning of Separation*.

21. Wormuth, *Origins*, 149, 151–152.

22. *Ibid.*, 191.

23. Gwyn, *Meaning of Separation*, 71, 72, 73, 74; Wormuth, *Origins*, 191, 193; Vile, *Constitutionalism*, 57, 58, 59. See also: Locke, *Treatise*, Ch. 11, secs. 134–142, 88–96.

24. Wormuth, *Origins*, 179. In 1698, Anthony Hammond "protested against a House of Commons 'abounding with officers' because this would obstruct the House in its important duty of 'calling ill ministers to account'." Quoted in Wormuth, *Origins*, 179.

25. Locke, *Treatise*, secs. 131 and 136, 85, 90–91.

26. Wormuth, *Origins*, 193.

27. The Act of Settlement of 1701 promoted judicial independence by providing for permanent judicial tenure contingent on good behavior. The act provided that, "Judges Commissions be made *Quam diu se bene Gesserint* and their Salaries ascertained and established but upon the Address of both Houses of Parliament it may be lawful to remove them." 12 and 13 Will. and Mar., c. 2 (1701). These provisions were reaffirmed at 1 Geo. III, c. 23 (1760) and 1 Edw. VII, c. 5 (1901). See also: Wormuth, *Origins*, 194–195.

28. Gwyn, *Meaning of Separation*, 98; Vile, *Constitutionalism*, 68–69.

29. Wormuth, *Origins*, 75–76; Gwyn, *Meaning of Separation*, 85–86, 88, 92, 138–141 [John Trenchard's *"Incomparable Preface" to His Short History of England* (1698)]; Henry St. John, Viscount Bolingbroke, *Works*, ed. David Mallet (1754; Hildesheim, Germany: George Olms Verlagsbuchhandlung, 1968), Vol. 1, 296 ("Remarks on The History of England").

30. Gwyn, *Meaning of Separation*, 85–86, 138–141.

31. Vile, *Constitutionalism*, 68–69, 71, 74.

32. Gwyn, *Meaning of Separation*, 98.

33. Sir William Blackstone, *Commentaries on the Laws of England*, ed. George Sharswood (Philadelphia: J.B. Lippincott Co., 1859), Vol. 1, 267–268: hereinafter cited as Blackstone, *Commentaries*. Although Blackstone recognizes that judicial power is delegated by the Crown, he cites the statute of 13 Will. III, c. 2, which grants the judiciary life tenure, and the statute of 1 Geo. III, c. 23, which confirmed the earlier statute. Blackstone argues that the two statutes were essential in promoting judicial independence and "the impartial administration of justice." Blackstone, *Commentaries*, 267–268.

34. Charles de Secondat, Baron de Montesquieu, *Spirit of The Laws*, ed. Robert M. Hutchins, *Great Books of The Western World*, Vol. 38 (Chicago: Encyclopedia Britannica, Inc., 1952), Book XI, Ch. 6, 74: hereinafter cited as Montesquieu, *Spirit of The Laws*. See also: Vile, *Constitutionalism*, 85–86.

35. Gwyn, *Meaning of Separation*, 111.

36. Montesquieu, *Spirit of The Laws*, Book XI, Chs. 1–3, 68–69; Vile, *Constitutionalism*, 81–82; Gwyn, *Meaning of Separation*, 101–102.

37. Montesquieu, *Spirit of The Laws*, Book XI, Ch. 6, 74. Although Montesquieu favored judicial independence, he did not rely on the judiciary to resolve conflict between the legislature and the executive. At a time when the scope of governmental power was more limited than it is today, Montesquieu believed that the judiciary's primary role would be to regulate essentially private conduct and rights rather than public conflict. See also: Gwyn, *Meaning of Separation*, 107; Vile, *Constitutionalism*, 88–89.

38. Gwyn, *Meaning of Separation*, 113. Montesquieu's model of the constitution of liberty represents a highly idealized version of British constitutional development after the Glorious Revolution. By 1730 the British system was moving toward parliamentary responsibility of the ministries. See, for example, Sir Robert Walpole's speech to the House of Commons, February 1, 1739, and Lord North's remarks to the House of Lords, December 14, 1778, reprinted in part in W.C. Costin and J. Steven Watson, eds., *The Law and Workings of The Constitution, 1660–*

1914 (London: Adam and Charles Black, 1952), Vol. 1, 217–218, 238: hereinafter cited as Costin, *Law and Workings.*

39. Montesquieu, *Spirit of The Laws,* Book XI, Ch. 4, 69.

40. Vile, *Constitutionalism,* 128.

41. *Ibid.,* 128, 132, 133.

42. From a letter to Richard Henry Lee (November 15, 1775), quoted in Vile, *Constitutionalism,* 133.

43. Wood, *Creation,* 222–229; Malcolm Sharp, "The Classical View of The Separation of Powers," *University of Chicago Law Review,* 2 (April 1935): 385–436, 395–396: hereinafter cited as Sharp, 2 *Chicago L. Rev.*

44. Vile, *Constitutionalism,* 132–133; Edward S. Corwin, "The Progress of Constitutional Theory between the Declaration of Independence and the Meeting of the Philadelphia Convention," *American Historical Review,* 30 (April 1925): 511–536, 513–514: hereinafter cited as Corwin, 30 *Amer. Hist. Rev.* The Pennsylvania Constitution of September 28, 1776, for example, provided for a unicameral assembly and a supreme executive council and president rather than a governor. See: Frances N. Thorpe, ed., *The Federal and State Constitutions* (Washington, D.C.: Government Print. Off., 1909), Vol. 5, 3081–3092: hereinafter cited as Thorpe, *Federal and State Constitutions.*

45. See: Vile, *Constitutionalism,* 133–152, for an excellent discussion of the acceptance of balanced government and the separation of powers in the states between 1776 and 1787.

46. See: *The Articles of Confederation,* Article 6 and Article 9, in Sol. Bloom, Director General, United States Sesquicentennial Commission, *History of the Formation of the Union under the Constitution* (Washington, D.C.: Government Print. Off., 1941), 534–535, 536–538: hereinafter cited as Bloom, *Formation of The Union.*

47. Corwin, 30 *Amer. Hist. Rev.,* 514. In settling judicially cognizable cases or controversies, some legislative acts specifically set aside "any usage, custom, or law to the contrary not withstanding." Corwin, 30 *Amer. Hist. Rev.,* 514.

48. *Ibid.,* 515.

49. *Ibid.;* Wood, *Creation,* 150–151, 154–155; Sharp, 2 *Chicago L. Rev.,* 417.

50. Sharp, 2 *Chicago L. Rev.,* 395–396, 397, 399, 402, from Thomas Jefferson's *Notes on Virginia* (1782), a letter from Thomas Jefferson to Edward Carrington (Paris: August 4, 1787), and a letter from Thomas Jefferson to John Adams (Paris: September 28, 1787); Charles Warren, *The Making of The Constitution* (Boston: Little, Brown & Co., 1937), 46: hereinafter cited as Warren, *Making.* From a letter from John Jay to Thomas Jefferson (August 18, 1786), and a letter from James Madison to Thomas Jefferson (March 19, 1786).

51. Wood, *Creation,* 228–229, 230–231.

52. Sharp, 2 *Chicago L. Rev.,* 419.

53. *Ibid.;* Max Farrand, ed., *The Records of The Federal Convention* (New Haven, Conn.: Yale Univ. Press, Vols. 1–3, 1911; Vol. 4, 1937), Vol. 1, 20–21, 30, 33, 35 (the Virginia Plan), 108 (John Dickinson), 291–292 (the Hamilton Plan), and Vol. 3, 612 (the New Jersey Plan): hereinafter cited as Farrand, *Federal Convention.*

54. Sharp, 2 *Chicago L. Rev.*, 407, 411–412.

55. *U.S. Constitution*, Art. 1, Sec. 8, Cl. 16 and Art. 1, Sec. 10, Cl. 3. Although debate on the militia clause was sharply divided between advocates of state and national power, both sides apparently assumed that the states would in fact be the first to respond to sudden attacks on the United States. See: Farrand, *Federal Convention*, Vol. 1, 332 (Sherman), Vol. 2, 330–331 (Elseworth), 386–387 (Madison), Vol. 3, 118–119 (Charles Pinckney, "Observations on the Plan of Government Submitted to the Federal Convention"), 207–209 (Luther Martin, "General Information," before the Maryland Legislature, November 29, 1787), 259 (Luther Martin, "Defense of Gerry," *Maryland Journal*, January 18, 1788), 318–319 (Madison, Debate in The Virginia Convention, June 14, 1788), and 420–421 (Gouverneur Morris to Moss Kent, January 12, 1815).

56. *U.S. Constitution*, Art. 1, Sec. 10; Farrand, *Federal Convention*, Vol. 3, 548 (James Madison, "Preface to The Debates in The Convention of 1787," from Gilpin, *Documentary History of The Constitution*, Vol. 3, 1840). Madison observes:

> In certain cases the authy. of the Confederacy was disregarded, as in violations not only of the Treaty of peace; but of Treaties with France & Holland, which were complained of to Congs.
> In other cases the Fedl authy was violated by Treaties & wars with Indians, as by Geo:by troops, raised & kept up. witht. the consent of Congs. as by Massts by compacts witht. the consent of Congs. as between Pena. and N. Jersey, and between Virga. & Maryd. From the Legisl: Journals of Virga. it appears, that a vote to apply for a sanction of Congs. was followed by a vote agst. a communication of the Compact to Congs.

57. As Oliver Elseworth of Connecticut said to the convention on August 17, 1787, "[T]here is a material difference between the cases of making *war*, and making *peace*. It should be more easy to get out of war, than into it." Farrand, *Federal Convention*, Vol. 2, 319.

58. *U.S. Constitution*, Art. 1, Sec. 8, Cls. 1, 11, 12, 13, 14, 15, and 16.

59. See: William Van Alstyne, "Congress, the President, and the Power to Declare War: A Requiem for Vietnam," *University of Pennsylvania Law Review*, 121 (November 1972): 1–28, 7, 9: hereinafter cited as Van Alstyne, 121 *Pennsylvania L. Rev.*; Raoul Berger, "War-Making by the President," *University of Pennsylvania Law Review*, 121 (November 1972): 29–86, 39–41, 78–79, 82: hereinafter cited as Berger, 121 *Pennsylvania L. Rev.*; Arthur Bestor, "Separation of Powers in the Domain of Foreign Affairs: The Intent of the Constitution Historically Examined," *Seton Hall Law Review*, 5 (Spring 1974): 527–665, 594–596: hereinafter cited as Bestor, 5 *Seton Hall L. Rev.*; Charles A. Lofgren, "War-Making under the Constitution," *Yale Law Journal*, 81 (March 1972): 672–707, 679–680, 685, 695, 697: hereinafter cited as Lofgren, 81 *Yale L. J.*

60. Alexander Hamilton, John Jay, and James Madison, *The Federalist*, ed. Edward Mead Earle (New York: Modern Library, n.d.), 322–323 (No. 48, Madison): hereinafter cited as Hamilton, *Federalist*.

61. *Ibid.*, 455 (No. 70, Hamilton).

62. *Ibid.*, 468–469 (No. 72, Hamilton); Farrand, *Federal Convention*, Vol. 3, 111; *U.S. Constitution*, Art. 2, Secs. 2 and 3.

63. Bestor, 5 *Seton Hall L. Rev.*, 532.

64. Hamilton, *Federalist*, 505 (No. 78, Hamilton).

65. *Ibid.*, 504 (No. 78, Hamilton).

66. Although much evidence, including colonial practice, exercise of constitutional review by the states' judiciary, some of the Framers' views, and the language of the Constitution's supremacy clause (Art. 6, Cl. 2), supports the Federal judiciary's exercising such power vis-à-vis Congress and the President, the historic basis and the Convention's intentions remain problematic. "The people who say the Framers intended [judicial review] are talking nonsense," Edward Corwin once remarked, adding, "and the people who say they did not intend it are [also] talking nonsense." *U.S. Congress, Senate, Committee on the Judiciary*, Hearings on Reorganization of the Federal Judiciary, on S. 1392, 75th Congress, 1st Session, Part 2, March 17 to March 20, 1937, 176.

67. James G. Randall, *Constitutional Problems under Lincoln*, rev. ed. (Urbana, Ill.: Univ. of Illinois Press, 1951), 25: hereinafter cited as Randall, *Constitutional Problems*; *Ex parte Milligan*, 71 U.S. (4 Wall.) 2, 120–121. As Justice Davis observed in his opinion, speaking for a majority:

> The Constitution of the United States is a law for rulers and people, equally in war and in peace, and covers with the shield of its protection all classes of men, at all times, and under all circumstances. No doctrine, involving more pernicious consequences, was ever invented by the wit of man than that any of its provisions can be suspended during any of the great exigencies of government.

68. Blackstone, *Commentaries*, Vol. 1, 253.

69. *Ibid.*, 257.

70. *Ibid.*

71. *Ibid.*

72. *Ibid.*, 257–258.

73. *Ibid.*, 258–259.

74. *Ibid.*, 258.

75. *Ibid.*, 262.

76. *Ibid.*, 262–263.

77. *Ibid.*, 263–264.

78. *Ibid.*, 265–266.

79. Francis L. Coolidge, Jr., "The Warmaking Powers: The Intentions of the Framers in the Light of Parliamentary History," *Boston University Law Review*, 50 (Spring 1970): 5–18, 6: hereinafter cited as Coolidge, 50 *Boston L. Rev.*; see also: 25 Edw. I, c. 5–6, The Confirmation of Charters, (1297).

80. Coolidge, 50 *Boston L. Rev.*, 6; see also: 27 Edw. III, c.1.

81. Coolidge, 50 *Boston L. Rev.*, 7; Thomas F. Eagleton, *War and Presidential Power: A Chronicle of Congressional Surrender* (New York: Liveright, 1974), 14–

15: hereinafter cited as Eagleton, *War and Presidential Power*; see also: 3 Car. I, c. 1 (1628).

82. Coolidge, 50 *Boston L. Rev.*, 7; see also: 17 Car. II, c. 1 (1665); a similar appropriation was passed in 1666 for the specific purpose of supporting the King's war, 18 & 19 Car. II, c. 1 (1666).

83. Coolidge, 50 *Boston L. Rev.*, 7, 8; see also: 31 Car. II, c. 1 (1679).

84. "An Act Declaring the Rights and Liberties of the Subject and Settling the Succession of the Crowne," 1 Will. & Mar., Sess. 2, c. 2 (1688). The Bill of Rights provided, among other things, that the Crown could not tax without parliamentary consent. In addition, the Crown was prohibited from maintaining a standing army in England during peacetime without parliamentary consent.

85. Eagleton, *War and Presidential Power*, 14–15.

86. "Lord Mansfield's Speech," in *The Parliamentary History of England*, Vol. 16, 1765–1771 (London: T.C. Hansard, 1803): 251–313, 266–267. This speech "in Behalf of The Constitution Against The Suspending and Dispensing Prerogative," was actually written by Mr. Macintosh with the assistance of Lords Temple and Lyttleton: hereinafter cited as 16 *Parliamentary History*.

87. *Ibid.*, 267.

88. *Ibid.*, 271.

89. Mansfield does not deny the King's prerogative. Rather, he argues that royal prerogative does not include the power to suspend or dispense with the standing law. Indeed, the Bill of Rights denied the Crown's power to suspend law without parliamentary consent. See: 1 Will. & Mar., Sess. 2., c. 2.

90. Raoul Berger, *Executive Privilege: A Constitutional Myth* (Cambridge, Mass.: Harvard Univ. Press, 1974), 51: hereinafter cited as Berger, *Executive Privilege*.

91. 71 U.S. (4 Wall.) 2, 121 (1866); see also Chief Justice Charles Evans Hughes' opinion for the Court in *Home Building and Loan Association* v. *Blaisdell*, 290 U.S. 398, 425 (1933):

> Emergency does not create power. Emergency does not increase granted power or remove or diminish the restrictions imposed upon power granted or reserved. The Constitution was adopted in a period of grave emergency. Its grants of power to the Federal Government and its limitations of the power of the states were determined in the light of emergency and they are not altered by emergency.

Hughes admitted, however, that emergencies may furnish the occasion for the exercise of the broad powers that are delegated to government. 290 U.S. 398, 426; see also: Arthur M. Schlesinger, Jr., *The Imperial Presidency* (Boston: Houghton Mifflin Co., 1973), 9: hereinafter cited as Schlesinger, *Imperial Presidency*.

92. Bestor, 5 *Seton Hall L. Rev.*, 565–567, 568–569.

93. *Articles of Confederation*, Article 6 and Article 9 in Bloom, *Formation of The Union*, 535, 536–537.

94. *Ibid.*, Article 9, 537.

95. *Ibid.*, Article 8, 535, and Article 9, 537–538.

96. *Ibid.*, Article 9, 538.

97. Despite limitations on the powers of the states to appoint ambassadors, enter into treaties, lay imposts or duties, maintain ships of war in peacetime, maintain an army (except for an armed and disciplined militia), and engage in offensive war, even Justice Story recognized that congressional powers were "greatly restricted in their exercise." Joseph Story, *Commentaries on the Constitution of the United States*, 2nd ed. (Boston: Charles C. Little & James Brown, 1851), Vol. 1, Book 2, Ch. 3, Sec. 237, 165: hereinafter cited as Story, *Commentaries on The Constitution*. Chapter 3 contains Story's analysis of the Articles of Confederation.

98. The overwhelming weight of evidence suggests that the states retained most governmental power. As George Washington wrote in 1785, "In a word the confederation appears to me to be little more than a shadow without the substance; and Congress a nugatory body, their ordinances being little attended to." In Story, *Commentaries on The Constitution*, Vol. 1, Book 2, Ch. 4, Sec. 247, 169. In peacetime, Story observed, the Confederation "was possessed of but a delusive and shadowy sovereignty [i.e., governmental power], with little more than the empty pageantry of office." Story, Vol. 1, Book 2, Ch. 4, Sec. 245, 167.

Most modern commentators agree that in theory and fact the states retained real governmental power. See, for example: Raoul Berger, "The Presidential Monopoly of Foreign Relations," *University of Michigan Law Review*, 71 (November 1972): 1–58: hereinafter cited as Berger, 71 *Michigan L. Rev.*; Berger, 121 *Pennsylvania L. Rev.*, 29–86; Claude H. Van Tyne, "Sovereignty in The American Revolution: An Historic Study," *American Historical Review*, 12 (April 1907): 529–545: hereinafter cited as Van Tyne, 12 *Amer. Hist. Rev.*; Corwin, 30 *Amer. Hist. Rev.*, 511–536; Maurice Kelman, "Brief for Constitutional Lawyers' Committee on Undeclared War as Amicus Curiae, *Massachusetts* v. *Laird*," *Wayne Law Review*, 17 (January–February 1971): 67–151: hereinafter cited as Kelman, 17 *Wayne L. Rev.*; Homer Hockett, *The Constitutional History of The United States* (New York: Macmillan Co., 1939): hereinafter cited as Hockett, *Constitutional History*; Merrill Jensen, *The Articles of Confederation* (Madison, Wisc.: Univ. of Wisconsin Press, 1940): hereinafter cited as Jensen, *Articles of Confederation*; Merrill Jensen, *The New Nation: A History of the United States During the Confederation 1781–1789* (New York: Alfred A. Knopf, 1958): hereinafter cited as Jensen, *New Nation*.

Even Justice Sutherland, an advocate of inherent presidential power in foreign affairs, admits that the states defied the treaty of peace with Great Britain (1783) and ignored congressional "resolutions declaring that the state legislatures had no power to enact laws construing treaties or restraining or controlling their operation, or execution. . . ." George Sutherland, *Constitutional Power and World Affairs: Columbia University Lectures* (New York: Columbia Univ. Press, 1919), 159: hereinafter cited as Sutherland, *Constitutional Power*. The Massachusetts Bill of Rights (1780), principally authored by John Adams, reflects the prevailing attitude that, while the states had delegated specific powers to Congress, they retained sovereign governmental power. See: Henry S. Commager, *Documents of American History*, 7th ed. (New York: Meredith Publishing Co., 1963), 108: hereinafter cited as Commager, *Documents*.

There are some nineteenth-century commentators, however, who suggest that beginning with the Declaration of Independence the American people has existed continuously as a sovereign nation. Their views reflect late nineteenth-century attitudes toward national sovereignty and American post–Civil War responses to theories of secession. See, for example: Israel Andrews, *Manual of The Constitution of The United States* (New York: Van Antwerp, Bragg & Co., 1874), 21, 34, 36–37, 46: hereinafter cited as Andrews, *Manual of The Constitution*; H. Van Holst, *The Constitutional and Political History of The United States*, Vol. 1, 1750–1833 (Chicago: Callaghan & Co., 1899), 5, 6, 9, 23: hereinafter cited as Van Holst, *Constitutional History*.

99. In his *Draft of a Constitution for Virginia* (1783), Jefferson defined executive power as the power to administer government, which is distinguished from prerogative power. "By Executive powers," Jefferson wrote, "we mean no reference to those powers exercised under our former government by the crown as of its prerogative; . . . We gave him [the governor] those powers only which are necessary to carry into execution the laws. . . ." Julian P. Boyd, ed., *The Papers of Thomas Jefferson*, Vol. 6 (Princeton, N.J.: Princeton Univ. Press, 1952), 298–299: hereinafter cited as Boyd, *Papers of Jefferson*; see also: Berger, *Executive Privilege*, 51–52; Schlesinger, *Imperial Presidency*, 8, 9.

100. In surrendering his commission, Washington remarked: "I have now the honor of offering my sincere congratulations to Congress, and of presenting myself before them, to surrender into their hands the trust committed to me. . . ." *Journals of The Continental Congress*, Vol. 25, 1783 (Washington: Government Print. Off., 1922), 837: hereinafter cited as *Journals of The Continental Congress*; U.S. Congress, Senate, Committee on Foreign Relations, Hearings on S. 731, S.J. Res. 18, and S.J. Res. 59, 92nd Congress, 1st Session, March to October, 1971 (Washington, D.C.: Government Print. Off., 1972), 78: hereinafter cited as *Senate, Committee on For. Rel.*, Hearings on S. 731.

101. Van Tyne, 12 *Amer. Hist. Rev.*, 539, 545.

102. *Ibid.*, 539–540, 541, 542.

103. Bestor, 5 *Seton Hall L. Rev.*, 570, 571, 573; Letter by Edmund Randolph to the delegates of the Virginia Ratifying Convention (October 16, 1787), in Paul Ford, ed., *Pamphlets on the Constitution of the United States* (1888; reprinted, New York: Da Capo Press, 1968), 259–276: hereinafter cited as Ford, *Pamphlets*.

104. Warren, *Making*, 6–14, wherein the author quotes extensively from the correspondence and writings of contemporary politicians and statesmen.

105. *Ibid.*, 14.

106. George Washington, *The Writings of George Washington*, ed. Jared Sparks (Boston: Little, Brown & Co., 1858), Vol. 9, December 1783–April 1789, 187–188: hereinafter cited as Washington, *Writings*.

107. John Jay, *The Correspondence and Public Papers of John Jay*, ed. Henry P. Johnston (New York: G.P. Putnam's Sons, 1891), Vol. 3, 1782–1793, 205: hereinafter cited as Jay, *Correspondence*.

108. These views were also reflected in Rufus King's correspondence with Jonathan Jackson (September 1786):

It must not be understood that these remarks authorize an opinion that a monarchy would promote the happiness of the people of America—far, very far from it. But they show this; if wise and prudent men discerning the imperfections of the present Governments, do not in season and without fear, propose suitable remedies, the causes which changed the Governments alluded to may, and probably will, change those of America.

Proceedings of The Massachusetts Historical Society, October 1915–June 1916, Vol. 49 (Boston: University Press, 1916), 89.

109. *Senate, Committee on For. Rel.*, Hearings on S. 731, 78.

110. Alfred H. Kelly and Winfred A. Harbison, *The American Constitution: Its Origin and Development* (New York: W.W. Norton & Co., 1948), 102: hereinafter cited as Kelly, *American Constitution*.

111. *Ibid.*, 107.

112. Gilbert L. Lycan, *Alexander Hamilton and American Foreign Policy* (Norman, Okla.: Univ. of Oklahoma Press, 1970), 22: hereinafter cited as Lycan, *Alexander Hamilton*.

113. *Ibid.*, 24, 68.

114. Hamilton, *Federalist*, 86–95 (No. 15, Hamilton). Hamilton notes that "The great and radical vice in the construction of the existing Confederation" is the lack of national power vis-à-vis the states. The consequence of this lack of power is that congressional enactments " . . . are mere recommendations which the states observe or disregard at their option." Hamilton, *Federalist*, 89–90.

115. Warren, *Making*, 20–21.

116. *Ibid.*, 22–23.

117. *Ibid.*, 30–32.

118. James Madison, *The Papers of James Madison*, ed. Henry D. Gilpin (Mobile, Alabama: Allston Mygatt, 1842), 589 (Debates of the Congress of the Confederation, February 21, 1787): hereinafter cited as Madison, *Papers*.

119. Merrill Jensen, *Articles of Confederation*, 130, 141. At least the convention's nationalists argued that Congress represented the people of the United States, which evaded the states' actual exercise of sovereign powers.

120. Schlesinger, *Imperial Presidency*, 5; Berger, *Executive Privilege*, 56; Warren, *Making*, 173–174. But see: Alexander Hamilton's argument for a strong executive in Hamilton, *Federalist*, 463–468 (No. 71, Hamilton).

121. Wood, *Creation*, 403–407.

122. Hamilton, *Federalist*, 53–62 (No. 10, Madison).

CHAPTER 2 (PAGES 31 TO 59)

1. For a summary of the debate on constitutional construction, see: W. Taylor Reveley, III, "Presidential War-Making: Constitutional Prerogative or Usurpation," *Virginia Law Review* 55 (November 1969): 1243–1305, 1250–1257: hereinafter cited as Reveley, 55 *Va. L. Rev.* For an example of the literalist or "filiopietistic" view, as Reveley describes this approach, see: Berger, 121 *Pennsylvania L. Rev.* In contrast to the filiopietistic view, see: Myres S. McDougal and Asher Lans, "Treaties and Congressional-Executive or Presidential Agreements of National Pol-

icy," *Yale Law Journal* 54 (Part 1, March 1945): 181–351, and (Part II, June 1945): 534–615: hereinafter cited as McDougal and Lans, 54 *Yale L. J.* McDougal and Lans write, "The geographical isolation, the jealousies, and the separatist movements of 1787 are now of significance only to historians or to those who seek to convert the Constitution into a Procrustean bed. 'The dead cannot bind the living.'"

2. W. Taylor Reveley, III, "Constitutional Allocation of the War Powers between the President and Congress: 1787–1788," *Virginia Journal of International Law* 15 (Fall 1974): 73–147, 78–79, 83: hereinafter cited as Reveley, 15 *Va. J. of Int'l. Law.*

3. Jonathan Elliot, ed., *The Debates in the Several State Conventions on the Adoption of the Federal Constitution*, etc., 2nd ed., 5 Vols. (Philadelphia: J.B. Lippincott Co., 1836): hereinafter cited as Elliot, *Debates in the State Conventions.* See, for example: Patrick Henry's speech to the Virginia Convention of June 5, 1788, in Elliot, Vol. 3, 58–60; George Mason's speech to the Virginia Convention of June 18, 1788, in Elliot, Vol. 3, 496; Luther Martin's address, *Genuine Information*, of November 29, 1787, in Farrand, *Federal Convention*, Vol. 3, 218.

4. Farrand, *Federal Convention*, Vol. 2, 318.

5. *Ibid.*, 318–319.

6. Reveley, 15 *Va. J. of Int'l. Law*, 76.

7. *Ibid.*

8. In a letter from Gouverneur Morris to Timothy Pickering (December 22, 1814), quoted in Reveley, 15 *Va. J. of Int'l Law*, 77; also see: Elliot, *Debates in the State Conventions*, Vol. 1, 507.

9. Eagleton, *War and Presidential Power*, 10; William Whiting, *War Powers under the Constitution of the United States*, 43rd ed. (Boston: Lee and Shepard, Publishers, 1871), 39–40: hereinafter cited as Whiting, *War Powers*; Berger, *Executive Privilege*, 64–65, 65–66, 67, 68; William B. Spong, Jr., "Can Balance be Restored in the Constitutional War Powers of the President and Congress?" *University of Richmond Law Review* 6 (Fall 1971): 1–47, 4: hereinafter cited as Spong, 6 *Richmond L. Rev.*; Thomas F. Eagleton, "Congress and the War Powers," *Missouri Law Review* 37 (Winter 1972): 1–32, 4: hereinafter cited as Eagleton, 37 *Mo. L. Rev.*

10. Farrand, *Federal Convention*, Vol. 2, 143, 145, 168.

11. *Ibid.*, 182 (Madison's *Notes*, August 6)

12. *Ibid.*, 172 (Comm. of Detail IX), 185 (Madison's *Notes*, August 6).

13. *Ibid.*, 313 (Journal, August 17).

14. *Ibid.*, 318 (Madison's *Notes*, August 17).

15. *Ibid.*

16. *Ibid.*

17. *Ibid.*, 319 (Madison's *Notes*, August 17).

18. *Ibid.*

19. See, for example: James G. Randall, *Lincoln the President: Midstream* (New York: Dodd Mead & Co., 1952), Vol. 3, 132–134: hereinafter cited as Randall, *Lincoln the President*; Carl Sandburg, *Abraham Lincoln: The War Years* (New York: Harcourt, Brace & Co., 1939), 4 Vols., Vol. 1, 419–420, 634–636; Vol. 2, 545; Vol. 4, 24: hereinafter cited as Sandburg, *Abraham Lincoln.*

20. J.F. Maurice, Lt. Col., *Hostilities without Declaration of War: From 1700 to 1870* (London: Her Majesty's Stationery Office, 1883), 3–8, 20–26: hereinafter cited as Maurice, *Hostilities without Declaration of War*. Colonel Maurice describes and enumerates various wars fought before 1799 without a declaration of war.

21. Lofgren, 81 *Yale L. J.*, 695–696; but, see: Barry M. Goldwater, "Opinion: Whose Power Is War Power," *Foreign Policy*, No. 8 (Fall 1972): 33–36: hereinafter cited as Goldwater, 8 *Foreign Policy*; *U.S. Congress, House of Representatives, Committee on Foreign Affairs, Subcommittee on National Security Policy and Scientific Development*, Hearings on Congress, the President, and the War Powers, June 18–August 5, 1970 (Washington, D.C.: Government Print. Off., 1970), 301: hereinafter cited as *H.R., Comm. on For. Aff.*, Hearings on War Powers. See: Testimony of Nicholas deB. Katzenbach, former U.S. Attorney General, before the Committee.

22. Schlesinger, *Imperial Presidency*, 21; Howard A. Nash, *The Forgotten Wars, 1798–1805: The Role of the U.S. Navy in the Quasi-War with France and the Barbary Wars, 1798–1805* (South Brunswick, N.J.: A.S. Barnes & Co., 1961), 55–56, 59, 64–67: hereinafter cited as Nash, *Forgotten Wars*.

23. *Bas* v. *Tingy*, 4 U.S. (4 Dall.) 37, 40, 41, 42 (1800); *Talbot* v. *Seeman*, 4 U.S. (4 Dall.) 34 (1800).

24. 4 U.S. (4 Dall.) 37, 43 (1800).

25. *Ibid.*, 45, 46.

26. In addition to *Bas* v. *Tingy* and *Talbot* v. *Seeman*, in *Little* v. *Barreme*, 6 U.S. (2 Cranch) 170 (1804), the Court suggests that Congress can limit the power of executive officers (i.e., a naval officer) to seize ships on the high seas. Under an act of February 9, 1799, Congress authorized the seizure of ships bound *to*, but not sailing *from*, French ports. Inasmuch as Captain Little had seized the *Flying Fish* sailing from a French port, Jeremie, to St. Thomas, a neutral Danish port, the captain had violated the President's orders issued in pursuance to the statute. One can infer that Congress has the power to authorize limited hostilities and control the scope of such hostilities, although the Court's decision does not involve a direct confrontation between Congress and the President. See: *Little* v. *Barreme*, 6 U.S. (2 Cranch) 170, 175–177 (1805).

27. See: Justice Jackson's concurring opinion in *Youngstown Sheet and Tube Co.* v. *Sawyer*, 343 U.S. 579, 635–638 (1952). Justice Jackson specifies three different contingencies under which presidential action can occur. Justice Jackson's analysis of these contingencies applies to constitutional zones in which Congress and the President have concurrent powers. First, when the President acts pursuant to an express or implied congressional authorization, his authority is at its maximum since he possesses his own constitutional power as well as the power that Congress delegates. Second, when the President acts on his own authority (under Article 2), in the absence of any congressional delegation, his power is uncertain in the twilight zone. Third, when the President acts in conflict with the expressed or implied will of Congress, his power is "at its lowest ebb."

28. Berger, *Executive Privilege*, 78; Merlo Pusey, *The Way We Go to War* (Boston: Houghton Mifflin Co., 1969), 54: hereinafter cited as Pusey, *The Way We Go to War*; Nash, *Forgotten Wars*, 178–180; Albert Putney, "Executive Assumption of

the War-Making Power," *National University Law Review* 11 (May 1972): 1–41, 6–8: hereinafter cited as Putney, 11 *Nat'l. U. L. Rev.*

29. James D. Richardson, ed., *A Compilation of the Messages and Papers of the Presidents 1789–1897* (Washington, D.C.: Government Print. Off., 1897), Vol. 1, 327: hereinafter cited as Richardson, *Messages and Papers of the Presidents.*

30. Jacob K. Javits, *Who Makes War: The President Versus Congress* (New York: William Morrow & Co., 1973), 37–38, 40–41, 46–49: hereinafter cited as Javits, *Who Makes War*; Abraham D. Sofaer, "The Presidency, War, and Foreign Affairs: Practice under the Framers," *Law and Contemporary Problems* 40 (Spring 1976): 12–38, 21–26: hereinafter cited as Sofaer, 40 *L. & Contemp. Prob.*

31. 2 Stat. 129, Ch. 4, 129–130 (1802). In response to Jefferson's request for authority to deal with the Tripolitan pirates, Congress passed "An Act for the protection of the Commerce and Seamen of the United States, against the Tripolitan Cruisers" that was almost as plenary in authority as the Gulf of Tonkin Resolution. The act authorized the President to " . . . employ such of the armed vessels of the United States as may be judged requisite by the President of the United States, for protecting effectually the commerce and seamen thereof on the Atlantic ocean, the Mediterranean and adjoining seas." 2 Stat. 129, 130, Ch. 4 (1802).

32. Stephen C. Blyth, *History of the War Between the United States and Tripoli and Other Barbary Powers* (Salem, Mass.: Salem Gazette Office, 1806), 115–125: hereinafter cited as Blyth, *History of the War Between the U.S. and Tripoli*; Nash, *Forgotten Wars*, 287–289.

33. See: unknown compiler, *The Life of the Late General William Eaton* (Brookfield, Mass.: E. Merriam & Co., 1813): hereinafter cited as Eaton, *Life of Gen. Eaton.* This work contains General Eaton's correspondence during the Barbary Wars.

34. Sofaer, 40 *L. & Contemp. Prob.*, 27. Sofaer argues that Eaton's mission was an offensive one and that Jefferson, backed by a congressional majority, employed presidential power aggressively, as had Adams, while feigning obeisance to congressional authority to control offensive warfare.

35. *U.S. Congress, Senate, Committee on Foreign Relations*, Report on Security Agreements and Commitments Abroad, 91st Congress, 2nd Session, 1970 (Washington, D.C.: Government Print. Off., 1970), 3: hereinafter cited as *Senate, Comm. on For. Rel.*, Report on Security Agreements.

36. See: *U.S. Congress, Senate, Committee on Foreign Relations*, Hearings on Agreement of Friendship between the United States of America and Spain, 91st Congress, 2nd Session, August 6, 1970 (Washington, D.C.: Government Print. Off., 1970): hereinafter cited as *Senate, Comm. on For. Rel.*, Hearings on Agreement of Friendship.

37. *U.S. Congress, Senate, Committee on Foreign Relations*, Hearings before the Committee on Foreign Relations on S. 440, War-Powers Legislation, 93rd Congress, 1st Session, April 11 and 12, 1973 (Washington, D.C.: Government Print. Off., 1973): hereinafter cited as *Senate, Comm. on For. Rel.*, Hearings on S. 440; *Senate, Comm. on For. Rel.*, Hearings on S. 731; Daniel S. Cheever and H. Field Haviland, Jr., *American Foreign Policy and the Separation of Powers* (Cambridge, Mass.: Harvard Univ. Press, 1952), 128–129: hereinafter cited as Cheever and

Haviland, *American Foreign Policy*; Francis O. Wilcox, "The President's Authority to Send Armed Forces Abroad," *Proceedings of the American Society of International Law* 1951 (April 26–28, 1951): 20–43: hereinafter cited as Wilcox, 1951 *Amer. Soc. of Int'l. L.*

Although the preceding works argue that the NATO treaty is a nonself-excuting treaty, which does not alter the constitutional relationship between Congress and the President, some scholars argue that it is self-executing, which implies that the President has power to dispatch U.S. armed forces to Europe under the treaty without further congressional authorization. See, for example: Cheever and Haviland, *American Foreign Policy*, 131, 134.

Still other scholars take the position that, while the President has independent authority to dispatch U.S. armed forces abroad, only Congress can commit them to war. See, for example: Pusey, *The Way We Go to War*, 85–86; Dorothy Schaffter and Dorothy M. Matthews, *The Powers of the President as Commander in Chief of the Army and Navy of the United States*, H.R. Doc. No. 443, 84th Congress, 2nd Session, 1956 (Washington, D.C.: Government Print. Off., 1956), 82–85: hereinafter cited as Schaffter, *Powers of the President*; Wilcox, 1951 *Amer. Soc. of Int'l. L.*, 21–22.

38. *U.S., Department of Defense, Office of the Assistant Secretary for Public Affairs*, Press Release No. 98–79, March 6, 1979; Berger, *Executive Privilege*, 140–141, 142.

39. Eagleton, *War and Presidential Power*, 17, 18; Robert S. Hirschfield, ed., *The Power of the Presidency: Concepts and Controversy* (New York: Atherton Press, 1968), 11, 12: hereinafter cited as, Hirschfield, *Power of the Presidency*; Binkley, *President and Congress*, 30–31, 31–32; William W. Crosskey, *Politics and the Constitution in the History of the United States* (Chicago: Univ. of Chicago Press, 1953), Vol. 2, 417–419: hereinafter cited as Crosskey, *Politics and the Constitution*; Milton, *Presidential Power*, 8.

40. Crosskey, *Politics and the Constitution*, Vol. 2, 443, 465, 466.

41. Elias Huzar, *The Purse and the Sword: Control of the Army by Congress through Military Appropriations* (Ithaca, N.Y.: Cornell Univ. Press, 1950), 18, 22, 23: hereinafter cited as Huzar, *Purse and the Sword*.

42. Huzar, *Purse and the Sword*, 22.

43. Warren, *Making*, 475–477; see also: Story, *Commentaries on the Constitution*, Vol. 1, Chapter 14, especially secs. 905–931, 629–652, for the pre-1937 construction of the general-welfare clause.

44. See: Crosskey, *Politics and the Constitution*, for a broad construction of the general-welfare clause, Vol. 1, 497–498, 501–508.

45. Farrand, *Federal Convention*, Vol. 2, 329 (Madison's *Notes*, August 18).

46. *Ibid.*, 330 (Madison's *Notes*, August 18).

47. *Ibid.*, 341 (Madison's *Notes*, August 20).

48. *Ibid.*, 509 (Madison's *Notes*, September 5).

49. *Ibid.*, 505 (*Journal*, September 5), 509 (Madison's *Notes*, September 5).

50. *Ibid.*, 632–633 (Madison's *Notes*, September 15), 635 (King, September 15).

51. *Ibid.*, Vol. 3, 207 (Luther Martin, *Genuine Information*, November 29, 1787).

52. Hamilton, *Federalist*, 156 (No. 25, Hamilton).

53. *Ibid.*, 153, 157, 158.

54. *Ibid.*, 159 (No. 26, Hamilton); see also: 261–262 (No. 41, Madison).

55. *Ibid.*, 160–161, 163 (No. 26, Hamilton).

56. *Ibid.*, 164.

57. Bloom, *Formation of the Union*, 537.

58. Story, *Commentaries on the Constitution*, Vol. 2, Ch. 21, Sec. 119F, 102.

59. Blackstone, *Commentaries*, Vol. 1, 262.

60. 13 Car. II, c. 6 (1661).

61. Blackstone, *Commentaries*, Vol. 1, 414–415.

62. *Ibid.*, 416.

63. Farrand, *Federal Convention*, Vol. 1, 293 (Madison's *Notes*, June 18).

64. Hamilton, *Federalist*, 156–157 (No. 25, Hamilton).

65. Farrand, *Federal Convention*, Vol. 2, 388 (Madison's *Notes*, August 23) and Vol. 3, 209 (Luther Martin, *Genuine Information*, November 29, 1787).

66. Farrand, *Federal Convention*, Vol. 3, 207–209 (Luther Martin, *Genuine Information*, November 29, 1787); Vol. 2, 385 (Elbridge Gerry), 386 (Oliver Elseworth and Roger Sherman), and 329–330 (Madison's *Notes*, August 18).

67. See: John Marshall's argument in *McCulloch* v. *Maryland*, 17 U.S. (4 Wheat.) 316, 412–424 (1819).

68. See: Thomas Jefferson's restrictive view of the necessary-and-proper clause, which appears in his *Opinion on the Constitutionality of a National Bank*, February 15, 1791, in Thomas Jefferson, *The Writings of Thomas Jefferson*, ed. Paul L. Ford (New York: G.P. Putnam's Sons, 1889), Vol. 5, 1788–1792, 287: hereinafter cited as Jefferson, *Writings*.

69. See: William W. Van Alstyne, "The Role of Congress in Determining Incidental Powers of the President and the Federal Courts: A Comment on the Horizontal Effect of the Sweeping Clause," *Law and Contemporary Problems* 40 (Spring 1976): 102–134, 116–117: hereinafter cited as Van Alstyne, 40 *L. & Contemp. Prob.*, for a broad construction of the necessary-and-proper clause; but, see: Warren, *Making*, 486–488, who argues that the Framers had a fairly limited interpretation of this clause. The necessary-and-proper clause, according to Warren, neither adds to nor detracts from the powers vested in Congress. Although Hamilton and Madison argue similarly in *Federalist*, Nos. 33 and 44, their writings seem a rather disingenuous attempt to disarm the anti-Federalist opponents who believed that the sweeping clause could be used to vitiate the states' powers.

70. Hamilton, *Federalist*, 293–294 (No. 44, Madison).

71. *Ibid.*, 198–201 (No. 33, Hamilton), 200–201 (No. 33, Hamilton), 294–295 (No. 44, Madison).

72. Warren, *Making*, 487.

73. Farrand, *Federal Convention*, Vol. 2, 633 (Madison's *Notes*, September 15).

74. *Ibid.*, 640 (according to Farrand, this document is from George Mason's copy of the September 12 draft of the Constitution, and is reprinted from Rowland's *Life of George Mason*, Vol. 2, 387–390.)

75. Van Alstyne, 40 *L. & Contemp. Prob.*, 116–117, 118, 133.

76. *Ibid.*, 119.

194   UNDECLARED WAR

77. Farrand, *Federal Convention*, Vol. 3, 363; Jefferson, *Writings*, Vol. 5, 1788–1792, 286–287.

78. See: argument of counsel for the State of Maryland in *McCulloch* v. *Maryland*, 17 U.S. (4 Wheat.) 316, 363–377 (1819).

79. Van Alstyne, 40 *L. & Contemp. Prob.*, 133–134.

80. *Ibid.*, 133.

81. Farrand, *Federal Convention*, Vol. 1, 64–69 (Madison's *Notes*, June 1), 79–81 (Madison's *Notes*, June 2), 85–89 (Madison's *Notes*, June 2), 97–105 (Madison's *Notes*, June 4).

82. *Ibid.*, Vol. 1, 66 (Madison's *Notes*, June 1).

83. *Ibid.*

84. Milton, *Presidential Power*, 8.

85. Warren, *Making*, 441–442.

86. Eagleton, *War and Presidential Power*, 17; Clinton Rossiter, *The American Presidency*, 2nd ed. (New York: Harcourt, Brace & World, 1960), 75–76: hereinafter cited as Rossiter, *American Presidency*.

87. Farrand, *Federal Convention*, Vol. 4, 18–19 (revised Mason manuscript of June 4).

88. Both the narrow and broad construction of Article 2's vesting clause are examined in the following works: Hirschfield, *Power of the Presidency*, 214–215; Edward S. Corwin, "The Steel Seizure Case: A Judicial Brick without Straw," *Columbia University Law Review* 53 (January 1953): 53–66, 53: hereinafter cited as Corwin, 53 *Columbia L. Rev.*; Corwin, *Total War*, 11; James Grafton Rogers, *World Policing and the Constitution* (Boston: World Peace Foundation, 1945), 14: hereinafter cited as Rogers, *World Policing and the Constitution*; Clarence Berdahl, *War Power of the Executive in the United States* (Champaign, Ill.: University of Illinois, Studies in the Social Sciences, Vol. 9, March–June 1920), 11–14: hereinafter cited as Berdahl, *War Power of the Executive*.

89. Farrand, *Federal Convention*, Vol. 3, 111.

90. See note 88, *supra*.

91. See: Justice Sutherland's majority opinion in *U.S.* v. *Curtiss-Wright Export Corp.*, 299 U.S. 304, 319–322 (1936).

92. Elliot, *Debates in the State Conventions*, Vol. 2, the New York and Pennsylvania Conventions; Vol. 3, the Virginia Convention; Vol. 4, the North Carolina and South Carolina Conventions.

93. Javits, *Who Makes War*, 22–24; Gilbert L. Lycan, *Alexander Hamilton and American Foreign Policy* (Norman, Okla.: Univ. of Oklahoma Press, 1970), 152, 153–154, 158–159: hereinafter cited as Lycan, *Alexander Hamilton and American Foreign Policy*; Binkley, *Powers*, 40–41.

94. Javits, *Who Makes War*, 28–31; Alexander De Conde, *The Quasi-War: The Politics and Diplomacy of the Undeclared War with France, 1797–1801* (New York: Charles Scribner's Sons, 1966), 70–72, 80, 85, 87, 89, 170: hereinafter cited as De Conde, *The Quasi-War*; Nash, *Forgotten Wars*, 50–52.

95. Javits, *Who Makes War*, 49–51; Pusey, *The Way We Go to War*, 54–55; Robert Leckie, *The Wars of America* (New York: Harper & Row, 1968), 6–8: hereinafter cited as Leckie, *Wars of America*; Edward S. Corwin, *The President's Con-*

trol of Foreign Relations (Princeton, N.J.: Princeton Univ. Press, 1917), 132, 133–135: hereinafter cited as Corwin, *President's Control of Foreign Relations*; Blyth, *History of the War Between the U.S. and Tripoli*, 93–94.

96. Farrand, *Federal Convention*, Vol. 1, 244–245 (Madison's *Notes*, June 15), 246 (Yates, June 15), 247 (King, June 15).

97. Elliot, *Debates in the State Conventions*, Vol. 3, 58–60. This view was also expressed by Luther Martin (*Genuine Information*, November 29, 1787), in Farrand, *Federal Convention*, Vol. 3, 218; George Mason (in the Virginia Convention, June 18, 1788), in Elliot, *Debates in the State Conventions*, Vol. 3, 496.

98. Both Madison and Butler expressed their fears of presidential military dictatorship to the Federal Convention on September 7. See: Farrand, *Federal Convention*, Vol. 2, 540–541 (Madison's *Notes*, September 7). On June 9, 1788, Patrick Henry expressed the same thought to the Virginia Convention, in Elliot, *Debates in the State Conventions*, Vol. 3, 160–161.

99. Farrand, *Federal Convention*, Vol. 1, 292 (Madison's *Notes*, June 18); Vol. 2, 157 (according to Farrand, this document is in Wilson's handwriting, and is probably from the New Jersey or Paterson Plan).

100. *Ibid.*, Vol. 2, 343 (Madison's *Notes*, August 20).

101. *Ibid.*, 185 (Madison's *Notes*, August 6).

102. Congress could, of course, delegate the power to call the militia (national guard) into the Federal service to the President, as it did in the Militia Acts of 1792 and 1795. See: 1 Stat. 264, Ch. 28, 264–265 (1792) and 1 Stat. 424, Ch. 36, 424–425 (1795).

103. Farrand, *Federal Convention*, Vol. 1, 64–66 (Madison's *Notes*, June 1).

104. Francis D. Wormuth, "The Nixon Theory of the War Power: A Critique," *California Law Review* 60 (May 1972): 623–703, 631, 643–645: hereinafter cited as Wormuth, 60 *California L. Rev.*

105. Ernest R. May, ed., *The Ultimate Decision: The President as Commander in Chief* (New York: George Braziller, 1960), 14–15: hereinafter cited as May, *Ultimate Decision.*

106. Farrand, *Federal Convention*, Vol. 2, 341 (Madison's *Notes*, August 20).

107. Patrick Henry to the Virginia Convention, June 5, 1788, in Elliot, *Debates in the State Conventions*, Vol. 3, 58–60.

108. Richardson, *Messages and Papers of the Presidents*, Vol. 6, 728–749 (Andrew Johnson's Message to the U.S. Senate, responding to Articles of Impeachment, March 23, 1868). Johnson viewed the Tenure of Office Act of 1867 as an unconstitutional interference with his duty as President to faithfully execute the law; *New York Times*, 25 September 1920, 1, and 26 September 1920, 1. Woodrow Wilson refused to carry out the mandate of Section 34 of the Jones Merchant Marine Act of 1920 because he regarded its provisions as an unconstitutional interference with his authority as President. Wilson denied that Congress had the legislative power to require the President to abrogate treaties.

109. Richardson, *Messages and Papers of the Presidents*, Vol. 2, 652 and 654; Vol. 6, 23.

110. *Ibid.*, Vol. 5, 634.

111. *Ibid.*, Vol. 6, 23.

112. 10 U.S.C. secs. 332, 333–334.

113. See: 16 *Parliamentary History*, 251–313; see also: Bill of Rights, 1 Will. & Mary, Sess. 2, c. 2 (1688).

114. *Youngstown Sheet and Tube Co.* v. *Sawyer*, 343 U.S. 579, 587 (1952); but see: Franklin D. Roosevelt's "Message to the Congress Asking for Quick Action to Stabilize the Economy," (September 7, 1942), in which the President threatened to act if Congress did not enact legislation by October 1 stabilizing prices on agricultural commodities. Roosevelt's statement is virtually a claim of prerogative to act in the name of the public interest:

> I ask the Congress to take this action by the first of October. Inaction on your part by that date will leave me with an inescapable responsibility to the people of this country to see to it that the war effort is no longer imperiled by threat of economic chaos.
>
> In the event that the Congress should fail to act, and act adequately, I shall accept the responsibility, and I will act.
>
> The President has the powers, under the Constitution and under Congressional Acts, to take measures necessary to avert a disaster which would interfere with the winning of the war.
>
> The American people can be sure that I will use my powers with a full sense of my responsibility to the Constitution and to my country. The American people can also be sure that I shall not hesitate to use every power vested in me to accomplish the defeat of our enemies in any part of the world where our own safety demands such defeat.
>
> When the war is won, the powers under which I act automatically revert to the people—to whom they belong.

In Samuel I. Rosenmen, ed., *The Public Papers and Addresses of Franklin D. Roosevelt*, 1942 (New York: Harper & Brothers Publishers, 1950), 364–365: hereinafter cited as Rosenman, *Papers and Addresses of Franklin D. Roosevelt*.

115. *Myers* v. *U.S.*, 272 U.S. 52, 291, 292, 293 (1926).

116. See, for example: *Holtzman* v. *Schlesinger*, 484 F. 2d 1307 (2nd Cir.), order stayed 414 U.S. 1321 (1973); *Commonwealth of Mass.* v. *Laird*, 451 F. 2d 26 (1st Cir. 1971); *DaCosta* v. *Laird*, 448 F. 2d (2nd Cir. 1971); *Orlando* v. *Laird*, 443 F. 2d 1039 (2nd Cir. 1971); *Berk* v. *Laird*, 429 F. 2d 302 (2nd Cir. 1970); *Mottola* v. *Nixon*, 318 F. Supp. 538 (N.D. Calif. 1970); *Davi* v. *Laird*, 318 F. Supp. 478 (W.D. Va. 1970); *Morse* v. *Boswell*, 289 F. Supp. 812 (D. Md. 1968); *Velvel* v. *Johnson*, 287 F. Supp. 846 (D. Kan. 1968).

117. On the argument for judicial abstention and self-restraint, see, for example: Robert F. Nagel, "Separation of Powers and the Scope of Federal Equitable Remedies," *Stanford Law Review* 30 (April 1978): 661–724: hereinafter cited as Nagel, 30 *Stanford L. Rev.*; Edward H. Levi, "Some Aspects of Separation of Powers," *Columbia Law Review* 76 (April 1976): 371–391: hereinafter cited as Levi, 76 *Columbia L. Rev.*; Jesse H. Choper, "The Supreme Court and the Political Branches: Democratic Theory and Practice," *University of Pennsylvania Law Re-*

view 122 (April 1974): 810–858: hereinafter cited as Choper, 122 *Pa. L. Rev.*;
Philippa Strum, *The Supreme Court and "Political Questions": A Study in Judicial Evasion* (Tuscaloosa, Alabama: University of Alabama Press, 1974): hereinafter cited as Strum, *Supreme Court and Political Questions*; Kenneth F. MacIver, Jr., Beverly M. Wolff, and Leonard B. Locke, "The Supreme Court as Arbiter in the Conflict between Presidential and Congressional War-Making Powers," *Boston University Law Review* 50 (Spring 1970): 78–116: hereinafter cited as MacIver, 50 *Boston L. Rev.*; Alexander M. Bickel, *The Least Dangerous Branch* (Indianapolis, Ind.: Bobbs-Merrill Co., 1962): hereinafter cited as Bickel, *Least Dangerous Branch*; Robert H. Jackson, *The Struggle for Judicial Supremacy* (New York: Alfred A. Knopf, 1949): hereinafter cited as Jackson, *Judicial Supremacy*; Charles G. Post, Jr., *The Supreme Court and Political Questions* (Baltimore: Johns Hopkins University Studies in Historical and Political Science, Johns Hopkins Press, 1936), Vol. 54, No. 4: hereinafter cited as Post, *Supreme Court and Political Questions*; Maurice Finkelstein, "Judicial Self-Limitation," *Harvard University Law Review* 37 (January 1924): 338–364: hereinafter cited as Finkelstein, 37 *Harvard L. Rev.*; James B. Thayer, "The Origin and Scope of the American Doctrine of Constitutional Law," *Harvard University Law Review* 7 (October 1893): 129–156: hereinafter cited as Thayer, 7 *Harvard L. Rev.*

128. On the argument for judicial review and intervention see, for example: William R. Bishin, "Judicial Review in Democratic Theory," *Southern California Law Review* 50 (September 1977): 1099–1137: hereinafter cited as Bishin, 50 *Southern Cal. L. Rev.*; Edwin B. Firmage, "The War Powers and the Political-Question Doctrine," *University of Colorado Law Review* 49 (Fall 1977): 65–101: hereinafter cited as Firmage, 49 *Colorado L. Rev.*; Wormuth, 60 *Cal. L. Rev.*; Jerome A. Barron, "The Ambiguity of Judicial Review: A Response to Professor Bickel," *Duke Law Journal* 1970 (June 1970): 591–604: hereinafter cited as Barron, 1970 *Duke L. J.*; Michael E. Tigar, "Judicial Power, the 'Political-Question Doctrine,' and Foreign Relations," *U.C.L.A. Law Review* 17 (June 1970): 1135–1179: hereinafter cited as Tigar, 17 *U.C.L.A. L. Rev.*; Lawrence R. Velvel, *Undeclared War and Civil Disobedience: The American System in Crisis* (New York: Dunellen Publishing Co., 1970): hereinafter cited as Velvel, *Undeclared War*; Paul G. Kauper, "The Supreme Court: Hybrid Organ of State," *Southwestern Law Journal* 21 (1967): 573–590: hereinafter cited as Kauper, 21 *Southwestern L. J.*; Herbert Wechsler, "Toward Neutral Principles of Constitutional Law," *Harvard University Law Review* 73 (November 1959): 1–35: hereinafter cited as Wechsler, 73 *Harvard L. Rev.*; Eugene V. Rostow, "The Democratic Character of Judicial Review," *Harvard University Law Review* 66 (December 1952): 193–224: hereinafter cited as Rostow, 66 *Harvard L. Rev.*; C. Perry Patterson, "Judicial Review as a Safeguard to Democracy," *The Georgetown University Law Journal* 29 (April 1941): 829–857: hereinafter cited as Patterson, 29 *Georgetown L. J.*

CHAPTER 3 (PAGES 60 TO 83)

1. See, for example, Justice Felix Frankfurter's opinion in *Colegrove v. Green*, 328 U.S. 549, 552, 554, 556 (1946), in which Justices Reed and Burton concurred,

and Justice Frankfurter's dissenting opinion in *Baker* v. *Carr*, 369 U.S. 186, 267, 269–270 (1962), in which Justice Harlan concurred; see also Felix Frankfurter, "John Marshall and the Judicial Function," *Harvard Law Review* 69 (December 1955): 217–238, 227–228: hereinafter cited as Frankfurter, 69 *Harvard L. Rev.*

2. Learned Hand, *The Bill of Rights* (Cambridge, Mass.: Harvard Univ. Press, 1958), 73: hereinafter cited as Hand, *Bill of Rights*.

3. See Herbert Wechsler, "Toward Neutral Principles of Constitutional Law," *Harvard Law Review* 73 (November 1959): 1–35, 15–16, 19: hereinafter cited as Wechsler, 73 *Harvard L. Rev.*

4. Hamilton, *Federalist*, 502–511 (No. 78, Hamilton).

5. In a recent article, William Bishin attempts to reconcile judicial review to democratic values, but fails to acknowledge the theoretical distinction between liberal and democratic values in American society. See William R. Bishin, "Judicial Review in Democratic Theory," *Southern California Law Review* 50 (September 1977): 1099–1137, 1102–1103, 1105–1107, 1108: hereinafter cited as Bishin, 50 *S. Cal. L. Rev.*; see also Jesse H. Choper, "The Supreme Court and the Political Branches: Democratic Theory and Practice," *University of Pennsylvania Law Review* 122 (April 1974): 810–858, 816, 829: hereinafter cited as Choper, 122 *Pa. L. Rev.*; Eugene V. Rostow, "The Democratic Character of Judicial Review," *Harvard Law Review* 66 (December 1952): 193–224, 194–195,197, 210: hereinafter cited as Rostow, 66 *Harvard L. Rev.*

6. Bishin, 50 *S. Cal. L. Rev.*, 1116–1118; see also F.A. Hayek, *The Constitution of Liberty* (Chicago: Univ. of Chicago Press, 1960), Ch. 12, especially 177–182: hereinafter cited as Hayek, *Constitution of Liberty*.

7. See, for example, Corwin, 30 *Amer. Hist. Rev.*, especially 521–527; *U.S. Congress, Senate, Committee on the Judiciary*, Hearings on Reorganization of the Federal Judiciary, on S. 1392, 75th Congress, 1st Sess., Part 2, March 17 to March 20, 1937, 176.

8. Corwin, 30 *Amer. Hist. Rev.*, 522–523.

9. *Ibid.*, 514; Wood, *Creation*, 150–151, 154–155; Sharp, 2 *Chicago L. Rev.*, 395–396, 397, 399, 402, 417; Warren, *Making*, 46.

10. Sharp, 2 *Chicago L. Rev.*, 395–396, 397, 399, 402, 417; Warren, *Making*, 46.

11. Farrand, *Federal Convention*, Vol. 2, 76 (Madison's *Notes*, July 21).

12. *Ibid.*, 78 (Madison's *Notes*, July 21).

13. *Ibid.*, 93 (Madison's *Notes*, July 23).

14. *U.S. Congress, Senate, Committee on the Judiciary*, Hearings on S. 1392, 176.

15. See *Stuart* v. *Laird*, 5 U.S. (1 Cranch) 308, 309 (1803); *Hollingsworth* v. *Virginia*, 3 U.S. (3 Dal.) 378, 382 (1798); *Hylton* v. *U.S.*, 3 U.S. (3 Dal.) 171, 175 (1796).

16. Leonard B. Rosenberg, "Constitutional Supremacy: An Early Advocate of Judicial Review," *Duquesne Law Review* 7 (Summer 1969): 515–541, 527, 528, 529: hereinafter cited as Rosenberg, 7 *Duquesne L. Rev.*

17. *Marbury* v. *Madison*, 5 U.S. (1 Cranch) 137, 176, 178, (1803).

18. *Ibid.*, 179.

19. *Ibid.*, 178–179.

20. *Cohens* v. *Virginia*, 19 U.S. (6 Wheat.) 264, 404 (1821).

21. Wechsler, 73 *Harvard L. Rev.*, 1, 6, 7.

22. See Choper, 122 *Pa. L. Rev.*; Rostow, 66 *Harvard L. Rev.*

23. See *Wesberry* v. *Sanders*, 376 U.S. 1 (1964); *Reynolds* v. *Sims*, 377 U.S. 533 (1964).

24. Choper, 122 *Pa. L. Rev.*, 810–811, 830; Bishin, 50 *S. Cal. L. Rev.*, 1102–1103.

25. See *Minersville School District* v. *Gobitis*, 310 U.S. 586 (1940); *Hirabayashi* v. *United States*, 320 U.S. 81 (1943); *Korematsu* v. *United States*, 323 U.S. 214 (1944).

26. See *West Virginia State Board of Education* v. *Barnette*, 319 U.S. 624 (1943); *Ex parte Endo*, 323 U.S. 283 (1944).

27. Rostow, 66 *Harvard L. Rev.*, 195; Eugene V. Rostow, "The Supreme Court and the People's Will," *Notre Dame Lawyer* 33 (August 1958): 573–596, 576, 578: hereinafter cited as Rostow, 33 *Notre Dame Lawyer*; C. Perry Patterson, "Judicial Review as a Safeguard to Democracy," *The Georgetown Law Journal* 29 (April 1941): 829–857, 847–848: hereinafter cited as Patterson, 29 *Georgetown L. J.*

28. Rostow, 66 *Harvard L. Rev.*, 195, 197, 198; Rostow, 33 *Notre Dame Lawyer*, 577; Edward H. Levi, "Some Aspects of the Separation of Powers," *Columbia Law Review*, 76 (April 1976), 371–391, 386–387: hereinafter cited as Levi, 76 *Columbia L. Rev.*

29. Rostow, 66 *Harvard L. Rev.*, 212–213, 223–224.

30. Bickel, *Least Dangerous Branch*, 16, 18, 19. Bickel argues that judicial review runs counter to the electoral process. By interfering with the policy decisions of popularly elected representatives, the Federal courts frustrate the people's policy preferences. Bickel obviously ignores the internal organization and structure of Congress, which often attenuate the relationship between popular preferences and congressional policy decisions. Furthermore, Bickel assumes that one can identify and translate popular choices into governmental policy on specific issues. Both congressional organization and the low saliency and visibility of most issues cast doubt on Bickel's assumptions.

31. James B. Thayer, "The Origin and Scope of the American Doctrine of Constitutional Law," *Harvard Law Review* 7 (October 1893): 129–156, 135, 136, 138: hereinafter cited as Thayer, 7 *Harvard L. Rev.*

32. *Ibid.*, 142.

33. *Ibid.*

34. Hand, *Bill of Rights*, 73–74.

35. Justice Robert H. Jackson also argues that government by lawsuit means testing the entire social process by a single standard, namely, that of the law. Decisions based on legally acceptable arguments and legally admissible evidence exclude much valuable economic, political, and social data necessary to make intelligent public policy. See Jackson, *Judicial Supremacy*, 291, 292.

36. See Justice Frankfurter's dissenting opinion in *Baker* v. *Carr*, 369 U.S. 186, 268, 282, 289, 295 (1962). See also Justice John Marshall Harlan's dissenting opinion at 337; see also Firmage, 49 *Colo. L. Rev.*, 74.

37. See Justice Frankfurter's opinion in *Colegrove* v. *Green*, 328 U.S. 549, 555,

556 (1946); see also Strum, *Supreme Court and Political Questions*, 18; Jack W. Peltason, *Federal Courts in the Political Process* (Garden City, N.Y.: Doubleday & Co., 1955), 10: hereinafter cited as Peltason, *Federal Courts*.

38. Strum, *Supreme Court and Political Questions*, 18; Peltason, *Federal Courts*, 10.

39. Jackson, *Judicial Supremacy*, 322; Bickel, *Least Dangerous Branch*, 184.

40. Strum, *Supreme Court and Political Questions*, 130.

41. On changes that have occurred in the constitutional as well as statutory requirements for standing to sue, see Lee A. Albert, "Justiciability and Theories of Judicial Review: A Remote Relationship," *Southern California Law Review* 50 (September 1977): 1139–1177: hereinafter cited as Albert, 50 *S. Cal. L. Rev.*; Joseph J. Giunta, "Standing, Separation of Powers, and the Demise of the Public Citizen," *American University Law Review* 24 (Spring 1975): 835–876: hereinafter cited as Giunta, 24 *American U. L. Rev.*

42. Fritz W. Scharpf, "Judicial Review and the Political Question: A Functional Analysis," *Yale Law Journal* 75 (March 1966): 517–597, 536–537: hereinafter cited as Scharpf, 75 *Yale L. J.*

43. Unlike other techniques of abstention such as standing, ripeness, and certiorari, which represent a short-term retreat, according to Scharpf, invocation of the political question means that the courts abandon their responsibility to define the law in a particular area. Scharpf, 75 *Yale L. J.*, 537–538; see also Julie M. Myers, "The Political Question Doctrine—*O'Brien* v. *Brown* and *Keane* v. *National Democratic Party*," *De Paul Law Review* 22 (Summer 1973): 887–897, 888: hereinafter cited as Myers, 22 *De Paul L. Rev.*

44. Scharpf, 75 *Yale L. J.*, 537–538.

45. For a statement of the classical view, see Wechsler, 73 *Harvard L. Rev.*, especially at 9; on the prudential view, see Bickel, *Least Dangerous Branch*; Thayer, 7 *Harvard L. Rev.*

46. Louis Henkin, "Is There a 'Political-Question' Doctrine?" *The Yale Law Journal* 85 (April 1976): 597–625, 598, 601, 606: hereinafter cited as Henkin, 85 *Yale L. J.*; "Limiting Judicial Review of Congressional Exclusion with the Political-Question Doctrine," *Utah Law Review* 1969 (January 1969): 182–195, 188–189, 191, 191–192: hereinafter cited as Anonymous, 1969 *Utah L. Rev.*; Scharpf, 75 *Yale L. J.*, 538–539.

47. *Luther* v. *Borden*, 48 U.S. (7 How.) 1 (1849); Myers, 22 *De Paul L. Rev.*, 889.

48. Anonymous, 1969 *Utah L. Rev.*, 188–189.

49. *Ibid.*, 191–192; Frederick G. McKean, "Border Lines of Judicial Power," *Dickinson Law Review* 48 (October 1943): 1–21, 10–11, 12: hereinafter cited as McKean, 48 *Dickinson L. Rev.*

50. Henkin, 85 *Yale L. J.*, 606.

51. Scharpf, 75 *Yale L. J.*, 541.

52. Bickel, *Least Dangerous Branch*, 261; Strum, *Supreme Court and Political Questions*, 142–143; Melville F. Weston, "Political Questions," *Harvard Law Review* 38 (January 1925): 296–333, 299, 301: hereinafter cited as Weston, 38 *Harvard L. Rev.*

53. Bickel, *Least Dangerous Branch*, 112, 125–126, 206.

54. Strum, *Supreme Court and Political Questions*, 102.

55. Bickel, *Least Dangerous Branch*, 184; Strum, *Supreme Court and Political Questions*, 18; Peltason, *Federal Courts*, 10.

56. See Justice Frankfurter's opinion in *Colegrove* v. *Green*, 328 U.S. 549, 552–556 (1946). At the very least, Frankfurter fears that the public will perceive that the judiciary is less than neutral, which he believes will vitiate public confidence in the courts and impair the judicial function.

57. Bickel, *Least Dangerous Branch*, 184.

58. *Ibid.*; Maurice Finkelstein, "Judicial Self-Limitation," *Harvard Law Review* 37 (January 1924): 338–364, 346, 347–348: hereinafter cited as Finkelstein, 37 *Harvard L. Rev.* Finkelstein suggests that the courts are reluctant to decide cases on their constitutional merits when the consequences are vast, unpredictable, and beyond judicial control.

59. *Korematsu* v. *United States*, 323 U.S. 214 (1944).

60. *Ibid.*, 244.

61. *Ibid.*, 245, 246, 247, 248.

62. Bickel, *Least Dangerous Branch*, 205.

63. Post, *Supreme Court and Political Questions*, 113–114, 115–116, 116–117.

64. *Ex parte Merryman*, 17 F. Cas. 144 (C.C.D. Md. 1861) (No. 9, 487).

65. Robert F. Cushman, ed., *Cases in Constitutional Law*, 4th ed. (Englewood Cliffs, N.J.: Prentice-Hall, Inc., 1975), 100: hereinafter cited as Cushman, *Cases in Constitutional Law*.

66. Strum, *Supreme Court and Political Questions*, 4, 10, 22–23, 32, 103, 104, 143.

67. Post, *Supreme Court and Political Questions*, 101–102.

68. *Ibid.*; Bickel, *Least Dangerous Branch*, 184.

69. Among the many articles on the legality of the Vietnam War, the following examine the arguments for and against judicial intervention and decision on the merits of presidential conduct of war without a congressional declaration of war: Anonymous, "War in Cambodia—Political Question," *The Albany Law Review* 38 (1974): 245–264: hereinafter cited as Anonymous, 38 *Albany L. Rev.*; Patrick M. Norton, "Justiciability—Veto Power—Standing," *Harvard International Law Journal* 15 (Winter 1974): 143–157: hereinafter cited as Norton, 15 *Harvard Int'l. L. J.*; Raul R. Tapia, John P. James, and Richard O. Levine, "Congress Versus the Executive: The Role of the Courts," *Harvard Journal on Legislation* 11 (February 1974): 352–403: hereinafter cited as Tapia, 11 *Harvard J. on Legis.*; R. Brooke Jackson, "The Political Question Doctrine: Where Does It Stand after *Powell* v. *McCormack*, *O'Brien* v. *Brown* and *Gilligan* v. *Morgan*," *Colorado Law Review* 44 (May 1973): 477–511: hereinafter cited as Jackson, 44 *Colo. L. Rev.*; Anonymous, "Requisite Congressional Approval of Vietnam War: Inferred from Mutual Participation of Congress with President in Conduct Thereof," *Fordham Law Review* 40 (March 1972): 661–671: hereinafter cited as Anonymous, 40 *Fordham L. Rev.*; Jack W. London, "Separation of Powers—Executive Branch Acting with Constitutional Authority in Conducting Extended Combat Activities When Supported by Congressional Appropriations and Conscript Laws," *Texas International Law*

Forum 6 (Winter 1971): 346–352: hereinafter cited as London, 6 *Texas Int'l. L. Forum*; Kenneth F. MacIver, Jr., Beverly M. Wolff, and Leonard B. Locke, "The Supreme Court as Arbiter in the Conflict between Presidential and Congressional Warmaking Powers," *Boston University Law Review* 50 (Spring 1970, Special Issue): 78–116: hereinafter cited as MacIver, 50 *Boston U. L. Rev.*; Anonymous, "Power to Declare War, Etc.," *Georgia Law Review* 5 (Fall 1970): 181–194: hereinafter cited as Anonymous, 5 *Georgia L. Rev.*; Michael P. Malakoff, "The Political Question and the Vietnam Conflict," *University of Pittsburgh Law Review* 31 (Spring 1970): 504–513: hereinafter cited as Malakoff, 31 *Pittsburgh L. Rev.*

70. Firmage, 49 *Colo. L. Rev.*, 74–75; Strum, *Supreme Court and Political Questions*, 10, 103, 104, 111–112, 130, 131, 142–143.

71. Strum, *Supreme Court and Political Questions*, 2 and 140–141; Finkelstein, 39 *Harvard L. Rev.*, 237, 242; Ralph J. Bean, "The Supreme Court and the Political Question: Affirmation or Abdication," *West Virginia Law Review* 71 (February 1969): 97–134, 99: hereinafter cited as Bean, 71 *W. Va. L. Rev.*

72. Scharpf, 75 *Yale L. J.*, 529.

73. *Ibid.*, 587.

74. *Ibid.*, 596.

75. Wechsler, 73 *Harvard L. Rev.*, 7–8, 9.

76. Scharpf, 75 *Yale L. J.* 529–530, 567–583.

77. Bickel, *Least Dangerous Branch*, 112, 128, 235, 240, 244.

78. See Yaron Z. Reich, "*United States* v. *A.T.&T.*: Judicially Supervised Negotiation and Political Questions," *Columbia Law Review* 77 (April 1977): 466–494: hereinafter cited as Reich, 77 *Columbia L. Rev.*

79. *Baker* v. *Carr*, 369 U.S. 186, 210 (1962).

80. *Ibid.*, 210–211.

81. *Ibid.*, 211.

82. Jackson, 44 *Colo. L. Rev.*, 500–501, 505.

83. *Baker* v. *Carr*, 369 U.S. 186, 217 (1962).

84. Jackson, 44 *Colo. L. Rev.*, 505.

85. *Baker* v. *Carr*, 369 U.S. 186, 211 (1962); Firmage, 49 *Colo. L. Rev.*, 67, 78, 79; see also Lawrence R. Velvel, "The War in Vietnam: Unconstitutional, Justiciable, and Jurisdictionally Attackable," *Kansas Law Review* 16 (1968): 449–503(e): hereinafter cited as Velvel, 16 *Kan. L. Rev.*

86. *Baker* v. *Carr*, 369 U.S. 186, 211 (1962).

87. See Firmage, 49 *Colo. L. Rev.*, 74, 75; Bickel, *Least Dangerous Branch*, 184; Strum, *Supreme Court and Political Questions*, 19; Scharpf, 75 *Yale L. J.*, 567; Finkelstein, 37 *Harvard L. Rev.*, 346; Peltason, *Federal Courts*, 10; Bean, 71 *W. Va. L. Rev.*, 106; H.G. Peter Wallach, "Restraint and Self-Restraint: The Presidency and the Courts," *Capitol University Law Review* 7 (1977): 59–74, 65: hereinafter cited as Wallach, 7 *Capitol U. L. Rev.*

88. *Baker* v. *Carr*, 369 U.S. 186, 214 (1962).

89. Wormuth, 60 *Cal. L. Rev.*, 681.

90. MacIver, 50 *Boston U. L. Rev.*, 78; Wormuth, 60 *Cal. L. Rev.*, 681; Jackson, 44 *Colo. L. Rev.*, 491–492, who argues that the Federal courts reached the merits to determine whether congressional acts meet the constitutional action necessary to

sustain presidential military conduct; London, 6 *Texas Int'l. L. Forum*, 347–349, makes the same point as the preceding article; Anonymous, 40 *Fordham L. Rev.*, 662, 668–669; Anonymous, 5 *Georgia L. Rev.*, 186–188.

91. Wormuth, 60 *Cal. L. Rev.*, 684–685; Anonymous, 5 *Georgia L. Rev.*, 189.

92. *Baker v. Carr*, 369 U.S. 186, 213–214 (1962).

93. *Ibid.*, 214; Firmage, 49 *Colo. L. Rev.*, 81.

94. Emergency Price Control Act of 1942, Ch. 26, Sec. 1(b), 56 Stat. 23 (1942); see also *Yakus v. U.S.*, 321 U.S. 414, 424–425 (1944).

95. *Baker v. Carr*, 369 U.S. 186, 214 (1962); *Chastleton Corp. v. Sinclair*, 264 U.S. 543, 547–548 (1924), in which the Court asserted its power to determine whether the emergency, upon which the operation of the Act of October 22, 1919, regulating rents in the District of Columbia, depended, still existed.

96. *Baker v. Carr*, 369 U.S. 186, 217 (1962).

97. *Ibid.*; Wormuth, 60 *Cal. L. Rev.*, 680, 685–686; Velvel, *Undeclared War*, 146; Tigar, 17 *U.C.L.A. L. Rev.*, 1167, 1170; Firmage, 49 *Colo. L. Rev.*, 66, 81; Velvel, 16 *Kan. L. Rev.*, 480–481; Anonymous, 40 *Fordham L. Rev.*, 665; Anonymous, 5 *Georgia L. Rev.*, 186–187.

98. MacIver, 50 *Boston U. L. Rev.*, 88–89; Velvel, *Undeclared War*, 136–138; Anonymous, 40 *Fordham L. Rev.*, 667, 668–669; Malakoff, 31 *Pittsburgh L. Rev.*, 507–509; Maurice Kelman, "Brief for Constitutional Lawyers' Committee on Undeclared War as *Amicus Curiae, Massachusetts v. Laird*," *Wayne Law Review* 17 (January–February 1971): 67–151, 117: hereinafter cited as Kelman, 17 *Wayne L. Rev.* But see Jackson, 44 *Colo. L. Rev.*

99. MacIver, 50 *Boston U. L. Rev.*, 90–91; Velvel, *Undeclared War*, 147–8; Malakoff, 31 *Pittsburgh L. Rev.*, 509–510; Kelman, 17 *Wayne L. Rev.*, 117.

100. MacIver, 50 *Boston U. L. Rev.*, 91–92; Velvel, *Undeclared War*, 139–141; Malakoff, 31 *Pittsburgh L. Rev.*, 510; Kelman, 17 *Wayne L. Rev.*, 117.

101. Jackson, 44 *Colo. L. Rev.*, 481; MacIver, 50 *Boston U. L. Rev.*, 92–93; Wormuth, 60 *Cal. L. Rev.*, 681–682; Firmage, 49 *Colo. L. Rev.*, 100; Velvel, *Undeclared War*, 139–141; Malakoff, 31 *Pittsburgh L. Rev.*, 511; Kelman, 17 *Wayne L. Rev.*, 117.

102. Tapia, 11 *Harvard J. on Legis.*, 396–397; Wallach, 7 *Capitol U. L. Rev.*, 64; Berger, *Executive Privilege*, 330–332.

103. *Baker v. Carr*, 369 U.S. 186, 215 (1962).

104. *Powell v. McCormack*, 395 U.S. 486 (1969). Justice Stewart dissented largely because he believed that the case had become moot when the Ninetieth Congress passed into history.

On the lowering of the political-question barrier, see Berger, *Executive Privilege*, 327; Anonymous, 38 *Albany L. Rev.*, 253–254.

105. On the lowering of the political-question barrier by an "activist" Supreme Court, see Henkin, 85 *Yale L. J.*, 604–605, 606; Strum, *Supreme Court and Political Questions*, 94–95; Albert, 50 *S. Cal. L. Rev.*, 1170.

On broader criteria for standing, as a means of lowering procedural barriers to judicial review, see *Flast v. Cohen*, 392 U.S. 83 (1968); *Association of Data Processing Service Organizations v. Camp*, 397 U.S. 150 (1970); *Sierra Club v. Mor-*

ton, 405 U.S. 727 (1972); *U.S.* v. *SCRAP*, 412 U.S. 669 (1973); see also Albert, *S. Cal. L. Rev.*, 1147–1151; Giunta, 24 *American U. L. Rev.*, 838–839, 856–865.

But see the following cases, which suggest that the Court has returned to narrower criteria of standing that require a concrete, particularized, and differentiated adversarial interest: *U.S.* v. *Richardson*, 418 U.S. 166 (1974); *Schlesinger* v. *Reservists Committee to Stop the War*, 418 U.S. 208 (1974); see also Giunta, 24 *American U. L. Rev.*, 866–871, 874.

106. *Powell* v. *McCormack*, 395 U.S. 486, 516–518 (1969).

107. *Ibid.*, 548–549 (1969).

108. Jackson, 44 *Colo. L. Rev.*, 480–482; Berger, *Executive Privilege*, 327; Malakoff, 31 *Pittsburgh L. Rev.*, 512; Anonymous, 38 *Albany L. Rev.*, 253, 254. In his opinion, Warren also suggests that invocation of the political question may also rest on the availability of judicial remedies.

109. *Powell* v. *McCormack*, 395 U.S. 486, 520 (1969).

110. *United States* v. *Nixon*, 418 U.S. 683 (1974); see also *Nixon* v. *Sirica*, 487 F. 2d 700 (D.C. Cir. 1973), in which the court, sitting en banc, in a per curiam opinion, rejected the President's unqualified claim of privilege, i.e., his claim of absolute discretion to withhold material subpoenaed in a criminal case.

111. *United States* v. *Nixon*, 418 U.S. 683, 697 (1974).

112. Anonymous, "The Supreme Court, 1973 Term," *Harvard Law Review* 88 (November 1974): 41–280, 58: hereinafter cited as Anonymous, 88 *Harvard L. Rev.*; H. King McGlaughon, Jr., "Executive Privilege: Tilting the Scales in Favor of Secrecy," *North Carolina Law Review* 53 (December 1974): 419–430, 422: hereinafter cited as McGlaughon, 53 *N.C. L. Rev.*; Gerald Gunther, "Judicial Hegemony and Legislative Autonomy: The Nixon Case and the Impeachment Process," *U.C.L.A. Law Review*, 22 (October 1974): 30–39, 34–35: hereinafter cited as Gunther, 22 *U.C.L.A. L. Rev.*; Kenneth L. Karst and Harold W. Horowitz, "Presidential Prerogative and Judicial Review," *U.C.L.A. Law Review*, 22 (October 1974): 47–67, 55–58: hereinafter cited as Karst, 22 *U.C.L.A. L. Rev.*

113. *United States* v. *Nixon*, 418 U.S. 683, 703 (1974).

114. *Ibid.*, 705.

115. *Ibid.*, 706.

116. *Ibid.*, 710–711.

117. *Ibid.*, 711; see also *U.S.* v. *Reynolds*, 345 U.S. 1, 10 (1953).

118. *U.S.* v. *Nixon*, 418 U.S. 683, 706, 710–711 (1974).

119. McGlaughon, 53 *N.C. L. Rev.*, 429–430, in which the author argues that the privilege recognized by the Court places such an extraordinary burden on the person seeking evidentiary material in a criminal proceeding that *Nixon* could contribute to executive secrecy; Raoul Berger, "The Incarnation of Executive Privilege," *U.C.L.A. Law Review* 22 (October 1974): 4–29, 26–29: hereinafter cited as Berger, 22 *U.C.L.A. L. Rev.* Berger argues that the *Reynolds-Nixon* dicta preclude *in camera* inspection of sensitive national-security information, which contributes to governmental secrecy. He concludes that such secrecy may become a vehicle for conspiracy and concealment of crime.

120. *U.S.* v. *Nixon*, 418 U.S. 683, 707 (1974).

121. *Ibid.*, 704.

122. Robert F. Nagel, "Separation of Powers and the Scope of Federal Equitable Remedies," *Stanford Law Review* 30 (April 1978): 661–724, 688: hereinafter cited as Nagel, 30 *Stanford L. Rev.*

123. *Youngstown Sheet and Tube Co.* v. *Sawyer*, 343 U.S. 579, 635, 637 (1952).

124. William P. Rogers, "Congress, the President, and the War Powers," *California Law Review* 59 (September 1971): 1194–1214: hereinafter cited as Rogers, 59 *Cal. L. Rev.*; Clinton Rossiter, *American Presidency*, 57; Glendon A. Schubert, Jr., *The Presidency in the Courts* (Minneapolis, Minn.: Univ. of Minnesota Press, 1957), 273: hereinafter cited as Schubert, *Presidency in the Courts*; Paul D. Carrington, "Political Questions: The Judicial Check on the Executive," *Virginia Law Review* 42 (1956): 175–201, 195: hereinafter cited as Carrington, 42 *Va. L. Rev.*

125. Nagel, 30 *Stanford L. Rev.*, 690–691.

126. *Ibid.*, 697–698, 702–704.

CHAPTER 4 (PAGES 84 TO 109)

1. See *Sarnoff* v. *Connally*, 457 F. 2d 809 (9th Cir. 1972), cert. denied sub nom. *Sarnoff* v. *Schultz*, 409 U.S. 929 (1972); *Luftig* v. *McNamara*, 373 F. 2d 664 (D.C. Cir. 1967); *Atlee* v. *Laird*, 347 F. Supp. 689 (E.D. Pa. 1972); *Meyers* v. *Nixon*, 339 F. Supp. 1388 (S.D. N.Y. 1972); *Davi* v. *Laird*, 318 F. Supp. 478 (W.D. Va. 1970); *Switkes* v. *Laird*, 316 F. Supp. 358 (S.D. N.Y. 1970); *U.S.* v. *Sisson*, 294 F. Supp. 515 (D. Mass. 1968); *U.S.* v. *Sisson*, 294 F. Supp. 511 (D. Mass. 1968); *Velvel* v. *Johnson*, 287 F. Supp. 846 (D. Kan. 1968); *U.S.* v. *Mitchell*, 246 F. Supp. 874 (D. Conn. 1965).

But see the following cases, which approached a decision on the merits: *Commonwealth of Mass.* v. *Laird*, 451 F. 2d 26 (1st Cir. 1971); *Da Costa* v. *Laird*, 448 F. 2d 1386 (2nd Cir. 1971); *Orlando* v. *Laird*, 443 F. 2d 1039 (2nd Cir. 1971); *Berk* v. *Laird*, 429 F. 2d 302 (2nd Cir. 1970); *Drinan* v. *Nixon*, 364 F. Supp. 854 (D. Mass. 1973); *Mottola* v. *Nixon*, 318 F. Supp. 538 (N.D. Calif. 1970).

See also *Holtzman* v. *Schlesinger*, 361 F. Supp. 553 (E.D. N.Y. 1973), which enjoined the government from continuing its bombing of Cambodia, rev'd *Holtzman* v. *Schlesinger*, 484 F. 2d 1307 (2nd Cir. 1973).

2. See Justice Douglas, dissenting in *Holmes* v. *U.S.*, cert. denied 391 U.S. 936, 946–947 (1968); see also *Velvel* v. *Nixon*, cert. denied 396 U.S. 1042 (1970); *Kalish* v. *U.S.*, cert. denied 396 U.S. 835 (1969).

3. In *Holmes* v. *U.S.*, 391 U.S. 936, 949 (1968), Douglas concluded:

> I think we owe to those who are being marched off to jail for maintaining that a declaration of war is essential for conscription an answer to this important undecided constitutional question.

4. See, for example, Scharpf, 75 *Yale L. J.*, 17–20; Joel Grossman and Richard S. Wells, *Constitutional Law and Judicial Policy Making* (New York: John Wiley and Sons, 1972), 563–564: hereinafter cited as Grossman, *Constitutional Law*; C.

Herman Prichett, *The American Constitution*, 3rd ed. (New York: McGraw-Hill, 1977), 271–272: hereinafter cited as Pritchett, *American Constitution*; Rossiter, *American Presidency*, 56; Clinton Rossiter, *The Supreme Court and the Commander in Chief* (Ithaca, N.Y.: Cornell Univ. Press, 1951), 127–128: hereinafter cited as Rossiter, *Supreme Court and Commander in Chief*; Schubert, *Presidency in the Courts*, 4, 315, 347, 348.

5. *United States* v. *Curtiss-Wright Export Corp.*, 299 U.S. 304, 318 (1936).

6. *Ibid.*

7. *Ibid.*

8. In his opinion in *United States* v. *Robel*, 389 U.S. 258, 263–264 (1967), Chief Justice Warren specifically rejected the idea that such incantations preclude judicial review. While he recognized the need for judicial deference to Congress, Warren remarked, " . . . the phrase 'war power' cannot be invoked as a talismanic incantation to support any exercise of congressional power which can be brought within its ambit. '[E]ven the war power does not remove constitutional limitations safeguarding essential liberties.'" In addition to the specific limitations of the Bill of Rights, the separation of the congressional war powers from the office of commander in chief ranks among the constitutional limitations safeguarding essential liberties and constitutional government.

9. Figures 4.1–4.3 were adapted from Donald E. King and Arthur B. Leavens, "Curbing the Dog of War," *Harvard International Law Journal* 18 (Winter 1977): 55–96, 63: hereinafter cited as King, 18 *Harvard Int'l. L. J.*; see note 20, *infra*.

10. See *Schecter Poultry Corp.* v. *United States*, 295 U.S. 495 (1935); *Panama Refining Co.* v. *Ryan*, 293 U.S. 388 (1935); *Homebuilding and Loan Association* v. *Blaisdell*, 290 U.S. 398 (1933); *Hampton, J.W., Jr., & Co.* v. *United States*, 276 U.S. 394 (1928).

11. *United States* v. *Curtiss-Wright Export Corp.*, 299 U.S. 304, 318–320 (1936).

12. *Reid* v. *Covert*, 354 U.S. 1, 5–6, 14 (1957).

13. *Ibid.*, 6, 8–9, 16–17.

14. Grossman, *Constitutional Law*, 555–556; Rossiter, *American Presidency*, 56; Rossiter, *Supreme Court and Commander in Chief*, 126–131; Schubert, *Presidency in the Courts*, 4, 315, 347, 348.

15. *Korematsu* v. *United States*, 323 U.S. 214, 246 (1944).

16. *Ex parte Merryman*, 17 F. Cas. 144 (C.C.D. Md. 1861) (No. 9,487).

17. *Youngstown Sheet and Tube Co.* v. *Sawyer*, 343 U.S. 579, 637 (1952).

18. *Ibid.*, 642. Jackson rejected the government's argument that the President could invest himself with the war powers by committing armed forced to foreign hostilities.

19. Eagleton, *War and Presidential Power*, 10; Berger, *Executive Privilege*, 39–40; Spong, 6 *Richmond L. Rev.*, 4; Eagleton, 37 *Mo. L. Rev.*, 4.

20. See King, 18 *Harvard Int'l. L. J.*, 58–63. King and Leavens array military conduct along a continuum that includes peacetime deployments, actions that threaten war, and acts of war. Their continuum is based on (1) the magnitude of hostilities, which is a function of scale and duration, and (2) the "political content" of military conduct. As the authors admit, however, few uses of military force are

apolitical. Moreover, the political content of military actions depends on the context as well as the perceptions and subjective evaluations of international actors. The dispatch of a U.S. fleet to participate in NATO training exercises in the Baltic, for example, can have high political content in relation to internal unrest in Poland. Given the empirical and theoretical difficulty of arraying events according to their political content, Figure 4.3 arrays military and diplomatic actions solely according to their magnitude, i.e., scale (of escalation) and duration.

21. *Youngstown Sheet and Tube Co.* v. *Sawyer*, 343 U.S. 579, 635 (1952).

22. *Ibid.*, 635–637.

23. *Ibid.* 637.

24. *Ibid.*

25. *Ibid.*, 662.

26. *Ibid.*, 637.

27. *Ibid.*, 638.

28. *Ibid.*, 653–654.

29. *Ibid.*, 637, 640.

30. *Ibid.*, 635, 645.

31. *Duncan* v. *Kahanamoku*, 327 U.S. 304 (1946); *Ex parte White*, 66 F. Supp. 982 (D. Hawaii 1944).

32. *Duncan* v. *Kahanamoku*, 327 U.S. 304, 309, 310, 311–312 (1946). In a separate concurring opinion, Justice Murphy also noted that the military emergency had long since passed by the time Duncan was tried in a provost court on March 2, 1944. 327 U.S. 304, 326–328, 329–330. Chief Justice Stone observed that if a military threat existed it had long since passed. Indeed, the military authorities had reopened places of amusement as early as December 24, 1941, an indication that the immediate threat of invasion was over. 327 U.S. 304, 336–337.

33. *Ex parte White*, 66 F. Supp. 982, 984–985 (D. Hawaii 1944).

34. *Youngstown Sheet and Tube Co.* v. *Sawyer*, 343 U.S. 579, 645–646 (1952).

35. *Ibid.*, 597.

36. *Ibid.*, 594–597, 645.

37. *Bas* v. *Tingy*, 4 U.S. (4 Dall.) 37 (1800); *Talbot* v. *Seeman*, 4 U.S. (4 Dall.) 34 (1800).

38. See the opinions of Justices Washington, Chase, and Paterson at 4 U.S. (4 Dall.) 37, 40, 43, 45, respectively.

39. *Ibid.*, 43.

40. *Ibid.*, 40, 41.

41. *Ibid.*, 39, 40, 41, 42, 43–44, 45–46.

42. *Little* v. *Barreme*, 6 U.S. (2 Cranch) 170 (1804).

43. *Ibid.*, 172–173, 175.

44. *Ibid.*, 175–176; "An Act further to suspend the Commercial Intercourse between the United States and France, and the dependencies thereof," 1 Stat. 613, 615, Ch. 2, Sec. 5 (1799).

45. *Little* v. *Barreme*, 6 U.S. (2 Cranch) 170, 177–178 (1804).

46. *Ibid.*

47. *Ibid.*, 179.

48. *Brown* v. *U.S.*, 12 U.S. (8 Cranch) 110 (1814).

49. *Ibid.*, 121–122.

50. See Justice Story's dissenting opinion in *Brown* v. *U.S.*, 12 U.S. (8 Cranch) 110, 150 (1814). Story had pronounced the circuit court's opinion as circuit justice in *The Emulous*, 8 F. Cas. 697, 703–704 (C.C. D. Mass. 1813) (No. 4,479).

51. *Brown* v. *U.S.*, 12 U.S. (8 Cranch) 110, 125–126 (1814).

52. *Ibid.*

53. *Ibid.*, 126–127, 128–129. According to Marshall, when war occurs " . . . the question, what shall be done with enemy property in our country, is a question rather of policy than of law." 12 U.S. (8 Cranch) 110, 128. Only Congress can determine the policy question since the Constitution vests the auxiliary war powers exclusively in the legislature. 12 U.S. (8 Cranch) 110, 128–129.

54. *Ibid.*, 145, 148–149.

55. *Ibid.*, 145.

56. *Ibid.*, 149–150.

57. *Ibid.*, 147.

58. *Ibid.*, 152.

59. *Foster* v. *Neilson*, 27 U.S. (2 Pet.) 253 (1829).

60. *United States* v. *Smith*, 27 F. Cas. 1192 (C.C. D. N.Y. 1806) (No. 16,342).

61. *Ibid.*, 1243–1244.

62. 1 Stat. 381, 384, Ch. 50 (1794).

63. *United States* v. *Smith*, 27 F. Cas. 1192, 1196 (C.C. D. N.Y. 1806) (No. 16,342).

64. *Ibid.*, 1230.

65. *Ibid.*, 1230–1231, 1243.

66. 1 Stat. 424, Ch. 36 (1795).

67. *United States* v. *Smith*, 27 F. Cas. 1192, 1230 (C.C. D. N.Y. 1806) (No. 16,342).

68. *Ibid.*, 1229, 1230, 1231.

69. *Durand* v. *Hollins*, 8 F. Cas. 111 (C.C. S.D. N.Y. 1860) (No. 4,186).

70. *Ibid.*, 112.

71. *Ibid.*

72. *Ibid.*

73. *Ibid.*

74. On Lincoln's assumption of dictatorial power during the Civil War, see Rossiter, *American Presidency*, 99–101; Binkley, *Powers*, 133; Upton, *Military Policy*, 229–230.

75. Binkley, *President and Congress*, 136.

76. 25 U.S. (12 Wheat.) 19 (1827); 1 Stat. 424, Ch. 36 (1795).

77. See Carl B. Swisher, *American Constitutional Development* (New York: Houghton Mifflin Co., 1943), 295–296: hereinafter cited as Swisher, *American Constitutional Development*; Charles C. Tansill, "War Powers of the President of the United States with Special Reference to the Beginning of Hostilities," *Political Science Quarterly* 45 (March 1930): 1–55, 52–53: hereinafter cited as Tansill, 45 *Political Science Q.*

78. Binkley *President and Congress*, 136, 138.

79. *The Parkhill*, 18 F. Cas. 1187, 1196–1197 (D.C. E.D. Pa. 1861) (No. 10,755a).

80. *Ibid.*, 1189.

81. *Ibid.*, 1191.

82. *Ibid.*, 1191, 1197, 1194–1195.

83. *Ibid.*, 1195.

84. *Ibid.*, 1196–1197.

85. *Ibid.*, 1197.

86. *Ibid.*, italics added.

87. *Ibid.*

88. *The Prize Cases*, 67 U.S. (2 Black) 635, 674–682 (1863).

89. *The Amy Warwick*, 1 F. Cas. 815 (D.C. D. Mass. 1862) (No. 344); *The Crenshaw*, 6 F. Cas. 803 (C.C. S.D. N.Y. 1861) (No. 3,384); *The Hiawatha*, 12 F. Cas. 95 (D.C. S.D. N.Y. 1861) (No. 6,451).

90. *The Prize Cases*, 67 U.S. (2 Black) 635, 668, 668–669 (1863).

91. *Ibid.*, 670.

92. *Ibid.*, 688–689, 690–693.

93. *Ibid.*, 692.

94. *Ibid.*, 697–698.

95. *Ibid.*, 697.

96. *Hanger* v. *Abbott*, 73 U.S. (6 Wall.) 532 (1868); *Levy* v. *Stewart*, 78 U.S. (11 Wall.) 244 (1871); *The Protector*, 79 U.S. (12 Wall.) 700 (1872).

97. *The Protector*, 79 U.S. (12 Wall.) 700, 701–702 (1872).

98. *Matthews* v. *McStea*, 91 U.S. 7, 9 (1875).

99. *Ibid.*, 13.

100. *Ibid.*, 11.

101. *Ibid.*

102. *Williams* v. *Bruffy*, 96 U.S. 176 (1877).

103. *Ibid.*, 188–190, 192.

104. *Ibid.*, 189–190.

CHAPTER 5 (PAGES 110 TO 134)

1. See Justice Grier's opinion in *The Prize Cases*, 67 U.S. (2 Black) 635, 669 (1863).

2. On August 2, 1964, three North Vietnamese patrol boats launched a torpedo and machine-gun attack on the U.S. destroyer *Maddox*. Two days later, on August 4, the U.S. Government claims that a second encounter occurred between North Vietnamese patrol boats and the destroyers *Maddox* and *C. Turner Joy*. On August 5, President Lyndon B. Johnson ordered reprisal raids, which were carried out that day. See *U.S. Congress, House of Representatives, Committee on Armed Services*, United States–Vietnam Relations, 1945–1967, A Study Prepared by The Department of Defense, 12 vols. (Washington, D.C.: Government Print. Off., 1971), Book 4, Part 4, c. 2. (b), "Evolution of the War: Military Pressures against North Vietnam, July–October 1964," 5–11: hereinafter cited as *Pentagon Papers*.

3. Beginning in 1954, Congress authorized direct military assistance to Cambodia, Laos, and Vietnam. See Mutual Security Act of 1954, Ch. 937, Sec. 121, 68 Stat. 832, 837 (1954); Foreign Assistance Act of 1961, 75 Stat. 424 (1961). Under these two acts, Congress authorized direct military, economic, technical, and other assistance to Indochina between 1954 and 1964. By June 30, 1962, Congress had authorized $996,000,000 in direct military assistance to Indochina, of which $760,000,000 went to Vietnam. Between 1954 and 1964 Congress also authorized $1,698,000,000 in nonmilitary assistance to Vietnam. See *Congressional Quarterly Almanac, 1963*, Vol. 19 (Washington, D.C.: Congressional Quarterly, Inc., 1963), 299: hereinafter cited as *C.Q. Almanac*; *Congress and The Nation, 1945–1964*, Vol. 1 (Washington, D.C.: Congressional Quarterly, Inc., 1965), 166: hereinafter cited as *Congress and The Nation*. Congress supported every American President, from Harry Truman to Lyndon Johnson, in his initiative to provide military and other assistance to Vietnam, Laos, and Cambodia.

4. See *C.Q. Almanac, 1967*, Vol. 23 (1968), 946; *U.S. Congress, Senate, Committee on Foreign Relations*, Report on Security Agreements and Commitments Abroad, 91st Congress, 2nd Session, December 21, 1970 (Washington, D.C.: Government Print. Off., 1970), 3: hereinafter cited as *Senate, Comm. on For. Rel.*, Report on Security Agreements.

5. *Pentagon Papers*, Book 1, Part 4, A. 2, 10.

6. *Ibid.*, Book 1, Part 4, A. 2, 15. The number of U.S. military advisors increased from 70 in 1950 to 342 in 1954.

7. The Mutual Security Act of 1954, Ch. 937, Sec. 121, 68 Stat. 832, 837 (1954).

8. 101 *Cong. Rec.* 1060 (1955).

9. Although the United States wanted to include these nations as members of SEATO, such membership would have contravened the Geneva Agreements. Therefore, the SEATO signatories simply extended the treaty's protection to Laos, Cambodia, and Vietnam. See *Pentagon Papers*, Book 1, Part 4, A.1, 21 and A.3, ix–x.

10. *Ibid.*, Book 2, Part 4, A.4, 1.1.

11. *U.S. Congress, Senate, Committee on Foreign Relations*, Background Information Relating to Southeast Asia and Vietnam, 93rd Congress, 2nd Session, December 1974 (Washington, D.C.: Government Print. Off., 1975), 5: hereinafter cited as *Senate, Comm. on For. Rel.*, Background Information; *Pentagon Papers*, Book 2, Part 4, A.4, 6.1.PP.

12. *Senate, Comm. on For. Rel.*, Background Information, 6; *Pentagon Papers*, Book 2, Part 4, A.4, 6.1.QQ.

13. *Congress and the Nation*, 1969–1972, Vol. 3 (1973), 901.

14. *Senate, Comm. on For. Rel.*, Background Information, 19, 20, 21.

15. See Anthony Austin, *The President's War* (Philadelphia: J.B. Lippincott, 1971), 42–43, 100–102: hereinafter cited as Austin, *President's War*; *U.S. Congress, Senate, Senate Journal*, 88th Congress, 2nd Session (1964), 496; 110 *Cong. Rec.* 18399, 18443, 18444, 18445, 18446, 18555, 18470 (1964). Despite his growing concern about presidential power, Fulbright urged his colleagues to support the resolution, which he believed was calculated to prevent the spread of war.

16. On the purpose and function of the Southeast Asia Resolution, see Eugene

G. Windchy, *Tonkin Gulf* (Garden City, N.Y.: Doubleday & Co., 1971), especially 33–35, 326–327: hereinafter cited as Windchy, *Tonkin Gulf*; Kenneth N. Waltz, *Foreign Policy and Democratic Politics: The American and British Experience* (Boston: Little, Brown & Co., 1967), especially 289–290: hereinafter cited as Waltz, *Foreign Policy*; Austin, *President's War*, 84, 90–93, 94–95; Velvel, *Undeclared War*, 5–6; George E. Reedy, *The Twilight of the Presidency* (New York: World Publishing Co., 1970), 40: hereinafter cited as Reedy, *Twilight of the Presidency*; Van Alstyne, 121 *Pennsylvania L. Rev.*, 1, 9, 10; Philip B. Kurland, "The Impotence of Reticence," *Duke Law Journal* 1968 (August 1968): 619–636, 625: hereinafter cited as Kurland, *1968 Duke L. J.*; Eugene V. Rostow, "Great Cases Make Bad Law: The War-Powers Act," *Texas Law Review* 50 (May 1972): 833–900, 878, 880–881, 882–885: hereinafter cited as Rostow, 50 *Texas L. Rev.*; Eagleton, 37 *Mo. L. Rev.*, 14–15.

17. PL 88–408 [H.J. Res. 1145], 78 Stat. 384 (1964), approved by the President, August 10, 1964; Italics added.

18. Formosa Resolution of 1955, PL 84–4 [H.J. Res. 159], 69 Stat. 7, approved by the President, January 29, 1955; Middle East Resolution of 1957, PL 85–7 [H.J. Res. 117], 71 Stat. 5, approved by the President, March 9, 1957; see also 110 *Cong. Rec.* 18403–18404, 18409 (1964).

19. 110 *Cong. Rec.* 18399; Italics added.

20. *Ibid.*, 18443–18444.

21. Statements of Undersecretary of State Nicholas deB. Katzenbach, *U.S. Congress, Senate, Committee on Foreign Relations*, Hearings on S. Res. 151, 90th Congress, 1st Session, August 16–September 19, 1967 (Washington, D.C.: Government Print. Off., 1967), 82–83: hereinafter cited as *Senate, Comm. on For. Rel.*, Hearings on S. Res. 151.

22. *Senate, Comm. on For. Rel.*, Background Information, 66.

23. Richard M. Nixon, *The Public Papers of the Presidents of the United States, 1973* (Washington, D.C.: Government Print. Off., 1975), 18–20: hereinafter cited as Nixon, *Public Papers*; *Senate, Comm. on For. Rel.*, Background Information, 180.

24. *Senate, Comm. on For. Rel.*, Background Information, 90; U.S. Department of Defense, Comptroller, *Selected Manpower Statistics* (Washington, D.C.: Dep't. of Def., April 15, 1973), 37: hereinafter cited as *Selected Manpower Statistics*.

25. *Senate, Comm. on For. Rel.*, Background Information, 103; *New York Times*, 3 May 1970, 1, 2; *Idem.*, 4 May 1970, 1, 7.

26. *Senate, Comm. on For. Rel.*, Background Information, 142, 145, 151.

27. Nixon, *Public Papers, 1972*, (1974), 585.

28. *Senate, Comm. on For. Rel.*, Background Information, 173.

29. See the Defense Procurement Authorization Act, PL 91–121 [S. 2546], 83 Stat. 204 (1969); The Defense Appropriations Act, PL 91–171 [H.R. 15090], 83 Stat. 469 (1969).

30. The Foreign Military Sales Act, extension, PL 91–672 [H.R. 15628], 84 Stat. 2053, 2055 (1970); Nixon, *Public Papers, 1970*, (1971), 546, 547.

31. The Supplemental Foreign Aid Authorization Act, PL 91–652 [H.R. 19911],

84 Stat. 1942, 1943 (1971); The Defense Procurement Act, PL 91–441 [H.R. 17123], 84 Stat. 905, 910 (1970).

32. *Congress and the Nation, 1969–1972*, Vol. 3 (1973), 916.

33. See PL 92–129 [H.R. 6531], 85 Stat. 348, 360–361 (1971); PL 92–156 [H.R. 8687], 85 Stat. 423, 428, 430 (1971); Nixon, *Public Papers, 1971*, (1972), 1114.

34. The Defense Procurement Act, PL 92–436 [H.R. 15495], 86 Stat. 734, 738, (1972); *Congress and The Nation, 1969–1972*, Vol. 3 (1973), 929–930.

35. Nixon, *Public Papers, 1973*, (1975), 621–622; PL 93–52 [H.J. Res. 636], 87 Stat. 130, 134 (1973).

36. *Youngstown Sheet & Tube Co. v. Sawyer*, 343 U.S. 579, 637 (1952).

37. *Ibid.*, 635.

38. PL 88–408 [H.J. Res. 1145], 78 Stat. 384.

39. *Youngstown Sheet & Tube Co. v. Sawyer*, 343 U.S. 579, 637 (1952).

40. See, for example, Nixon, *Public Papers, 1970*, (1971), 405–410. In his address to the nation, Nixon warned the North Vietnamese

> . . . that if they continue to escalate the fighting when the United States is withdrawing its forces, I shall meet my responsibility as Commander in Chief of our Armed Forces to take the action I consider necessary to defend the security of our American men. . . . We will not allow American men by the thousands to be killed by an enemy from privileged sanctuaries; at 408.

Also see Henry Kissinger, *White House Years* (Boston: Little, Brown & Co., 1979), 497, 504–505: hereinafter cited as Kissinger, *White House Years*. Kissinger argues that the Cambodian invasion was " . . . an essentially defensive operation, limited in both time and space, . . . " whose purpose was to prevent massive infiltration along the Cambodian frontier during the Vietnamization process.

41. See William Shawcross, *Sideshow: Kissinger, Nixon, and the Destruction of Cambodia* (New York: Simon & Schuster, 1979), 144–148: hereinafter cited as Shawcross, *Sideshow*. Shawcross argues that the Cambodian incursion widened the war and was an offensive rather than a defensive measure.

42. *U.S. Congress, House of Representatives, Committee on Foreign Affairs*, Hearings on Congress, the President, and the War Powers, 91st Congress, 2d Session, June, July, and August 1970 (Washington, D.C.: Government Print. Off., 1970), 40–41, 158–159, 497–504: hereinafter cited as *House of Representatives, Comm. on For. Aff.*, Hearings on the War Powers; William D. Rogers, "The Constitutionality of the Cambodian Incursion," 175–186, in Richard A. Falk, ed., *The Vietnam War and International Law*, Vol. 3 (Princeton, N.J.: Princeton Univ. Press, 1972): hereinafter cited as Falk, *The Vietnam War*.

43. *House of Representatives, Comm. on For. Aff.*, Hearings on the War Powers, 157, 539–544, 545–549; William H. Rehnquist, "The Constitutional Issues—Administration Position," 163–174, in Falk, *The Vietnam War*; Robert H. Bork, "Commentary," 187, in Falk, *The Vietnam War*.

44. *Congress and The Nation, 1973–1976*, Vol. 4 (1977), 890–891.

45. *U.S. Congress, Senate, Special Committee on the Termination of the National Emergency*, Hearings, Part 1, Constitutional Questions Concerning Emergency Powers, 93rd Congress, 1st Session, April 11 and 12, 1973 (Washington, D.C.: Government Print. Off., 1973), 60–61: hereinafter cited as *Senate, Special Comm. on Nat'l. Emergency*, Hearings, Constitutional Questions; *Guide to Congress*, 2nd ed. (Washington, D.C.: Congressional Quarterly, Inc., 1976), 272: hereinafter cited as *Guide to Congress*.

46. See *Holtzman v. Schlesinger*, 361 F. Supp. 553 (E.D. N.Y.), rev'd 484 F. 2d 1307 (2nd Cir.), *order stayed* 414 U.S. 1321, *cert. denied* 416 U.S. 936 (1973); *Mottola v. Nixon*, 318 F. Supp. 538 (N.D. Calif. 1970), *rev'd* 464 F. 2d 178 (9th Cir. 1972); *Berk v. Laird* (1), 429 F 2d 302 (2nd Cir.), *aff'd Orlando v. Laird*, 443 F. 2d 1039 (2nd Cir.), *cert. denied* 404 U.S. 869 (1971); *Da Costa v. Laird*, 471 F. 2d 1386 (2nd Cir.), *cert. denied* 405 U.S. 979 (1972).

47. *Luftig v. McNamara*, 252 F. Supp. 819 (D. D.C. 1966), *aff'd* 373 F. 2d 664 (D.C. Cir), *cert. denied* 387 U.S. 945 (1967); *Mora v. McNamara*, 387 F. 2d 862 (D.C. Cir.), *cert. denied* 389 U.S. 934 (1967).

48. 373 F. 2d 664, 665, 665–666 (D.C. Cir. 1967).

49. *Velvel v. Johnson*, 287 F. Supp. 846 (D. Kan. 1968), *aff'd sub nom. Velvel v. Nixon*, 415 F. 2d 236 (10th Cir.), *cert. denied* 396 U.S. 1042 (1970); *United States v. Sisson* (1), 294 F. Supp. 511 (D. Mass. 1968); *Davi v. Laird*, 318 F. Supp. 478 (W.D. Va. 1970); *Meyers v. Nixon*, 339 F. Supp. 1388 (S.D. N.Y. 1972); *Atlee v. Laird*, 347 F. Supp. 689 (E.D. Pa. 1972)', *aff'd sub nom. Atlee v. Richardson*, 411 U.S. 911 (1973); *Drinan v. Nixon*, 364 F. Supp. 854 (D. Mass.), *aff'd* 502 F. 2d 1158 (1st Cir. 1973).

50. *Berk v. Laird* (1), 429 F. 2d 302 (2nd Cir.), *aff'd Orlando v. Laird*, 443 F. 2d 1039 (2nd Cir.), *cert. denied* 404 U.S. 869 (1971); *Orlando v. Laird*, 317 F. Supp. 1013 (E.D. N.Y. 1970); *Da Costa v. Laird*, 448 F. 2d 1386 (2nd Cir.), *cert. denied* 405 U.S. 979 (1972); *Massachusetts v. Laird*, 327 F. Supp. 378 (D. Mass.), *aff'd* 451 F. 2d 26 (1st Cir. 1971).

51. *Mottola v. Nixon*, 318 F. Supp. 538 (N.D. Calif. 1970), *rev'd* 464 F. 2d 178 (9th Cir. 1972); *Holtzman v. Schlesinger*, 361 F. Supp. 553 (E.D. N.Y.), *rev'd* 484 F. 2d 1307 (2nd Cir.), *order stayed* 414 U.S. 1321, *cert. denied* 416 U.S. 936 (1973).

52. 252 F. Supp. 819, 821 (D. D.C. 1966).

53. *Ibid.*, 819.

54. 373 F. 2d 664, 666 (D.C. Cir. 1967).

55. *Ibid.*, 665.

56. *Ibid.*, 665–666.

57. 287 F. Supp. 846, 848 (D. Kan. 1968).

58. *Ibid.*, 846, 850.

59. *Ibid.*

60. *Ibid.*, 852.

61. *Ibid.*, 852, 853.

62. 294 F. Supp. 511, 515 (D. Mass. 1968) (*Sisson* I). In addition to challenging the constitutionality of waging war without a congressional declaration of war, Sisson also questioned the legality of the war under various treaties and international

law. See *U.S.* v. *Sisson*, 294 F. Supp. 515 (D. Mass. 1968) (*Sisson* II). Finally, Sisson challenged the U.S. action in Vietnam as violating Article 51 of the United Nations Charter. See *U.S.* v. *Sisson*, 294 F. Supp. 520 (D. Mass. 1968) (*Sisson* III).

63. *Sisson* I, 294 F. Supp. 511, 512.

64. *Ibid.*, 512–513, 515.

65. *Ibid.*, 514.

66. *Ibid.*, 514, 515.

67. *Ibid.*, 515.

68. 318 F. Supp. 478, 484 (W.D. Va. 1970).

69. *Ibid.*, 479.

70. *Ibid.* Also see *Baker* v. *Carr*, 369 U.S. 186, 211–214 (1962), in which the Court enumerates a series of issues that raises political questions, e.g., whether a treaty is in force, whether the U.S. recognizes a foreign government, or whether hostilities exist. However, the Court argued that " . . . it is error to suppose that every case or controversy which touches foreign relations lies beyond judicial cognizance." At 211.

71. *Powell* v. *McCormack*, 395 U.S. 486, 521, 548 (1969).

72. *Ibid.*, 548–549.

73. 318 F. Supp. 478, 482, 483 (W.D. Va. 1970).

74. *Ibid.*, 480.

75. *Ibid.*

76. *Ibid.*, 481.

77. *Ibid.*, 480, 481.

78. *Ibid.*, 481.

79. *Ibid.*, 481–482.

80. *Ibid.*, 482.

81. *Ibid.*, 483.

82. 339 F. Supp. 1388, 1389–1391 (S.D. N.Y. 1972).

83. *Ibid.*, 1390.

84. *Ibid.*

85. *Atlee* v. *Laird*, 347 F. Supp. 689, 691, 705, 706 (E.D. Pa. 1972).

86. *Ibid.*, 692.

87. *Ibid.*

88. *C. & S. Airlines* v. *Waterman S.S. Corp.*, 333 U.S. 103, 111 (1948); See also: *Luther* v. *Borden*, 48 U.S. (7 How.) 1, 42, 47 (1849); *the Prize Cases*, 67 U.S. (2 Black) 635, 670 (1863); *Mississippi* v. *Johnson*, 71 U.S. (4 Wall.) 475, 499 (1867); *In re Biaz*, 135 U.S. 403, 432 (1890); *Oetjen* v. *Central Leather Co.*, 246 U.S. 297, 302 (1918).

89. 347 F. Supp. 689, 697, 701 (E.D. Pa. 1972).

90. *Ibid.*, 696.

91. *Ibid.*, 698.

92. See *Baker* v. *Carr*, 369 U.S. 186, 211–212 (1962).

93. 347 F. Supp. 689, 701 (E.D. Pa. 1972).

94. *Ibid.*, 700.

95. *Ibid.*, 703.

96. *Ibid.*, 705, 706, 707.

97. *Ibid.*, 702.
98. *Ibid.*
99. *Ibid.*, 702, 705, 707.
100. *Ibid.*, 703.
101. *Ibid.*, 704–705.
102. *Ibid.*, 705.
103. *Ibid.*, 706.
104. *Ibid.*, 708.
105. *Ibid.*, 709.
106. *Ibid.*, 710.
107. *Ibid.*, 711.
108. *Ibid.*
109. *Ibid.*, 712.
110. *Ibid.*
111. *Ibid.*, 713.
112. *Ibid.*; also see *Powell* v. *McCormack*, 395 U.S. 486, 549 (1969).
113. 347 F. Supp. 689, 707 (E.D. Pa. 1972).
114. *Ibid.*, 708.
115. *Ibid.*
116. *Cohens* v. *Virginia*, 19 U.S. (6 Wheat.) 264, 404 (1821).
117. 347 F. Supp. 689, 709 (E.D. Pa. 1972).
118. *Drinan* v. *Nixon*, 364 F. Supp. 854, 856 (D. Mass. 1973).
119. *Ibid.*, 855.
120. *Ibid.*, 856, 856–857.
121. *Ibid.*, 856, 857, 858.
122. *Ibid.*, 858; Italics added.
123. *Ibid.*
124. *Ibid.*, 858, 859.
125. *Ibid.*, 859.
126. *Ibid.*, 859–860.
127. *Ibid.*, 860, 866–867.
128. *Ibid.*, 860.
129. *Ibid.*
130. *Ibid.*, 862, 863–864.
131. *Ibid.*, 865.
132. *Ibid.*
133. See *Baker* v. *Carr*, 369 U.S. 186, 217 (1962).

Chapter 6 (pages 135 to 160)

1. 395 U.S. 486 (1969).
2. See, for example, Chief Judge Joseph Lord's dissenting opinion in *Atlee* v. *Laird*, 347 F. Supp. 689, 710 (E.D. Pa. 1972). Also see Judge William Sweigert's opinion in *Mottola* v. *Nixon*, 318 F. Supp. 538, 550–551 (N.D. Calif. 1970), Judge Orrin Judd's opinion in *Holtzman* v. *Richardson*, 361 F. Supp. 544, 551–552 (E.D.

N.Y. 1973), and Judge Charles Wyzanski's opinion in *Mitchell* v. *Laird*, 488 F. 2d 611, 614 (D.C. Cir. 1973).

3. 395 U.S. 486, 512, 517, 518–521, 548–549 (1969).

4. See President Nixon's message to Congress vetoing H.R. 7447, 93rd Congress, 1st Session (1973), the Second Supplemental Appropriations Act of 1973, as an interference with his Vietnamization and withdrawal programs, Nixon, *Public Papers, 1973* (1975), 621–622.

5. 488 F. 2d 611, 614, 616 (D.C. Cir. 1973).

6. *Ibid.*, 613. Citing *Mississippi* v. *Johnson*, 71 U.S. (4 Wall.) 475, 499–501 (1867) as authority, the district court dismissed the complaint against the President as an interference with the discretionary power that the Constitution confers exclusively on his office. The district court also dismissed the complaint against the secretary of defense and the other defendants, citing *Luftig* v. *McNamara*, 373 F. 2d 664 (D.C. Cir. 1967), as authority.

7. 488 F. 2d 611, 614 (D.C. Cir. 1973). Massachusetts District Judge Charles Wyzanski, sitting on the D.C. Circuit Court by designation, wrote the court's opinion, which rests on the assumption that beyond a measurable threshold, as determined by a war's magnitude and duration, the President's actions become aggressive or offensive rather than defensive in character.

8. *Ibid.*

9. *Ibid.*, 615. Also see the discussion of *Berk* v. *Laird, Orlando* v. *Laird*, and *Massachusetts* v. *Laird, infra.*

10. 488 F. 2d 611, 614–615 (D.C. Cir. 1973).

11. *Ibid.*, 615, italics added. Although numerous appropriations and authorization acts had ratified the President's military conduct, Judge Wyzanski argued that the legislative history demonstrated that Congress had not actually endorsed presidential action. In contrast to Wyzanski's reliance on legislative history, other Federal judges argued that the record was ambiguous while the language of the statutes was clear on its face. Under the circumstances, there was no need or justification for relying on the record. See Judge Mulligan's opinion in *Holtzman* v. *Schlesinger*, 484 F. 2d 1307, 1314 (2nd Cir. 1973) and Justice Jackson's concurring opinion in *Schwegman Brothers* v. *Calvert Distillers Corp.*, 341 U.S. 384, 395–396 (1951).

12. 488 F. 2d 611, 615 (D.C. Cir. 1973).

13. *Ibid.*, 616. In deferring to the executive, Judge Wyzanski accepted both functional and pragmatic rationale for judicial self-restraint. Unless presidential conduct amounts to a serious breach of faith, the courts should not interfere with delicate international negotiations and bargaining designed to resolve international conflict.

14. *Ibid.*, 614, 616.

15. See Circuit Judge Robert Anderson's opinion in *Berk* v. *Laird*, 429 F. 2d 302, 305 (2nd Cir. 1970).

16. *Orlando* v. *Laird*, 443 F. 2d 1039, 1043 (2nd Cir. 1971).

17. 429 F. 2d 302, 304, 306 (2nd Cir. 1970).

18. *Ibid.*, 305.

19. *Ibid.*

20. *Ibid.*, 305–306.

21. *Ibid.*, 305.

22. *Ibid.*, 306.

23. *Berk* v. *Laird*, 317 F. Supp. 715, 716 (E.D. N.Y. 1970).

24. *Ibid.*, 728–729.

25. *Ibid.*, 717–718.

26. *Ibid.*, 717.

27. *Ibid.*

28. *Ibid.*, 718, 721–722. Also see 5th Cong. Sess. 2, c. 48, 1 Stat. 561 (1798); 7th Cong. Sess. 1, c. 4, 2 Stat. 129 (1802); 13th Cong. Sess. 2, c. 90, 3 Stat. 230 (1815); 63rd Cong. Sess. 2 [H.J. Res. 251], 38 Stat. 770 (1914); PL 84–4 [H.J. Res. 159], 69 Stat. 7 (1955); PL 85–7 [H.J. Res. 117], 71 Stat. 5 (1957); PL 87–733 [S.J. Res. 230], 76 Stat. 697 (1962); [H. Con. R. 570], 76 Stat. 1429 (1962).

29. 317 F. Supp. 715, 723 (E.D. N.Y. 1970).

30. *Ibid.*, 727.

31. *Ibid.*

32. *Ibid.*, 728. In contrast to *Greene* v. *McElroy*, 360 U.S. 474, 506 (1958), Judd argued that Congress enacted appropriations bills with full knowledge of the government's purpose. Since Congress was aware of the government's policies, the appropriations acts constituted ratification of the President's military actions.

33. 317 F. Supp. 715, 728–729 (E.D. N.Y. 1970).

34. 317 F. Supp. 1013, 1016, 1018–1019 (E.D. N.Y. 1970). Judge Dooling argued that the existence of valid congressional authorization for the President's military conduct presented a "purely judicial question."

35. Inasmuch as an exclusive textual commitment of the power to declare war exists, only Congress can make the initial policy determination required by Article 1, Section 8 (Cl. 11). See *Powell* v. *McCormack*, 395 U.S. 486, 518–519 (1969).

36. 317 F. Supp. 1013, 1017, (E.D. N.Y. 1970). Strictly speaking, the commander-in-chief clause confers an office on the President. Whatever power the commander in chief possesses derives from the vesting, take-care, and other clauses of Article 2 in addition to the powers that Congress delegates to the President.

37. *Ibid.*, 1017, 1018; Also see King, 18 *Harvard Int'l. L. J.*, 58, 60, 63.

38. 317 F. Supp. 1013, 1018–1019, 1020 (E.D. N.Y. 1970). As King and Leavens observe, neither Judge Dooling nor any other Federal judge who employed the threshold theory defined the precise point at which a war requires joint congressional-presidential participation. King, 18 *Harvard Int'l. L. J.*, 60.

39. *Orlando* v. *Laird*, 443 F. 2d 1039, 1039–1040 (2nd Cir. 1971).

40. *Ibid.*, 1042–1043.

41. *Ibid.*, 1043.

42. *Ibid.*

43. *Ibid.*

44. 448 F. 2d 1368, 1369 (2nd Cir. 1971).

45. *Ibid.*

46. *Ibid.*, 1370.

47. 327 F. Supp. 378, 381 (D. Mass. 1971).

48. *Ibid.*, 380–381.

49. *Massachusetts* v. *Laird*, 451 F. 2d 26 (1st Cir. 1971).

50. *Ibid.*, 30–31, 34.

51. *Ibid.*

52. *Ibid.*

53. *Ibid.*, 31–32.

54. *Ibid.*, 32–33.

55. *Ibid.*, 34.

56. *Mottola* v. *Nixon*, 318 F. Supp. 538, 548–551, (N.D. Calif. 1970); *Holtzman* v. *Richardson*, 361 F. Supp. 544, 551–552 (E.D. N.Y. 1973); *Holtzman* v. *Schlesinger*, 361 F. Supp. 553, 561–562 (E.D. N.Y. 1973).

57. 318 F. Supp. 538, 550 (N.D. Calif, 1970). In *Youngstown Sheet & Tube Co.* v. *Sawyer*, 343 U.S. 579, 585, 587–588 (1952), the Court asserted its power to construe the President's authority, under the vesting and commander-in-chief clauses, to seize "private property in order to keep labor disputes from stopping production." At 587.

58. 318 F. Supp. 538, 550–552 (N.D. Calif. 1970).

59. *Ibid.*, 552.

60. *Ibid.*, 553, 554.

61. *Ibid.*, 553.

62. *Ibid.*

63. *Ibid.*, 554.

64. *Ibid.*, 541.

65. *Ibid.*, 541–542; 6 *United States Treaties* 81, 83; T.I.A.S. No. 3170. Article 4, Section 1 of the Southeast Asia Collective Defense Treaty provides that:

> Each Party recognizes that aggression by means of armed attack in the treaty area against any of the Parties or against any State or territory which the Parties by unanimous agreement may hereafter designate, would endanger its own peace and safety, and agrees that it will in that event act to meet the common danger *in accordance with its constitutional processes.* [Italics added.]

66. 318 F. Supp. 538, 542–543 (N.D. Calif. 1970).

67. *Ibid.*, 553.

68. *Ibid.*, 543.

69. *Ibid.*, 543–545.

70. *Ibid.*, 544.

71. *Ibid.*, 545.

72. On July 13, 1972, the Court of Appeals for the Ninth Circuit decided that Mottola and the other reservist-plaintiffs did not have standing to sue. Therefore, the court dismissed the complaint without determining any of the constitutional questions. See *Mottola* v. *Nixon*, 464 F. 2d 178 (9th Cir. 1972).

73. *Holtzman* v. *Richardson*, 361 F. Supp. 544, 551–552 (E.D. N.Y. 1973); *Holtzman* v. *Schlesinger*, 361 F. Supp. 553, 561–562 (E.D. N.Y. 1973).

74. 361 F. Supp. 553, 565–566 (E.D. N.Y. 1973).

75. See *Holtzman* v. *Schlesinger*, 484 F. 2d 1307 (2nd Cir. 1973), as analyzed in this chapter, *infra.*

76. 361 F. Supp. 544, 548–549, 550, 552 (E.D. N.Y. 1973).

77. *Ibid.*, 551.

78. See *Atlee* v. *Laird*, 347 F. Supp. 689 (E.D. Pa. 1972), *aff'd sub nom. Atlee* v. *Richardson*, 411 U.S. 911 (1973), chap. 5, *supra.*

79. 361 F. Supp. 544, 551 (E.D. N.Y. 1973).

80. *Ibid.*

81. *Ibid.*, 552.

82. 361 F. Supp. 553, 564–566 (E.D. N.Y. 1973).

83. *Ibid.*

84. See PL 91–441 [H.R. 17123], 84 Stat. 905, 910 (1970); PL 92–204 [H.R. 11731], 85 Stat. 716, 734 (1971); PL 92–436 [H.R. 15495], 86 Stat. 734, 738 (1972); PL 92–570 [H.R. 16593], 86 Stat. 1184, 1202–1203 (1972).

85. PL 91–652 [H.R. 19911], 84 Stat. 1942, 1943 (1971).

86. *Ibid.*, PL 92–226 [S. 2819], 86 Stat. 20, 30 (1972).

87. 361 F. Supp. 553, 562–563, 565 (E.D. N.Y. 1973).

88. *Ibid.*, 559; 119 *Cong. Rec.* 15317–15318, 21544 (1973).

89. 361 F. Supp. 553, 560 (E.D. N.Y. 1973); H.R. 9055, 93rd Congress, 1st Session, 119 *Cong. Rec.* 22363–22364 (1973); H.J. Res. 636, 93rd Congress, 1st Session, 119 *Cong. Rec.* 22636–22637 (1973).

90. 361 F. Supp. 553, 559 (E.D. N.Y. 1973); 119 *Cong. Rec.* 21777–21778 (1973). By a vote of 241–173, on June 27, the House of Representatives failed to override the President's veto. On the same day, the Senate accepted Senator Eagleton's amendment to a bill continuing an increase in the debt ceiling, H.R. 8410 (by a vote of 67–29), 119 *Cong. Rec.* 21661 (1973). The amendment provided that: "No funds heretofore or hereafter appropriated under any Act of Congress may be obligated or expended to support directly or indirectly combat activities in, over, or from the shores of Cambodia or in or over Laos by United States forces" 119 *Cong. Rec.* 21659 (1973). The amended bill was passed by a vote of 72–19, 119 *Cong. Rec.* 21708 (1973). Inasmuch as the Senate passed the amended bill subsequent to the President's veto, one can argue that the vote registered the Senate's continuing opposition to the bombing of Cambodia.

On June 29, the Senate voted to adopt an amendment to H.J. Res. 636 (the continuing appropriation for 1974) offered by Senator Fulbright (by a vote of 64–26) delaying the effective date of the cutoff until August 15, 119 *Cong. Rec.* 22325 (1973). The Senate then voted to delete Senator Eagleton's amendment (58–31), 119 *Cong. Rec.* 22326 (1973).

91. On June 30, the House of Representatives ended the stalemate by agreeing to the conference report on H.J. Res. 636 (continuing appropriations for 1974), by a vote of 266–75, 119 *Cong. Rec.* 22636–22637 (1973). While acceptance of the conference report ended the impasse, considerable disagreement exists on the vote's implications. Did Congress actually authorize continuing the bombing until August 15 or merely provide the government with essential appropriations for the fiscal year 1974?

92. 361 F. Supp. 553, 563, 565 (E.D. N.Y. 1973).

93. *Ibid.*, 564, 565.

94. *Ibid.*, 564, 565–566.

95. *Holtzman v. Schlesinger*, 484 F. 2d 1307, 1308 (2nd Cir. 1973).

96. *Holtzman v. Schlesinger*, 414 U.S. 1304 (1973), Justice Marshall's Denial of Application to Vacate Stay, Opinion in Chambers. Also see Bob Woodward and Scott Armstrong, *The Brethren: Inside the Supreme Court* (New York: Simon & Schuster, 1979), 277–279: hereinafter cited as Woodward and Armstrong, *The Brethren*. Since Woodward and Armstrong do not document their book, one should exercise caution in accepting their work as authoritative. Nevertheless, their brief account of *Schlesinger v. Holtzman* is consistent with Justice Marshall's and Justice Douglas' opinions.

97. 414 U.S. 1304, 1311–1312 (1973).

98. *Ibid.*, 1312–1313. Bob Woodward and Scott Armstrong also argue that Marshall was " . . . predisposed to stop the bombing . . . but thought that it would be irresponsible to do so if it were only to be reinstated by a majority who would refuse to decide the constitutionality of the war in Southeast Asia." At 277. Want of a majority and the impending cessation of hostilities on August 15 apparently explain Marshall's brief and cautious order refusing to stop the bombing of Cambodia. See Woodward and Armstrong, *The Brethren*, 277.

99. 414 U.S. 1304, 1314 (1973).

100. *Ibid.*, 1314–1315.

101. *Holtzman v. Schlesinger*, 414 U.S. 1316, 1317, 1318, 1319 (1973), Justice Douglas, On Reapplication to Vacate Stay, issued August 3, released August 4, 1973.

102. In *Holmes v. U.S.*, *cert. denied* 391 U.S. 936, 948–949 (1967), Douglas argued that the Court should have granted certiorari to decide whether the government has the constitutional authority to conscript men during peacetime, i.e., in the absence of a declaration of war. Douglas believed that this important question deserved more than a simple, unexplained denial of certiorari.

In *Massachusetts v. Laird*, 400 U.S. 886, 896, 897 (1970), Douglas exposed his disagreement with the majority, arguing that the President's power to conduct armed hostilities without a congressional declaration of war poses a justiciable rather than a political question. Douglas' review of standing and the political-question doctrine suggests that the Court's denial of certiorari rests on the assumption that the complaint could not surmount these procedural barriers.

Although Douglas had been dissenting from the Court's denials of certiorari since 1966, only Potter Stewart had joined the dissent in 1967. In *Massachusetts v. Laird*, John Marshall Harlan joined the dissenters. Nevertheless, Douglas could not command the fourth vote necessary to grant cert. Apparently, Douglas' natural allies, Brennan and Black, could not overcome the political-question barrier. According to Woodward and Armstrong, Black believed that the entire war power was committed to Congress and the President to the exclusion of the courts. Only Congress could limit presidential power to initiate and wage an undeclared war. Unlike Black, Brennan believed that the Court could determine the issue " . . . only if Congress explicitly opposed the war and the President continued to conduct it." See Woodward and Armstrong, *The Brethren*, 125–128.

Douglas's other dissents from denials of certiorari are: *Sarnoff v. Schultz*, 409 U.S. 929 (1972), with Brennan concurring; *DaCosta v. Laird*, 405 U.S. 979 (1972);

McArthur v. *Clifford*, 393 U.S. 1002 (1968); *Hart* v. *U.S.*, 391 U.S. 956 (1968); *Mora* v. *McNamara*, 389 U.S. 934 (1967), with Stewart concurring; *Mitchell* v. *U.S.*, 386 U.S. 972 (1966).

103. *Holtzman* v. *Schlesinger*, 414 U.S. 1316, 1318–1320 (1973).

104. *Schlesinger* v. *Holtzman*, 414 U.S. 1321 (1973). If one accepts Woodward and Armstrong's account, Justice Brennan proposed the telephonic conference in order to avoid the unusual and unseemly situation of one justice overruling another's order. See Woodward and Armstrong, *The Brethren*, 278.

105. 414 U.S. 1321, 1323–1326 (1973). According to Woodward and Armstrong, Douglas was so irritated by Marshall's violation of the Court's "six-man-quorum rule" that he referred to Marshall privately as a "spaghetti spine." See Woodward and Armstrong, *The Brethren*, 279.

106. 484 F. 2d 1307 (2nd Cir. 1973).

107. *Ibid.*, 1308–1313. See also *DaCosta* v. *Laird* (III), 471 F. 2d 1146, 1155 (2nd Cir. 1973).

108. 484 F. 2d 1307, 1313 (2nd Cir. 1973).

109. *Ibid.*, 1313, 1314.

110. *Ibid.*, 1315–1318.

111. *Ibid.*, 1318.

112. *Ibid.*, 1314, 1316, 1318.

113. *Ibid.*, 1316.

114. *Ibid.*, 1310, 1312.

115. *Ibid.*, 1314. Also see *Proverbs* 20, v. 18.

CHAPTER 7 (PAGES 161 TO 175)

1. Rostow, 66 *Harvard L. Rev.*, 195, 196; Rostow, 33 *Notre Dame Lawyer*, 576, 578; Patterson, 29 *Georgetown L. J.*, 847–848. Also see *Holtzman* v. *Richardson*, 361 F. Supp. 544 (E.D. N.Y. 1973).

2. See Van Alstyne, 40 *L. & Contemp. Prob.*, 102–134, for a broad construction of the necessary-and-proper clause; but, see Warren, *Making*, 486–488, who argues that the clause neither adds to nor detracts from the powers vested in Congress.

3. Farrand, *Federal Convention*, Vol. 2, 318, 319.

4. *Orlando* v. *Laird*, 317 F. Supp. 1013, 1017 (E.D. N.Y. 1970).

5. *Ibid.* Also see Wormuth, 60 *Cal. L. Rev.*, 631, 643–645; May, *Ultimate Decision*, 14–15; Farrand, *Federal Convention*, Vol. 2, 341.

6. Cheever and Haviland, *American Foreign Policy*, 128–129; Wilcox, 1951 *Amer. Soc, of Int'l. L.*, 20–43; Berger, *Executive Privilege*, 140–141, 142.

7. See, for example, Judge Tauro's opinion in *Drinan* v. *Nixon*, 364 F. Supp. 854, 859 (D. Mass. 1973), and Judge Wyzanski's opinion in *Mitchell* v. *Laird*, 488 F. 2d 611, 613–614 (D.C. Cir. 1973).

8. 110 *Cong. Rec.* 18443, 18444, 18445, 18446, 18470 (1964).

9. The vesting clause of Article 1 simply prohibits the delegation of powers that are subsequently conferred on Congress. Inasmuch as the declaration-of-war clause

also requires that Congress judge the necessity of initiating war, the legislature cannot transfer this discretionary authority to the President. See *Schecter Poultry Corp.* v. *U.S.*, 295 U.S. 495, 529–530 (1935), and *Panama Refining Co.* v. *Ryan*, 293 U.S. 388, 421 (1935). Although the prevailing view is that the delegation issue has long been settled by subsequent decisions that sustain broad delegations of power to the executive, e.g., *Yakus* v. *United States*, 321 U.S. 414 (1944), the Court has never sustained the transfer of the war power to the President. Moreover, several recent decisions suggest that the delegation issue could arise under appropriate circumstances. See *U.S.* v. *Yoshida International, Inc.*, 526 F. 2d 560 (C.C.P.A. 1975).

10. Speaking for a majority in *Youngstown Sheet & Tube Co.* v. *Sawyer*, Justice Black pointed to the dangers inherent in expanding the concept of "the theater of war" to encompass the domestic society, 343 U.S. 579, 587 (1952).

11. *United States* v. *Smith*, 27 F. Cas. 1192 (C.C. D. N.Y. 1806) (No. 16, 342).

12. See Harry S Truman, *Memoirs, Years of Trial and Hope, 1946–1952*, Vol. 2 (Garden City, N.Y.: Doubleday & Co., 1956), Chapter 22, 331–348: hereinafter cited as Truman, *Memoirs*.

13. PL 93–148 [H.J. Res. 542], 87 Stat. 555 (1973).

14. *Drinan* v. *Nixon*, 364 F. Supp. 854, 858, 859, 860, 862, 863–864, 865 (D. Mass. 1973).

15. 17 F. Cas. 144 (C.C. D. Md. 1861) (No. 9,487).

16. 68 U.S. (1 Wall.) 243 (1864).

17. 71 U.S. (4 Wall.) 2 (1866).

18. *Minersville School District* v. *Gobitis*, 310 U.S. 586 (1940); *West Virginia State Board of Education* v. *Barnette*, 319 U.S. 624 (1943).

19. *Hirabayashi* v. *United States*, 320 U.S. 81 (1943); *Korematsu* v. *United States*, 323 U.S. 214 (1944); but see *Ex parte Endo*, 323 U.S. 283 (1944).

20. 323 U.S. 214, 245–248 (1944).

21. Bickel, *Least Dangerous Branch*, 205.

Table of Cases

Index

DATE DUE
